WILLIAM R. HARPER'S
ELEMENTS OF HEBREW

BY

AN INDUCTIVE METHOD

NEW AND REVISED EDITION

BY

J. M. POWIS SMITH, Ph.D.

PROFESSOR OF OLD TESTAMENT LANGUAGE AND LITERATURE
IN THE UNIVERSITY OF CHICAGO

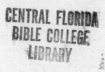
CHARLES SCRIBNER'S SONS
NEW YORK   CHICAGO   BOSTON

PREFACE

The sixth edition of Harper's ELEMENTS OF HEBREW appeared in 1885. Since that time it has served the needs of large numbers of students beginning the study of Hebrew, and has gained for itself a secure position among elementary text-books. But during the past thirty-five years much progress has been made in the study of Hebrew grammar, of which Harper's ELEMENTS remained unaware. The late President Harper himself was, of course, fully conscious of this, and frequently expressed his eagerness to bring out a new edition of the ELEMENTS. The pressure of official duties, however, and his premature death denied him this privilege.

The value of the Harper manner of approach to the study of Hebrew has been so clearly demonstrated in the experience of successive generations of students that the perpetuation of the text-books in which it is embodied seems called for. To this end the present revision has been undertaken. Effort has been made to preserve the form and method of the original as far as possible. The changes incorporated in the new edition are only such as seem demanded by the present status of our knowledge of Hebrew and Semitic grammar. The more important of these changes may be noted here.

(1) The half-open syllable has been eliminated, as was suggested by Sievers (*Metrische Studien*, vol. I, p. 22), and approved by Gesenius-Kautzsch (*Hebr. Grammatik*, 28th ed., 1909). (2) A beginning has been made along the line of bringing Hebrew grammar into accord with the results of the modern study of phonetics. This involves some marked changes in the treatment of the Hebrew vowel-system; but it seems well to make this departure, even in a book for beginners, since beginners are entitled to protection from known errors; and further because many students in our best colleges are learning the newer phonetic principles and will welcome them as old friends when they find them in this new field. (3) A frank acceptance has been accorded the biliteral explanation of the so-called ע״ע and ע״ו

3

verbs and nouns. This point of view seems more nearly in accordance with the facts, and likewise makes the study of these forms simpler for beginners. The biliteral hypothesis has not been carried as far here as it might well be in a more advanced grammar, its application being confined to the more apparent cases, for the sake of simplicity.

It remains to express my sense of obligation to two of my colleagues. Professor Ira Maurice Price has read the work both in manuscript and in proof, and has done much to insure accuracy in printing. To Professor Martin Sprengling, who read the book in manuscript, I am especially grateful for numerous and valuable suggestions, the acceptance of which will, I trust, greatly increase the worth of the book. Its errors are my own; I cannot hope to have escaped error in the presentation of a subject beset with so much that is problematical. "To err is human; to forgive, divine!" I can hope only that the present edition may give a new lease of life to this work of my greatest teacher.

J. M. Powis Smith.

The University of Chicago, Jan. 1, 1921.

PREFACE TO THE SIXTH EDITION

The first edition of the ELEMENTS was issued in July, 1881; the second, in October, 1882; the third, in February, 1883; the fourth, in November, 1883; the fifth, in November, 1884. All these editions, the first excepted, were printed from one set of plates, with only such changes and additions, from time to time, as the use of the same plates would permit. The peculiar circumstances of publication explained, although they could not excuse, the incomplete, and often imperfect, treatment accorded in these editions to very many of the subjects. While the present edition lays no claim to completeness, or to freedom from error, it will certainly be found more nearly complete and perfect than preceding editions. The author can only regret that regular and special duties of a most exacting nature, have not permitted him to give that amount of time, or that attention to the preparation of the book, which justice to the subject, to those who may use the book, and to himself, demanded.

The present edition, which contains nearly one hundred additional pages, and is entirely re-written, differs considerably from the former editions, and radically from other grammars now in common use. Some of the distinguishing features of the grammar deserve, perhaps, special mention:

1) For the purpose, not of aiding the beginner to pronounce, but of teaching the exact force and value of the several consonant- and vowel-sounds, a minute system of transliteration has been employed, by which the attention of the student is directed from the very beginning to the details of the vowel-system. Too little, by far, is made in Hebrew study, of the vowel-system, without a correct knowledge of which all effort is merely groping in darkness.

2) A tolerably exhaustive treatment, more complete perhaps than any that has yet appeared in English, is given of the various vowel-sounds. Each sound is treated separately, the laws which regulate its occurrence and the grammatical forms in which it appears being carefully noted.

5

3) Certain important distinctions, not heretofore generally recognized by American teachers, are indicated throughout the grammar; e. g., (a) the tone-long é (‏ֵ‎), heightened from ă, which is seen in Segholates, in ‏לְ"ה‎ Imperfects and Participles, and elsewhere; (b) the naturally long e (‏ֵי‎) contracted from ay, which occurs in plural nouns before the pronominal suffixes ‏ךְ‎, ‏ךָ‎, and in certain Imperfects before ‏נָה‎; (c) the ô obscured from â, as distinguished from the ô = aw.

4) Instead of adopting a new Paradigm-word for each class of weak verbs, the verb ‏קְטֵל‎ is retained, with such variation as the particular weak verb under consideration demanded; e. g., ‏עְטֵל‎ for the ‏פ'‎ guttural verb, ‏קְטֹט‎ for the ‏ע"ע‎ verb, ‏קוּל‎ for the ‏ע"ו‎ verb. There can be no objection to this method. Many grammarians have adopted it in the treatment of noun-formation. Experience has shown that, in this way, men learn the verb more rapidly and more thoroughly.

5) In the treatment of the strong verb, the student is referred, in every case, to the primary form or ground-form from which the form in use has arisen in accordance with the phonetic laws of the language. That treatment which starts with stems having the form which occurs in the Perf. 3 m. sg., or Impf. 3 m. sg., is, at the same time, unscientific and unsatisfactory. The bugbear of Hebrew grammar is the weak verb. Nor will it be otherwise so long as the effort is made to explain the forms of weak verbs from those of the strong verb. How absurd, for example, to derive ‏יָקוּם‎ from a form like ‏יִקְטֹל‎; but how simple to derive it from a form like ‏יַקְטֵל‎, the ground-form of ‏יִקְטֹל‎. Together with the form in use, the student should learn also the primary form from which the usual form is derived. This method will furnish a knowledge of the language, which will be not only more scientific, but also more lasting.

6) Particular attention is given to the subject of noun-formation, and on this is based the treatment of noun-inflection. The same method which would teach the primary forms of verbal stems, will also teach the primary forms of noun-stems.

7) That fiction of Hebrew grammarians, the connecting-vowel, has

been practically discarded. The Hebrew has no connecting-vowels. The vowels incorrectly called connecting-vowels are the relics of old case- or stem-endings. These case- or stem-endings, summarily disposed of in current grammars under the head of "paragogic" vowels, are restored to the position which their existence and occurrence demand.

But it is asked, What has a beginner to do with all this? Why should a grammar which proposes only to consider the "elements" of the language, take up these subjects? While this may do for specialists, of what service is it to him who studies Hebrew only for exegetical purposes? Our reply is this :—

1) The experiment of teaching men something about Hebrew grammar, of giving them only a superficial knowledge, has been tried for half a century; and it has failed. Men instructed in this manner take no interest in the study, learn little or nothing of the language, and forget, almost before it is learned, the little that they may have acquired. If for no other reason, the adoption of a new system is justified by the lamentable failure of the old to furnish any practical results.

2) Those who take up the study of Hebrew are men, not children. Why should they not learn, as they proceed, the explanation of this or that fact? Why should the student be told that the Infinitive Construct (קְטֹל) is formed from the Absolute (קָטוֹל) by rejecting the pretonic qāmĕç? Is it not better that he should learn at once that the ō of the Construct is from ŭ, while the ô of the Absolute is from â, and thus be enabled to grasp all the more firmly those two great phonetic laws of the language, *heightening* and *obscuration?*

3) The best way, *always*, to learn a thing is the right way, even if, at first, it is more difficult. If there *is* a difference between the ō of the Imperfect, Imperative and Infinitive Construct on the one hand, and the ô of the Infinitive Absolute and Participles on the other, what is gained by passing over it in silence?

4) In order to learn any subject, the student must be interested in that subject. Is he not more likely to be interested in an accurate, scientific treatment, than in an arbitrary, superficial treatment?

The treatment adopted in the ELEMENTS is an inductive one, so far as it was possible to make it such. In the discussion of each subject there are first given sufficient data, either in the way of words taken from the text, or of Paradigms, to form a basis for the work. The words cited are from the early chapters of Genesis, with which the student is supposed to be familiarizing himself, as the subjects are being taken up. Where these chapters furnished no suitable example, a word is taken from some other book, the chapter and verse being cited in each case. It is intended that the student shall feel in all his work that he is dealing with the actual facts of the language, and not with hypothetical forms. After the presentation of the "facts," the principles taught by these facts are stated as concisely as possible. While the book is an elementary treatise and, for this reason, does not aim to take up the exceptions and anomalies of the language, it will be found to contain a treatment of all that is essential, and to include everything of importance which can be classified. In the treatment of the strong and weak verbs, a list is given under each class of the more important verbs belonging to this class. This list may be used as an exercise, or merely for handy reference.

The author lays no claim to originality so far as concerns the material employed; there is indeed little room for originality in this line. In the matter, however, of arrangement, and of statement, he confidently believes that a kind of help is here afforded the student which cannot be found elsewhere.

In the work of preparation, the best and latest authorities have been freely used. Special acknowledgment is due the grammars of Bickell, Gesenius (Kautzsch), and Davidson; but valuable aid has been received from those of Green, Nordheimer, Kalisch, Land, Ewald, Olshausen, König, Stade, and Böttcher.

For his assistance in the preparation of the manuscript for the printer, and for many valuable suggestions, the author is indebted to Mr. Frederic J. Gurney, of Morgan Park. He desires also to express his thanks to Mr. C. E. Crandall, of Milton, Wis., for aid rendered by him in the verification of references and in the revision of the proof-sheets, and to Rev. John W. Payne, of Morgan Park, Ill., for the skill and care exhibited in the typographical finish and accuracy of the book. He is under obligations, still further, to Professors C. R.

Brown, of Newton Centre, S. Burnham, of Hamilton, E. L. Curtis, of Chicago, and F. B. Denio, of Bangor, for useful suggestions and corrections.

It is generally conceded that in America we are on the eve of a great revival in the department of Semitic study. It is the author's hope that this volume may contribute something toward this greatly needed awakening. Trusting that the new edition may be received with the same favor as those which have preceded it, and that its shortcomings will be as far as possible overlooked, he places the book, although with many misgivings, in the hands of those who favor the Inductive Method.

W. R. H.

Morgan Park, Ill., Sept. 1, 1885.

TABLE OF CONTENTS

PART FIRST—ORTHOGRAPHY.

11

PART FIRST—ORTHOGRAPHY

I. The Letters

1. Alphabet

Sign.	Equiv-alent.	Name.	Num. Value.		Sign.	Equiv-alent.	Name.	Num. Value.
1	א	'	'Å-lĕf	1	12	ל	l	Lå-mĕd	30
2	בּ	b	Bêθ	2	13	מ	m	Mêm	40
	[ב]	v	]		14	נ	n	Nûn	50
3	גּ	g	Gí-mĕl	3	15	ס	s	Så-mĕχ	60
	[ג]	ǧ	]		16	ע	'	'Å-yĭn	70
4	דּ	d	Då-lĕθ	4	17	פּ	p	Pê	80
	[ד]	đ =	th in this]			[פ]	f	]
5	ה	h	Hê	5	18	צ	ṣ	Ṣå-đê	90
6	ו	w	Wåw	6	19	ק	ḳ	Ḳôf	100
7	ז	z	Zå-yĭn	7	20	ר	r	Rêš	200
8	ח	ḥ	Ḥêθ	8	21	שׁ שׂ	š, ś	Šîn, Śîn	300
9	ט	ṭ	Ṭêθ	9	22	ת	t	Tåw	400
10	י	y	Yôd	10		[ת]	θ =	th in cloth]
11	כּ	k	Kåf	20					
	[כ]	χ	]						

1. The Hebrew language has twenty-two letters; these are consonants and are written from right to left.

2. The vowels in the "names" of the letters, given above, are sounded according to the English equivalents given in § 5. The "equivalents" for the consonants given above are rather to be regarded as symbols suggestive of the characters they represent than as exact reproductions.

3. The equivalent of each sign is the initial letter of its name.

4. The six consonants written with a dot in them are also written without the dot; but then they are changed in pronunciation, viz., ב = v; ג = ǧ; ד = đ; כ = χ; פ = f; ת = θ; see § 12.

17

2. Remarks on the Pronunciation of Letters

1. אֵת = 'ēθ (1:1)[1]; הָאָרֶץ = hå-'å̆-rĕṣ (1:1); אֱלֹהִים = 'elô-hîm (1:1); תְהוֹם = θᵉhôm (1:2).

2. עַל = 'ăl (1:2); עֶרֶב = 'ĕ-rĕv (1:5); רָקִיעַ = rå-ḳi(ă)' (1:6).

3. אֶחָד = 'ĕ-ḥåd (1:5); חֹשֶׁךְ = ḥŏ-šĕχ (1:2); מְרַחֶפֶת = mᵉrå-ḥĕ́-fĕθ (1:2).

4. קָרָא = ḳå-rå' (1:5); כִּי = kî (1:4); בֹּקֶר = bŏ-ḳĕr (1:5).

5. טוֹב = ṭôv (1:4); מִתַּחַת = mĭt-tă̆-ḥă̆θ (1:7); הַקָּטֹן = hăḳ-ḳå̆-ṭōn (1:16).

6. בְּרֵאשִׁית = bᵉrē'-šĭθ (1:1); וַיַּעַשׂ = wăy-yă̆-'ăś (1:7); חֹשֶׁךְ = ḥŏ-šĕχ (1:2).

7. עֵץ = 'ēṣ (1:11); תּוֹצֵא = tô-ṣē'(1:12); יִסְגֹּר = yĭs-gōr (2:21).

8. וְאֵת = wᵉ'ēθ (1:1); וָבֹהוּ = wå-vŏ-hû (1:2); וְרוּחַ = wᵉrû(ă)ḥ (1:2).

1. א (') is a laryngeal stop, made by bringing the edges of the larynx together, thus shutting off the emission of the breath; ה (h) is a "rough breathing," like h in how.

2. ע (') is a sound peculiar to the Semitic and made far down in the larynx; it is so difficult of utterance that no attempt is made to reproduce it here.

3. ח (ḥ) was a deep laryngeal; it is now generally pronounced like ch in the German Buch.

4. ק (ḳ) is a k-sound, but pronounced farther back on the palate than כ (k).

5. ט (ṭ) is a dental sound made with the tip of the tongue higher up than in the pronunciation of ת (t)[2].

6. שׁ (š) is pronounced like the English sh; שׂ (ś) is an ordinary s-sound, now indistinguishable from ס (s).

7. צ (ṣ) is a sharp hissing s-sound; more emphatic than the ordinary ס (s).

8. ו (w) is pronounced like w in water, and not like our v.

9. The spirant כ (χ) is pronounced like weak German ch in Kirche.

10. The spirant ג (ğ) is pronounced like g in German Tage.

---

[1] The chapter and verse in Genesis, in which a given word is found, are thus indicated; 1:1—meaning chapter 1, verse 1; 2:3—meaning chapter 2, verse 3, etc.

[2] In ordinary practice, ט and ת are scarcely, if at all, to be distinguished.

3. Remarks on the Forms of Letters

1. בְּרֵאשִׁית בָּרָא אֱלֹהִים אֵת־הַשָּׁמַיִם וְאֵת

2. (1:12) תּוֹצֵא | (1:2) פְּנֵי | (1:2) פְּנֵי | (1:1) אֱלֹהִים | (1:2) פְּנֵי | (1:4) כִּי
(1:11) עֵץ | (1:20) עוֹף | (1:4) בֵּין | (1:2) הַמַּיִם | (1:2) חֹשֶׁךְ

3. כּוֹכָבִים (3:24); (1:16) בִּדְגַת (1:28), פְּנֵי (1:2); דֶּרֶךְ
(1:11) הָיְתָה (1:2), חֹשֶׁךְ (1:2); וַיְהִי (1:3); בֵּין (1:4), זֶרַע
(1:6), רָקִיעַ (1:5); יוֹם (2:21), יִסְגֹּר (1:2); מַיִם (1:4), טוֹב
תּוֹצֵא (1:12); חֹשֶׁךְ (1:4), עֶשֶׂב (1:11).

1. Words are written from right to left, and may not be divided; when it is necessary to fill out a line, certain letters (א, ה, ל, ם, ת) are extended.

2. Five letters (כ, מ, נ, פ, צ) have two forms; the second (ך, ם, ן, ף, ץ) is used at the end of words.

3. Certain letters, very similar in form, are to be carefully distinguished: ם, ב, כ; כ, ב; ג, נ; ד, ר, ך; ה, ח, ת; ו, י; ז, ן; מ, ט; ם, ע, צ; שׁ, שׂ.

4. The Classification of Letters

	Labials.	Labio-Dentals.	Dentals.	Palatals.	Velars.	Laryngeals
Stops	פ ב		ט ת ד		ק כ ג	א
Fricatives	ו	פ ב	ת ד צ שׁ שׂ ז שׁ	י	כ ג	ע ח ה
Nasals	מ		נ			
Lateral			ל			
Rolled			ר			

Hebrew words consist of consonants and vowels as in all other languages. The use of the breath is fundamental in the production of these sounds. Vowels are produced by the relatively free, unobstructed emission of the breath, the modifications of vowel-sound being caused by varying positions of the vocal organs. Consonants, on the other hand, involve either a total or a partial obstruction of the breath. The Hebrew consonants, therefore, are classified on two bases: (1) the use of the breath in their production, (2) the vocal organs employed.

1. The first classification includes five groups of sounds:

a. The *Stops* which involve a complete stoppage of the breath.

b. The *Fricatives* produced by the friction of the breath escaping through some narrow passage.

Remark.—The Fricatives בֿ, גֿ, דֿ, כֿ, פֿ, תֿ may for convenience be designated spirants.

c. The *Nasal* sounds in which the breath is emitted through the nose.

d. The *Lateral* sound (ל *l*) in which the breath escapes along openings on one or both sides of the tongue.

e. The *Rolled* sound (ר *r*) in which the tongue rapidly taps the teeth or the ridge of the teeth, thus successively obstructing and freeing the passage of air.

2. The second classification, based on the organs of speech employed, falls into six sub-divisions:

a. The *Labials* proper involve the closing or partial closing of the lips.

b. The *Labio-Dentals*, a special variety of labials, are made by allowing the breath to escape with the front teeth placed upon the lower lip.

c. The *Dentals* are made with the tip of the tongue touching, or in close proximity to, the front teeth. Of these some bring the tip of the tongue close to the front teeth, or in contact with them, while with others the contact or approach is a little farther back on the tongue. The difference between בּ and בֿ, תּ and תֿ, גּ and גֿ, פּ and פֿ, דּ and דֿ, כּ and כֿ is that in the stops the breath is fully checked, while in the spirants the breath is allowed a partial outlet.

d. The *Palatal* consonant (י__*y*) involves the approach toward the highest part of the palate of that part of the tongue which is opposite the top of the palate.

e. The *Velars* involve contact between the tongue and the soft palate (velum). Of these ק is made the farthest back.

f. The *Laryngeals* involve action of the larynx which is not as yet clearly understood.

Note 1.—A third classification is generally recognized by students of phonetics: viz., *voiced* and *unvoiced* consonants. The former involve vibration of the vocal cords, the latter do not. Examples of voiced consonants are ב, ד, and of unvoiced, פ, ת. But for further details of phonetics the student may refer to G. Noël-Armfield, *General Phonetics for Missionaries and Students of Languages* (Cambridge: Heffer & Sons, 1915).

II. Vowels

5. The Vowel-Signs[1]

1. ‏מַב, חַת, חַם, עַל, מַ, הַשׁ; וָן, תָה, אָ, הָ, שָׁ, רָא, בְּ‏

2. ‏יֵשׁ, לֶם, מְק, מֵת, יִק, יָם; נִי, דִיל, כִּי, הִי, הִים, שִׁית‏

3. ‏שֵׁר, קֵר, רֵב, פֵּת, שֶׁךְ, רָץ; שֵׁ, מֵ, בֵּין, דֵּל, נֵי, רֵ‏

4. ‏יֵל, יִק, רֵם, לֶק, כָל; דוּ, בוּ, צוּ, יוּ, וּ, רוּ, הוּ‏

5. ‏עֵב, אַךְ, שֵׁם, כָּל, שֶׁל, תֵּ, לֵ, אוֹר, יוֹם, הוֹם‏

6. ‏הֵ, קֵ; אֵ, הֵ; עֵ, אֵ; מֵ, תֵ, פֵ, יֵ, וֵ, בְּ‏

1. ‏ـَ‎ is pronounced as *å* in *åll*; ‏ـَ‎ like *ă* in *class*.

2. ‏ـִי‎ is pronounced as *i* in *machine*; ‏ـِ‎ (*i. e.*, without a following ‏י‎), as *i* in *pin*.[2]

3. ‏ـֵי‎ or ‏ـֵ‎ is pronounced as *ey* in *they*; ‏ـֶ‎ as *e* in *met*.

4. ‏וּ‎ is pronounced as *oo* in *moon*; ‏ـֻ‎ as *u* in *put*.[2]

5. ‏וֹ‎ or ‏ـֹ‎ is pronounced as *o* in *note*; ‏ـָ‎ practically the same as *å* in *åll*, the same sign being used for both sounds.

6. *a.* ‏ـְ‎ is a very quickly uttered sound, as *e* in *below*, when the word is pronounced rapidly, so as to slur over the *e* and run the *b* and *l* almost (but not quite) together; thus—*b'low*, not *below*, nor *blow*; *p'lice*, not *police*, nor *plice*.

b. ‏ـֲ‎ (a combination of ‏ـְ‎ and ‏ـַ‎) is a little fuller in sound than ‏ـְ‎, and with a slight *ă* quality.

c. ‏ـֱ‎ (a combination of ‏ـְ‎ and ‏ـֶ‎) is a little fuller in sound than ‏ـְ‎, and with a slight *ĕ* quality.

d. ‏ـֳ‎ (a combination of ‏ـְ‎ (ŏ) and ‏ـָ‎) is a little fuller in sound than ‏ـְ‎, and with a slight *å* or *ŏ* quality.

6. The Vowel-Letters

Before the introduction[3] of vowel-signs (§ 5.), certain weak consonants, ‏א, ה, ו, י‎, were sometimes used to indicate the vowel-sounds, and hence were called *vowel-letters*:

---

[1] All *letters* in Hebrew are consonants; the alphabet contains no vowels. To supply the lack of vowels the above system of vowel-signs was introduced.

[2] Sometimes ‏ـִ‎ is written where ‏ـִי‎ was intended, and ‏ـֻ‎ where ‏וּ‎ was intended; in such cases ‏ـִ‎ is pronounced as ‏ـִי‎ (*i* in *machine*), and ‏ـֻ‎ as ‏וּ‎ (*oo* in *moon*).

[3] These signs were introduced between the sixth and eighth centuries A. D.

1. קָאם[1] = ḳâm; הָיְתָה = hå-yᵉθå (1 : 2); הָיָה = hăy-yå (1 : 20).

2. תֹהוּ = θō-hû (1 : 2); רוּחַ = rû(ă)ḥ (1 : 2); הָיוּ = hå-yû (1 : 15); אוֹר = 'ôr (1 : 3); טוֹב = ṭôv (1 : 4); יוֹם = yôm (1 : 5).

3. אֱלֹהִים = 'ᵉlô-hîm (1 : 1); רֵאשִׁית = rē'-šîθ (1 : 1); שְׁלִישִׁי = šᵉlî-šî (1 : 13); פְּנֵי = pᵉnê (1 : 2); שֵׁנִי = šᵉnê (1 : 16); בֵּין = bên (1 : 4).

4. יִהְיֶה = yĭh-yê (1 : 29); מִקְוֵה = mĭḳ-wê (1 : 10); אָהֳלֹה = 'öhᵒ-lô (12 : 8).

1. The a-sound was indicated, when medial, by the laryngeal א; when final, by the laryngeal ה.

Note 1.—Medial a (å or â) was indicated rarely; final å was generally, though not uniformly, indicated.[2]

Note 2.—The letter א, when the final letter of a root, does not belong here; since, in this case, it is not a vowel-letter, but has merely lost its consonantal character.

2. The sounds û and ô were indicated by ו.

Note.—Medial û and ô were generally indicated; final û and ô were always indicated.

3. The sounds î and ê were indicated by י.

Note.—Medial î and ê were generally indicated; final î and ê were always indicated.

4. The sounds ê and ô, when final, were frequently indicated by ה.

Note 1.—Only *long* vowels were thus indicated, and, with but few exceptions, besides å, only the naturally long (§ **30.**) vowels.

Note 2.—Vowels indicated thus are said to be written *fully;* when not thus indicated, they are said to be written *defectively.*

Note 3.—Briefly stated, the use of the vowel-letters may thus be put:

The vowels î and ê, medial and final, are represented by..........י.
The vowels û and ô, medial and final, are represented by........ו.
Final vowels, except î and û, are represented by...............ה.

Note 4.—In the later books of the Old Testament the *full* writing is more common than in the earlier books, the tone-long vowels (§ **31.**) being often thus represented.

---

[1] Hos. 10 : 14. [2] *Cf.* קֹלֵךְ (3 : 10); אָכְלָה (3 : 11).

7. The Classification of the Vowel-Sounds

The primary vowel-sounds in Hebrew are represented by the three vowels ă (—̇), ĭ (—̇), and ŭ (—̣). Of these ă is made with the widest opening of the vocal organs; ĭ is made with a narrower opening and with the breath striking the front of the hard palate; ŭ is also made with a narrow opening, but farther back in the mouth, and with rounding of the lips.

Closely related to the foregoing are five other sounds, viz., ĕ (—̇), ē (—̇), å (̣), ŏ (—̇), and ō (—̇). Of these, ĕ is midway between ă and ĭ, and may arise from either by *deflection*. Likewise å and ŏ are midway between ă and ŭ, and are so closely alike as to be represented by the same sign; å comes from ă under the influence of the tone by a *rounding* of the lips, while ŏ comes from ŭ without tonal influence by a lowering of the back of the tongue, which produces a greater opening as for the ă sounds—this may also be designated as *deflection*. The remaining two vowels, ē and ō, arise from ĭ and ŭ, respectively, under the influence of the tone; each of them is made farther back on the palate than its corresponding short vowel. Hence we shall speak of ē and ō as *lowered* respectively from ĭ and ŭ.

In addition to these vowel-sounds, there are two other classes, viz., those made by *lengthening* the primary vowel-sounds and those made by *reducing* them to their lowest terms.

The naturally long vowels are of three classes, viz., (1) those arising from *contraction*, e. g., ă + w = ô; (2) those arising in *compensation* for the quiescence or loss of a consonant, e. g., in יֹאמֶר the א has quiesced causing ă to become â, which was then rounded to ô; (3) those which acquired their length in the earliest stages of the language and are found as characteristic of certain formations, e. g., the ô of the Ḳăl active participle which has been rounded from â.

The *reduced* vowels are of two classes, viz., (1) the simple Šᵉwâ which is a neutral sound to which any one of the short vowels may be reduced, and (2) the compound Šᵉwâ which has a distinct form for each of the three short vowels, viz., —̇ from ă, —̇ from ĭ, and —̇ from ŭ.

The vowel-sounds, therefore, may be classified according to (1) their organic formation, (2) their quantity, (3) their nature, (4) their value:

1. Classified according to their *organic formation*, they are:

   a. A-class, including the *a*-vowels and those derived from them.

   b. I-class, including the *i*-vowels and those derived from them.

   c. U-class, including the *u*-vowels and those derived from them.

2. Classified according to their *quantity*, they are:

	a-class.	*i*-class.	*u*-class.
a. Short,	ⲧ ⲧ	ⲧ ⲧ	ⲧ ⲧ(ŏ)
b. Long,	ⲧ	ⲧ, ⲧ or ⲧ, ⲧ	ⲧ, ⲧ or ⲧ
c. Reduced,	ⲧ ⲧ	ⲧ ⲧ	ⲧ ⲧ

Note.—The vowels ⲧ and ⲧ are sometimes called doubtful; because, not infrequently, they are the defective writing of a long vowel.

3. Classified according to their *origin* or *nature*, they are:

   a. Pure .... ă;   ĭ;   ŭ.

   b. Deflected .... ĕ from ă;   ĕ from ĭ;   ŏ from ŭ.

   c. Attenuated .... ĭ from ă;

   d. Tone-Long .... å from ă;   ē from ĭ;   ō from ŭ.

   e. Naturally Long... { â;   î;   û.

   ô from â;   ê;   ô.

   ệ (= ⲧ or ⲧ)

   f. Reduced .... ᵉ and ᵃ; ᵉ and ᵉ; ᵉ and °.

4. Classified according to their *value* in inflection, they are:

   a. Changeable—viz., (1) all short vowels not followed by a consonant in the same syllable; (2) tone-long; (3) reduced.

   b. Unchangeable—viz., (1) short vowels followed by a consonant in the same syllable; (2) naturally long.

Note.—*Changeable* and *unchangeable* here apply only to changes of *quantity*, not of quality.

8. The Names of the Vowels

The following table presents the arrangement of the vowel-sounds according to their quantity (§ 7. 2), and at the same time gives the technical name of each sound.

Class.	Long.			Short.		Reduced.	
A-Class.	◌ָ â, å	Ḳâmĕṣ		◌ַ ă	Pă‏θ‏ăḥ	◌ְ ᵉ	Simple Šᵉwâ
	י◌ֶ ê	Sᵉğôl	◌ֶ			◌ֲ ᵃ	Ḥâṭêf-Pă‏θ‏ăḥ
I-Class.	◌ִ î	Ḥîrĕḳ	◌ִ ĭ	Ḥîrĕḳ	◌ְ ᵉ	Simple Sᵉwâ
	◌ֵ ê, ē	Ṣērê	◌ֶ ĕ	Sᵉğôl	◌ֱ ᵉ	Ḥâṭêf-Sᵉğôl
U-Class.	ו◌ û	Šûrĕḳ	◌ֻ ŭ	Ḳĭbbûṣ	◌ְ ᵉ	Simple Šᵉwâ
	◌ֹ ô, ō	Ḥôlĕm	◌ָ ŏ	Ḳâmĕṣ-Ḥâṭûf	◌ֳ ᵒ	Ḥâṭêf-Ḳâmĕṣ

9. Simple and Compound Šᵉwâ

1. וְ originally וֻ; בְּ originally בַּ; רָקִיעַ (1 : 15), but רְקִיעַ (1 : 6).

2. אֲשֶׁר (1 : 7); יַעֲזֹב־ (2 : 24); אֱלֹהִים (1 : 1); מוֹעֲדִים(1 : 14); לְקָחָהּ (2 : 23).

1. Simple Šᵉwâ (◌ְ) is a neutral sound which may arise from any of the short vowels and represents the minimum of vowel-sound. (For transliteration and pronunciation see § 5. 6. *a*).

2. Compound Šᵉwâ (◌ֲ, ◌ֱ, ◌ֳ) is a more audible sound than simple Šᵉwâ (§ 5. 6. *b. c. d.*), and is found, instead of simple Šᵉwâ, chiefly under laryngeals. Each of the three classes of vowels has its own distinctive compound Šᵉwâ.

10. Vocal Šᵉwâ

1. בְּרֵאשִׁית (1:1); תְּהוֹם (1:2); הָיְתָה (1:2); יִשְׁרְצוּ (1:20).

2. *a.* וַיְהִי = wăy-hî (1:3).

   b. בִּרְ־קִיעַ = bĭr-ḳi(ă)ʿ (1:15); מְלֹא־אוּ = mĭl-ʼû (1:28).

   c. יַעֲזֹב־ = yăʼᵃ-zŏv (2:24); לְקָחָהּ = lŭḳᵒ-ḥâ (2:23); יַעֲלֶה = yăʼᵃ-lê (2:6).

   d. בְּדְ־גֶת = bĭd-ğăθ (1:28); וַיְכַל = wăy-χăl (2:2); עָבְ־דָהּ = ʻŏv-dâh (2:15).

1. Vocal Šᵉwâ is always *initial, i. e.*, it goes with the *following* vowel to form a syllable.

2. Certain forms in which Šᵉwâ seems to waver between two sylla-

bles, and is consequently called *medial* by many grammarians, are to be treated as follows:

a. Forms with wâw-conversive (§ **70.**), where the dåğēš-förtē has disappeared, were originally pronounced like wăy-yᵉhî; but with the loss of the second yôd the vocal Šᵉwâ also disappeared; hence such forms are better pronounced as wăy-hî, etc., ay being treated as a diphthong.

b. Similarly Šᵉwâ is silent in such forms with prefixed prepositions as bĭr-ķî(ă)ʽ and lim-ʾô-rôθ and in forms like mil-ʾû.

Note.—This pronunciation is attested by such forms as לִנְפֹּל[1] and חָשְׁפִי.[2] That there was more or less variation in such cases, however, is clear from the variation in the use of dåğēš-lēnē in spirants after such a Šᵉwâ, from the fact that the Hebrew uses the same sign for a vocal Šᵉwâ and a silent Šᵉwâ, and from the testimony of the transliterations in the older strata of the Septuagint (§ **11.**). *Cf.* similar variations in spoken English, *e. g.*, tol-e-ra-ble and tol-rᵉble, con-side-ra-ble and con-sid-rᵉble; ath-letic and ath-e-letic.

c. In such forms as יַעֲזֹב, etc., the Šᵉwâ is only a helping vowel and does not affect the general situation; *cf.* the similar situation in such forms as שָׁלַחַתְּ, where the coming in of paθaḥ-furtive does not increase the number of syllables.

d. In forms with spirants after a so-called medial Šᵉwâ, the absence of the dåğēš is a survival from an earlier stage when a vowel-sound was heard before the spirant; *cf.* again שָׁלַחַתְּ, in which the presence of the later påθăḥ-furtive does not change the older hard sound of the *t*.

11. Silent Šᵉwâ

1. וַיִּקְרָא = wăy-yĭķ-râʾ (1:5); וַיַּבְדֵּל = wăy-yăv-dēl (1:7); מַבְדִּיל = măv-dîl (1:6).

2. *a.* חֹשֶׁךְ (1:4); בְּתוֹךְ (1:6); הַהֹלֵךְ (2:14).

  b. אַתְּ = ʾătt; נָתַתְּ = nå-θătt; קָטַלְתְּ = ķå-țălt.

Remark.—בְּרֵאשִׁית (1:1); וּבֵין (1:4); טוֹב (1:4); יוֹם (1:5); רָאשִׁים (2:10).

---

[1] Jer. 51:49.   [2] Isa. 47:2.

The simple Š⁰wâ (-⸳-), aside from its use to indicate a vowel-sound (§ 9.), appears frequently where it has no sound. It occurs thus:

1. Under all consonants standing in the *middle* of a word and closing a syllable (§ 26.).

2. Under a final letter, when that letter

    a. Is Kăf; or

    b. Is a consonant containing Dåğēš-fŏrtē or lēnē, or preceded by another consonant with Š⁰wâ.

3. Under an *initial* consonant in שְׁתֵּי, שְׁתַּיִם.

Remark.—The weak letters א, ה, ו, י, when quiescent, or used as vowel-letters (§ 6.), do not, of course, receive this silent Š⁰wâ.

Note 1.—Š⁰wâ under an *initial* consonant, whether of a word or of a syllable, is always *vocal*.

Note 2.—Š⁰wâ under a final consonant, whether of a word or of a syllable, is always *silent*.

III. Other Points

12. Dåǧēš-Lēnē

1. בְּרֵאשִׁית (1:1); הָיְתָה (1:2); וָבֹהוּ (1:2); בְּתוֹךְ (1:6);
מַבְדִּיל (1:6). יִסְגֹּר (2:21); בּוֹ פְרִי (1:29); עַל־פְּנֵי (1:2);

2. בְּדֶנֶת = bĭd-ğăθ (1:28); לְעָבְדָהּ = lᵉʻŏv-dåh (2:15).

3. כִּי בְּיוֹם (2:17); וּנְקֵבָה בָּרָא (1:27); בְּצַלְמוֹ בְּצֶלֶם (1:27);
תִּגְּעוּ בּוֹ פֶּן (3:3). רְדוּ בִּדְנַת (1:28);

1. The letters ב, ג, ד, כ, פ, ת, have two sounds. Their hard sound (b, g, d, k, p, t) is indicated by a point called Dåǧēš-lēnē, which they regularly receive whenever they do not immediately follow a vowel-sound.

Note 1.—As fricatives they are pronounced: ב = v; ד = d = th in *those*; פ = f in *fat* (cf. *ph* in *philosophy*); ת = θ = th in *thin*; כ = χ, like German *ch* in *Kirche*, but made farther forward; ג (= ǧ in German *Tage*) is not in ordinary practice distinguished from ג (= g).

Note 2.—To distinguish these six fricatives from the rest of the class thus named, we shall call them *Spirants*. The term spirant is commonly used in a wider sense than this, but for practical purposes we may confine it here to this definite usage.

2. These spirants without Dåǧēš-lēnē usually follow a vowel-sound, but sometimes the absence of the Dåǧēš persists even after the preceding vowel has disappeared.

Note.—The soft sound of these letters after preceding vowels is due to the failure to shut off completely the emission of the breath involved in the pronunciation of the vowel which would result in a stop (ד, ת, etc., cf. § 4.). Cf. the common Irish pronunciation of *lady* as *laðy*, and *better* as *bĕθĕr*.

3. When by a disjunctive accent (§ 23. 2. *a*) one of these letters is cut off from whatever may precede it, as at the beginning of a chapter, verse, or section of a verse, it does not immediately follow a vowel and hence takes Dåǧēš-lēnē.

29

13. Dăḡēš-Fŏrtē

1. הַשָּׁמַיִם = hăš-šă-mă-yĭm (1 : 1); הַמַּיִם = hăm-mă-yĭm (1 : 7);

הַיַּבָּשָׁה = hăy-yăb-bâ-šâ (1 : 9); הַמְּאֹרֹת = hăm-mᵉ'ô-rôθ
(1 : 16).

2. חַוָּה = hăw-wâ (3 : 20); מִתַּחַת = mĭt-tă-hăθ (1 : 7); הַבְּהֵמָה
= hăb-bᵉhē-mâ (1 : 25); הַדַּעַת = hăd-dă-'ăθ (2 : 17).

1. The doubling of a letter is indicated by a point in its bosom, called Dăḡēš-fŏrtē. Consonants may be doubled, however, only when they immediately follow a full vowel.

2. The point in Wâw and in the spirants is always Dăḡēš-fŏrtē, if preceded by a full vowel.

Note 1.—Dăḡēš-fŏrtē in a spirant serves also as Dăḡēš-lēnē, doubling the *hard*, not the *soft*, sound of the spirant.

Note 2.—A syllable whose final consonant has Dăḡēš-fŏrtē is called *sharpened* (§ 26. 2. N. 1).

Note 3.—A doubled letter is regularly preceded by a short vowel; this is generally a *pure* (§ 29. 1–3) vowel, seldom a deflected (§ 29. 4, 5) vowel.

14. Omission of Dăḡēš-Fŏrtē

1. וַיְכַל (2:2) *for* וַיְכַל; וַיְצַו (2:16) *for* וַיְצַו; אִם (2:24) *for* אִם.

2. וַיְהִי (1:3) *for* וַיְהִי; חַיָּתוֹ (1:24) *for* חַיָּתוֹ; לְקָחָה (2:23) *for* לְקָחָה.

3. הַהֹלֵךְ; הַחֹשֶׁךְ (1 : 4) *for* הַחֹשֶׁךְ; הָאוֹר (1 : 4) *for* הָאוֹר; הַהֹלֵךְ (2 : 14) *for* הַהֹלֵךְ.

1. Dăḡēš-fŏrtē is *always* omitted from a final vowelless consonant, there being nothing in this case to support the doubling.[1]

2. It is often omitted from medial consonants which have only a Šᵉwâ to support them. (But a spirant may not thus lose Dăḡēš-fŏrtē.)

3. It is always omitted from the laryngeals, א, ה, ח, ע, and ר.

Note 1.—When Dăḡēš-fŏrtē is omitted from a laryngeal and no compensation made for the loss by the strengthening of the preceding vowel, the Dăḡēš is said to be implied or understood.

---

[1] The only exceptions to this statement are אַתְּ *thou* (f.), and נָתַתְּ *thou* (f.) *didst give*.

Note 2.—Dåğēš may be thus implied in ח, ה, and ע, but not in א and ר.

Note 3.—The syllable preceding a consonant in which Dåğēš-fŏrtē is thus implied is really a closed syllable.

15. Kinds of Dåğēš-Fŏrtē

1. נָתַתִּי; יִנָּקֵהוּ for (1:9); יִקָּחֻ; מִן־תַּחַת for (1:7) מִתַּחַת
   (2:21) יֻקַּח; מִן־מֶן־נוּ for (3:22) מִמֶּנּוּ; נְתַנְתִּי for (1:29)
   for יִלְקַח.

2. יְקַדֵּשׁ (2:3); יְכַלּוּ (2:1); מִתְהַלֵּךְ (3:8); חַטָּאת (4:7);
   כִּנּוֹר (4:21).

3. לְקָחָה־זֹּאת (2:23); אֶעֱשֶׂה־לּוֹ (2:18); עֹשֶׂה־פְּרִי (1:12).

4. הַלְּבֵן (17:17); הַצְּפִינוֹ (Ex. 2:3); מִקְּדָשׁ (Ex. 15:17).

5. חָדְלוּ (Judg. 5:7); וַיֶּחֱלוּ (Job 29:21); יְצַתּוּ (Isa. 33:12).

6. אֵלֶּה (2:4); לָמָּה (4:6); הֵנָּה (6:2); [הֵמָּה].

1. When the doubling represents the combination of two similar, or the assimilation of two dissimilar consonants, the Dåğēš-fŏrtē is called *compensative.*

2. When the doubling is characteristic of a grammatical form, the Dåğēš-fŏrtē is called *characteristic.*

3. When by its use the initial letter of a word is joined to the final vowel of a preceding word, the Dåğēš-fŏrtē is called *conjunctive.*

4. When it is inserted in a consonant with Šᵉwâ, which is preceded by a short vowel, to make the Šᵉwâ audible, the Dåğēš-fŏrtē is called *separative.*

5. When the doubling strengthens or emphasizes the final tone-syllable of a section or verse, the Dåğēš-fŏrtē is called *emphatic.*

6. When the doubling gives greater firmness to the preceding vowel, the Dåğēš-fŏrtē is called *firmative.*

16. Mǎppiḳ and Råfê

1. לְאִישָׁה (2:15); לְשָׁמְרָה (2:15); לְעָבְדָהּ (1:24); לְמִינָהּ
   (3:6); עַמָּהּ (3:6); זַרְעָהּ (3:15).

2. וּמֵחֶלְבְּהֶן (4:4); לְקָחָהּ (2:23); בְּדִגַּת (1:26); לְמָיִם (1:6);
וַיַּהַרְגֵנְהוּ (4:8).

1. Măppîḳ (מַפִּיק extender) is a point placed in final ה, when
this letter is used as a consonant, and not as a vowel-letter.

Note.—Măppîḳ is written in MSS. also in א,[1] ו and י.

2. Râfê (רָפֶה rest) is a horizontal stroke placed over a letter, to
call particular attention to the *absence* of Dăğĕš or Măppîḳ.

17. Măḳḳēf

1. זַרְעוֹ־בּוֹ (1:5); וַיְהִי־עֶרֶב (1:3); יְהִי־אוֹר (1:2); עַל־פְּנֵי
(1:11).

2. יִמְשָׁל־בָּךְ (3:16); כָּל־נֶפֶשׁ (1:21); אֶת־הָאוֹר (1:4);
וְשֵׁם־הַנָּהָר (2:13).

1. Măḳḳēf (מַקֵּף binder) is a horizontal stroke placed between
two words, to indicate that they are to be pronounced together and
accented as if they formed but a single word.

2. If the former of two words, joined by Măḳḳēf, should contain a
long vowel in a closed syllable (§ 26. 2), such a vowel gives way to
a short vowel, or receives Méθĕğ (§ 18. 4).

18. Méθĕğ

1. הַכּוֹכָבִים (1:9); תֵּרָאֶה (1:7); הָרָקִיעַ (1:3); וַיְהִי־אוֹר
(1:16); הָאַרְבָּעִים (18:29).

2. בְּהִבָּרְאָם (2:4); תּוֹלְדוֹת (1:21); שָׁרְצוּ (1:2); הָיְתָה (2:4);
תֹּאכְלוּ (3:1).

3. הָאֲדָמָה (1:25); לְעֲשׂוֹת (1:26); נַעֲשֶׂה (2:3); לְקָחָה (2:23);
יַעֲשׂוּ (3:7).

4. בְּתוֹךְ־הַגָּן (3:3); עֵץ־הַגָּן (3:2); וְשֵׁם־הַנָּהָר (2:13);
תֵּת־כֹּחָהּ (4:12).

---

[1] A Măppîḳ in א is found in printed texts in Gen. 43 : 26; Lev. 23 : 17.

5. יְהְיֶה (1:29); יִהְיוּ (2:25); כִּהְיוֹתָם (4:8); יְחְיֶה (17:18);
וְחְיֶה (20:7).

6. וַיֵּצֵא (4:16); פַּדֶּנָה אֲרָם (24:9); וַיִּשָּׁבַע לוֹ (28:2).

Měθěǧ (מֶתֶג bridle) is a perpendicular line placed on the left side
of a vowel-point, to indicate that the syllable to which it belongs has
a secondary accent.[1] The following are its chief uses:

1. On the second syllable before the tone, but generally on the
third, if the second is closed (§ 26. 2).

2. With a long vowel followed by a vocal Šᵉwâ pretonic.

3. With all vowels before compound Šᵉwâ.

4. With a long vowel in a closed syllable, before Măḳḳēf.

5. With the first syllable of all forms of הָיָה and חָיָה in which
the ה and ח have Simple (i. e., silent) Šᵉwâ.

6. With an unaccented ⸗ in a final syllable; and to insure the
distinct enunciation of a vowel which otherwise might be neglected.

19. Ḳᵉrê and Kᵉθiv

1. הוֹצֵא (8:17) = הוֹצֵא; וייֹשֶׂם (24:33) = וַיִּישֶׂם; בגד (30:11)
= בְּגֶד.

2. הַוֹצֵא (8:17), read הֵיצֵא; וַיִּישֶׂם (24:33) = וייֹשֶׂם; בְּגֶד
(30:11), read בָּא גֵד.

3. הוא, to be read הִיא; יְהֹוָה, to be read אֲדֹנָי; יֱהֹוִה, to be
read אֱלֹהִים; נַעַר, to be read נַעֲרָה.

The Hebrew text was first written with consonants only. Not
until somewhere between 600 and 800 A. D. were the vowels written
with the consonants. Sometimes the vowels call for a different pronunciation from that indicated by the consonants; but usually the
vowels agree with the consonants as to pronunciation.

1. Kᵉθiv (כְּתִיב, written) is the term applied to the pronuncia-

---

[1] Mûnâḥ (·) is sometimes substituted for Měθěǧ.

tion of a word that is called for by the consonants of the text as distinguished from the vowels written with them.

2. Ḳᵉrê (קְרִי, *to be read*) is the term applied to the pronunciation of a word called for by the vowels supplied by the Massoretes (the name applied to those students of the Hebrew text who established the traditional pronunciation represented by the present vocalization of the text).

3. Some words are always read otherwise than as they are written. These are said to have a "perpetual Ḳᵉrê."

IV. The Accents

20. *The Place of the Accent*[1]

1. רֵאשִׁית (1:1); בָּרָא (1:1); שָׁמַיִם (1:1); הָאָרֶץ (1:1); חֹשֶׁךְ (1:2).

2. רֵאשִׁית (1:1); מָקוֹם (1:9); שָׁמַיִם (1:1); מַיִם (1:6); תַּחַת (1:9).

3. רֵאשִׁית (1:1); בָּרָא (1:1); מַבְדִּיל (1:6); יִקְרָא (2:23); מִתְהַלֵּךְ (3:8).

מַאֲכָל (2:9); יִקְרָא (1:5); אֶחָד (1:5); רָקִיעַ (1:6); תַּצְמִיחַ (3:18).

4. אֶרֶץ (1:10); חֹשֶׁךְ (1:2); דֶּשֶׁא (1:11); שֶׁרֶץ (1:20); עֵדֶן (2:8). אֶבֶן (1:20); נֶפֶשׁ (1:11); עֵשֶׂב (1:5); עֶרֶב (1:2); תֹהוּ (2:12).

1. The accent or tone may rest on the ultima, in which case the word is called Mĭlră'; or on the penult, in which case the word is called Mĭl'ēl; but never on the antepenult.

2. So far as the syllabification of a word is concerned, a closed syllable with a long vowel, or an open syllable with a short vowel, is, as a rule, accented (§ 28. 1. 2).

3. Uninflected words, and words receiving in inflection no endings, are accented on the ultima.

4. Nouns of the class called Seğolates, which are really monosyllabic (§ 89.), usually accent the characteristic vowel and not the helping vowel.

Note 1.—The place of the accent in *inflected* words, involving appendages, must be studied in connection with the subject of verbal and nominal inflection.

---

[1] The place of the accent is indicated in this grammer by the the the use of the accent ⟋. Words which are not thus indicated are to be accented on the ultima.

Note 2.—The term "accent" is used of the sign marking the syllable which receives the stress of voice; the term "tone" is used of the *stress* of voice.

21. Shifting of the Tone

1. לַיְלָה קָרָא (1:5); עָשָׂה פְרִי (1:11); תֹּאכַל לֶחֶם (3:19).

2. אַתָּה (4:7), but אַתָּה (3:11); אָנֹכִי (7:4), but אָנֹכִי (4:9).

3. וַיֹּאמֶר (1:3); וַיְבָרֶךְ (1:22); וַיִּיצֶר (2:7); וַיָּקָם (4:8).

4. וְאָכַלְתָּ ,וְהוֹצֵאתִי (3:18); וְהִכֵּיתִי (Ex. 3:20); וְהִצַּלְתִּי (Ex. 6:6).

1. The tone is often shifted from the ultima to the penult of a word which is followed closely by a monosyllable, or by a dissyllable accented upon the penult.

2. The tone is sometimes shifted in the case of words standing at the end of a clause or section, *i. e., in pause* (§ 38.).

3. Wāw Conversive with the Imperfect usually causes shifting of the tone from the ultima to the penult when the latter is an open syllable (§ 70.) and the former is closed.

4. Wāw Conversive with the Perfect often causes shifting of the tone from the penult to the ultima (§ 70.).

22. The Table of Accents

1. DISJUNCTIVES

Class I.—Emperors

1. סִלּוּק: Sĭllûk . . . . אָ
2. אַתְנָח 'Aθnâh . . . . אָ
3. סֶגֹלְתָּא Sᵉğōltå . . . . אֽ
4. שַׁלְשֶׁלֶת Šălšēlēθ . . . . אֽ

Class II.—Kings

5. זָקֵף קָטֹן Zâḳēf ḳåtōn . . אֵ
6. זָקֵף גָּדוֹל Zâḳēf ğådôl . . . אֵ
7. רְבִיעַ Rᵉvi(ă)' . . . . אֵ

Class III.—Dukes

8. פַּשְׁטָא Păštå . . . . אֽ
9. יְתִיב Yᵉθîv . . . . אֽ
10. טִפְחָא Tĭfḥå . . . . אֽ
11. תְּבִיר Tᵉvîr . . . . אֽ
12. זַרְקָא Zărḳå . . . . אֽ

Class IV.—Counts

13. גֶּ֜רֶשׁ Gĕrĕš............א֜ | 16. פָּ֡זֶר Påzēr............א֡

14. גֵּרְשַׁ֞יִם Gᵉråšȧyĭm.......א֞ | 17. קַרְנֵי פָרָה Ķărnê Fårå..א֟

15. לְגַרְמֶ֣הּ¹....א֣ | L⁰gărmēh¹....א֣ | | 18. תְּלִישָׁא גְדוֹלָה Tᵉlĭšå
                                             Gᵉdôlå....א

2. CONJUNCTIVES

Class V.—Servants

19. מֵרְכָ֥א Mĕrχå..........א֥ | 24. מַהְפָּ֤ךְ Măhpăχ........א֤

20. מֵרְכָ֦א כְפוּלָא Mĕrχå | 25. תְּלִישָׁא קְטַנָּה Tᵉlĭšå
    χᵉfûlå.......א֦ | Ķᵉṭănnå.......א֩

21. מוּנַ֣ח Mûnåḥ..........א֣ | 26. יֶרַח בֶּן־יוֹמוֹ Yĕråḥ bĕn
                                    yômô.......א

22. דַּרְגָּ֧א Dărgå..........א֧ | 27. מְאַיְלָא² Mᵉˀăy-yᵉlå²......א

23. קַדְמָ֨א Ķădmå........א֨

23. Remarks on the Table of Accents

1. The "Accents" were designed to have a threefold use:

a. To serve as musical notes in the cantillation of the Law and the Prophets in the synagogue;

b. To indicate the tone-syllable (*i. e.*, the syllable which is to be accented) of every word;

c. To show the relation sustained by each word to the other words in a clause or sentence.

2. Every accent is used as a sign of interpunction (§ 23. 1. *c*), to separate or join the several words of a sentence:

a. Disjunctives (those numbered 1–18 in the Table) mark a separation.

b. Conjunctives (those numbered 19–27 in the Table) mark a connection.

3. The Disjunctives vary in strength or power, and are accordingly divided into four ranks: Emperors, Kings, Dukes, Counts.

4. Those accents numbered 9 and 18 are *pre*-positive, *i. e.*, written

---

¹ Made up of Mûnåḥ and Pᵉsîḳ.

² Used for Mέθĕğ with words which have Sĭllûḳ or 'Aθnåḥ.

only on the first letter of a word, wherever the tone-syllable of that word may be.

5. Those accents numbered 3, 8, 12, 25 are *post*-positive, *i. e.*, written only on the last letter of a word, wherever the tone-syllable of that word may be.

6. The post-positive accents are repeated whenever their word is accented on the Penult, or has Păθăḥ-furtive (§ **42. 2.** *d*) under the last letter.

7. Sĭllûḳ may be distinguished from Mĕθĕ̆ǧ (§ **18.**), Păš̆tă from Ḳăḋmă, and Yᵉθîv from Măhpăχ by their position.

24. The Consecution of the More Common Accents

1. הָאָֽרֶץ׃ . . . . Gen. 1 : 1.

2. הָאָֽרֶץ׃ . . . . אֱלֹהִ֑ים . . . . Gen. 1 : 1.

3. כֵּֽן׃ . . . . לָרָקִ֫יעַ . . . . הָרָקִ֫יעַ . . . . Gen. 1 : 7.

   עַל־הָאָֽרֶץ׃ . . . . . . וְכִבְשֻׁ֑הָ . . . . אֱלֹהִ֔ים . . . . . . Gen. 1 : 28.

1. Every verse (Păsûḳ) is separated from the verse following by the sign ׃, called Sôf Păsûḳ (*end of the verse*); while the last word of every verse has on its tone-syllable the accent ⸱⸱, called Sĭllûḳ, which, in form, is like Mĕθĕ̆ǧ (§ **18.**).

Note.—Since Sĭllûḳ always stands on the last tone-syllable of a verse, while Mĕθĕ̆ǧ never stands on a tone-syllable, they are easily distinguished.

2. If the verse contain *two* primary sections, Sĭllûḳ marks the end of the *first*, while the end of the second is indicated by ⸱⸱, 'Aθnăḥ.

Note 1.—In the study of the accentuation of a verse one must begin with Sĭllûḳ, *i. e.*, at the end of the verse.

Note 2.—These accents have only relative power. The pauses marked are logical pauses.

3. If the verse contain *three* primary sections, Sĭllûḳ marks the end of the first; 'Aθnăḥ, the end of the second; while the end of the third is indicated by ⸱⸱, called Sᵉğōltă.

Note.—For an explanation of the repetition of ⸱⸱, see § **23. 6.**

4. Gen. 1 : 2...וָבֹהוּ......תְּהוֹם......אֱלֹהִים......הַמָּיִם : 4.

5. a. Gen. 1 : 14...הַשָּׁמַיִם........לְהַבְדִּיל........הַלַּיְלָה

b. Gen. 1 : 9...וַיֹּאמֶר אֱלֹהִים...אֶחָד............הַיַּבָּשָׁה

6. Gen. 1 : 1...בְּרֵאשִׁית....אֱלֹהִים....הַשָּׁמַיִם....הָאָרֶץ :

Gen. 1 : 4...אֶת־הָאוֹר כִּי־טוֹב....הָאוֹר......הַחֹשֶׁךְ :

Gen. 3:14...הַנָּחָשׁ....זֹאת. Gen. 1:28....אֹתָם. אֱלֹהִים...

4. When a *primary* section is large enough to be divided, or to contain a *secondary* section, the end of this secondary section, whether it stand in the primary section ruled by Sĭllûḳ or 'Aθnâḥ, is most frequently marked by ⸚, called Zâḳēf ḳâṭōn.

5. *a.* In secondary sections containing but a single word, where Zâḳēf ḳâṭōn would have been expected, Zâḳēf gâdôl, ⸚, is generally found instead.

b. A secondary section of less importance than that which is indicated by Zâḳēf ḳâṭōn is marked by ⸚, called Rᵉvî(ă)'.

6. The pause required by the rhythm before Sĭllûḳ and 'Aθnâḥ is marked by a disjunctive ⸗, called Ṭîfḥâ; that before Sᵉğōltâ, by ⸚, called Zărḳâ.

Note.—For the consecution of the remaining disjunctives see the Table of Consecution of Accents (§ 25.).

7. (1:2);........עַל־פְּנֵי הַמָּיִם : (1:1);........וְאֵת הָאָרֶץ : 7.

(1 : 4)........וּבֵין הַחֹשֶׁךְ :

8. (1:2);........עַל־פְּנֵי תְהוֹם (1 : 1);........בָּרָא אֱלֹהִים .8

(1 : 5)......קָרָא לַיְלָה

9. (3:3)......אֲשֶׁר בְּתוֹךְ־הַגָּן (3 : 14);......כִּי עָשִׂיתָ זֹּאת .9

7. The Conjunctive accent which always accompanies Sĭllûḳ is ⸗, called Mĕrχâ.

8. The Conjunctive accent which always accompanies 'Aθnâḥ is ⸗, called Mûnâḥ.

9. The Conjunctive accent which always accompanies Sᵉğōltâ is likewise Mûnâḥ.

25. A Table Showing the Consecution of the Accents

(table of accent symbols, with "or" alternatives in each bracketed group)

REMARKS ON THE TABLE

1. The Consecution of Sïllûḳ and 'Aθnâḥ, with the exception of the first conjunctive, is the same.

2. The *third* disjunctive preceding Sïllûḳ and 'Aθnâḥ, the *second* preceding Sᵉḡôltâ and Zâḳēf ḳâṭōn, and the *first* preceding Rᵉvî(ă)ʿ is Gérĕš, after which the consecution is the same for all.

3. This Gérĕš may be entirely omitted, in which case the servant of the preceding disjunctive will be present and will assume the functions of Gérĕš.

4. After Ḳădmâ the consecution may proceed either with Tᵉlîšâ Ḳᵉṭännâ (and its Mûnâḥ's) or, if there is a slight emphasis, with the disjunctive Tᵉlîšâ Ğᵉdôlâ (and its Mûnâḥ's).

5. Words standing between the Tᵉlîšâ Ḳᵉṭännâ or the Tᵉlîšâ Ğᵉdôlâ and the beginning of the section, will receive Mûnâḥ if they are closely related, but Pâzēr if there is a great emphasis. Words standing between Pâzēr and the beginning of the verse will receive Mûnâḥ.

Note.—Instead of Mûnâḥ, Lᵉḡármēh (*i. e.*, Mûnâḥ with Pᵉsîḳ (|⁻)) is substituted if there is a slight emphasis on the word.

6. Instead of Pâzēr, preceded by Mûnâḥ, there may be substituted Ḵărnê Fârâ, which is always preceded by Yĕrăḥ bĕn yômô. Other words will have Mûnâḥ.

Note 1.—This table exhibits in general the features of the prose system. There are, however, many exceptions. The poetic system is entirely different.

Note 2.—A few accents, occurring but seldom, are omitted from the table.

Note 3.—This very brief treatment of the accent aims only to introduce the student to a subject, which demands much careful study and investigation for its mastery. Reference may be made to Wickes, *A Treatise on the Accentuation of the Twenty-One so-called Prose Books of the Old Testament* (1886); *Idem, A Treatise on the Three so-called Poetical Books of the Old Testament, Psalms, Proverbs and Job* (1881).

V. Syllables

26. Kinds of Syllables

1. יְהִי (1:2); פְּנֵי (1:2); וְ־בֹ־הוּ (1:2); תָ־הוּ (1:2); בָּ־רָא (1:1); (1:3).

2. מַזְ־רִיעַ (1:11); טוֹב (1:4); בֵּין (1:4); מַבְ־דִיל (1:6); לִמְשֹׁל (1:18).

1. Syllables which end in a vowel-sound are called *open*.
2. Syllables which end in a consonant are called *closed*.

Note 1.—A *closed* syllable whose final consonant is doubled is called *sharpened*.

Note 2.—What seems to be an unaccented *open* syllable, with a short vowel, is of frequent occurrence; this is commonly called a half-open syllable; but it is better treated as closed (§ **10.**).

27. Syllabification

1. אֲשֶׁר (1:7); רְקִיעַ (1:20); וּ־מֵ־חָל־בְּ־הֶן (4:4).

2. וּ־בֵין (1:4); אֱלֹ־הִים (1:1); בְּרֵא־שִׁית (1:1); יִשְׁ־רְצוּ (1:20).

3. עֲרֹב (1:5) for עֶרֶב; יְרֹב (1:22) for יֶרֶב; וַיִּשְׁתְּ (9:21).

1. A word contains as many syllables as it has vowels; but Păθăḥ-furtive (§ **42. 2.** *d*), and Šᵉwâ do not form syllables.

2. Syllables must *begin* with a consonant, the only exception being the prefixed conjunction וּ; they *may* begin with two consonants, the first always having under it a vocal Šᵉwâ.[1]

Remark.—Syllables often occur which apparently begin with a Šᵉwâ. These are cases in which Šᵉwâ creeps in after a laryngeal as a transitional or liaison element linking the two syllables together and facilitating pronunciation of the laryngeal. The Šᵉwâ is better treated as belonging with the preceding laryngeal.

---

[1] There is a single exception to this remark, viz., שְׁתֵּי (Gen. 4 : 19) in which the Šᵉwâ is silent.

3. Syllables may end in *two* consonants, but only when these are strong. The harshness resulting from this combination is generally avoided by the insertion of a helping vowel (§ **36.**).

28. *Quantity of the Vowel in Syllables*

1. בָּרָא (1:1); בְּרֵא־שִׁית (1:1); מֵ־עַל (1:7); הָ־אֹור (1:4); הָ־יְתָה (1:2).

2. אֵת (1:1); מַבְ־דִּיל (1:6); מִקְ־וֵה (1:10); וַיִּקְ־רָא (1:5); מֵ־עַל (1:7).

3. הַשָּׁמַיִם (1:1); לְאִשָּׁה (2:22); אִמֹּו (2:24); יָקֻם (4:15).

4. (*a*). הַ־חֹשֶׁךְ (1:4);

   (*b*). נַעֲשֶׂה (1:26);

   (*c*). בִּרְקִיעַ (1:14); מִלְאוּ (1:22);

   (*d*). וַאדֹנִי (18:12).

5. בַּיִת (6:14); מַיִם (1:6); יֵרֶב (1:22); נַעַר (19:4).

1. The vowel of an unaccented open syllable must be long.

2. The vowel of a closed syllable must be short, unless it has the tone; when it has the tone, it *may be* long.

3. The vowel of the sharpened syllable is short, unless it has the tone; it is pure, *i. e.*, ă, ĭ, ŭ, and not deflected, *i. e.*, ĕ or ŏ.

4. Short vowels are often found in what appear to be unaccented open syllables, and are often called half-open syllables; but they are better treated as closed syllables. For example in (*a*) dåğēš-fŏrtē is implied or understood, thus making the syllable closed; in (*b*) the laryngeal once had no vowel (*cf.* תַּעֲדֶה[1]; יֵאָסֹר; נֶחְמָד [2:9]; and the Šᵉwâ is therefore only a secondary helping-element and does not affect the syllabification; in (*c*) the Šᵉwâ is to be treated as silent (*cf.* § **10.**); in (*d*) the laryngeal was once vocal and closed the syllable, and the short vowel persists even though the laryngeal has become quiescent (*cf.* § **10.**).

5. The vowel of an open accented syllable may be short.

---

[1] 1 Kgs. 20:14.   [2] Isa. 61:10.

VI. Euphony of Vowels[1]

29. *Short Vowels*

1. *a.* יַבְדֵּל (1:4); יַבָּשָׁה (1:9); יָמִים (1:10); חָיָה (1:20); מַזְרִיעַ (1:11).

b. אַף (1:7); מֵֽ־עַל (2:12); זָהָב (2:12); גַּן (2:8); הַחַיַּת־ (1:25); (3:1).

c. שַׁבַּת (2:3); לָקַח (2:22); דָּבַק (2:24); לָקַח (3:23); יִצְמַח (2:9).

d. הִשִּׁיאַנִי (3:13); אַיִן (2:5); דַּעַת (2:9); פַּעַם (2:23); שָׁמַיְמָה (24:32); בֵּיתָה (15:5).

e. מַאֲכָל (2:9); לַעֲבֹד (2:5); יַעֲלֶה (2:6); נַעֲשֶׂה (1:26).

2. *a.* יֶרֶב (1:22); אִשְׁתּוֹ (2:24); אִמּוֹ (2:24); הִנֵּה (1:29); יֶבֶן (2:22).

b. יִקְרָא (1:5); הַמְטִיר (2:5); לִמְשֹׁל (1:18); וְקִטְלוֹ; נִפְקְחוּ (3:5).

3. *a.* וַיְכַלּוּ (2:1); עֵירֻמִּים (3:7); לָקַח (3:23); יָקָם (4:24); [הֻקַּח].

1. The pure short ă is found:

   a. In unaccented closed, or sharpened syllables;

   b. In the closed syllable with secondary accent of nouns in the construct state, and a few monosyllabic nouns and particles;

   c. In the accented closed syllable of many verbal forms.

   d. (1) As the accented characteristic vowel of laryngeal and עַ״י Seġolates (§ 89.); (2) before the suffix נִי, and (3) sometimes before the locative ending הָ.

---

[1] This treatment is not intended to be exhaustive; it will be found practically complete, however, so far as general principles are concerned.

e. In a closed syllable with Méθěǧ (§ **18**. 3) before a compound Š^ewâ.

2. The pure short ĭ is found:

 a. In unaccented closed, and especially sharpened, syllables, and in some accented open syllables (§ **28**. 5); but

 b. That ĭ (─) which comes by attenuation or thinning (§ **36**. 4) from an original ă must be distinguished from an original ĭ, although it is subject to the same rules as the latter.

3. The pure short ŭ is found almost exclusively in unaccented sharpened syllables.

4. אֶת־ (1:4); וַיְבָרֶךְ (1:22); וַיָּשֶׂם (2:8); וַיְגָרֶשׁ (3:24); וַתֵּלֶד (4:1).

חֹשֶׁךְ (1:2); עֵשֶׂב (1:11); עֵזֶר (2:18); יֶרֶב (1:22); וַיִּבֶן (2:22). יֶדְכֶם [וַיֶּעֱטַל]; עֶבֶד; אֶרֶץ (9:2). נֶחְמָד (2:9);

5. כָּל־ (1:21); אָכְלָה (1:29); כֻּתֳּנֹות (3:21); רָחְבָּהּ (6:15); [הָקְטַל].

עָבְדָהּ (2:15); שָׁמְרָה (2:15); אָכָל־ (3:11); יַעֲזֹב־ (2:24).

4. The short *e*-sound ─ (ĕ), as a deflection from ă or ĭ, is found:

 a. In unaccented closed syllables in general.

 b. As an unaccented vowel in certain forms with wåw conversive.

 c. As a helping-vowel in Seǧolate nouns.

 d. As the characteristic accented vowel in Seǧolate forms.

 e. In unaccented closed syllables before laryngeals.

 Note 1.—There is also to be noticed the character of the ─ which appears in certain particles, *e. g.*, אֲשֶׁר, פֶּן, etc., and pronominal forms (כֵּן; כֶּם; תֶּן; תֶּם; אַתֶּם); the origin of which is obscure.

5. The short *o*-sound ─ (ŏ), deflected from and more common than ─ (ŭ) and sustaining to ─ and ─ (ō) the same relation that is sustained by ─ (ĕ) to ─ (ĭ) and ─ (ē), is found in unaccented closed syllables.

30. Naturally Long Vowels

1. *a.* נָע (4 : 14) = nâ'; שָׁת (4 : 25) = šâθ; [קָל = ḳâl].

   b. גִּנָּב=gănnâv[1]; מַתָּן=măttân[2]; כְּתָב=keθâv[3]; קְרָב=ḳerâv.[4]

   c. אֱלֹהִים (1 : 1) = 'elôhîm *for* 'elâhîm; יֹאמֶר (1 : 3) = yô'měr *for* yâ'měr; גְּדֹל (1 : 16)=gâdôl *for* gâdâl; אָכֹל (2 : 16) = 'âχôl *for* 'âχâl.

2. *a.* יִישָׁן (2:21); יִישָׁן = יֵישָׁן; (1:6); וִיהִי = וְיהִי; (2:7); יֵיצֶר = יִיצֶר; (2:21). יְהִי = וִיהִי.

   b. יָמִין = yâmîn[5]; חָסִיד = ḥâsîd[6]; מָשִׁיחַ = mâšî(ă)ḥ.[7]

   c. פִּילֶגֶשׁ;[8] קִטּוֹר *for* קְטוֹר.[9]

   d. צֻוֵּיתִי (3 : 17) *for* (עָשִׂיתָ); עָשִׂית (3 : 13) *for* עָשִׂית; צֻוֵּיתִי (צֻוֵּיתִי).

   e. הִשִּׂיא (3:13); הִגִּיד (3:11); יַלְבֵּשׁ (3:21); הִמְטִיר (2:5); הִבְדִּיל (1:18).

   f. מֵקִים (6 : 16); תָּשִׂים (9 :9);

3. *a.* קוּם;[11] יָקוּם;[10] תָּשׁוּב (3 : 19);

   b. הוּסַד=הֻוסַד;[12] בְּהוּ = בֹּהוּ (1 : 2); תֹּהוּ = תָּהוּ (1 : 2); הוּקַם.[13]

   c. אָרוּר (3 : 14); עָרוּם (3 : 1); הַבּוּרָה (4 : 23); כָּרוּב (3 : 24); רְכוּשׁ (12 : 5).

Naturally long vowels have arisen either (1) from contraction of a vowel and semivowel (*i. e.*, *y* or *w*), or (2) as the characteristic of certain nominal and verbal forms, or (3) in compensation.

    1. Naturally long â (⸗, seldom אָ), comparatively rare, is found:

    a. In certain forms of middle-vowel verbs (§ 86.) of which it is characteristic.

    b. In certain nominal forms, of which it is characteristic (§§ 91, 93.).

---

[1] Ex. 22 : 1, 6, 7.   [2] Gen. 34 : 12; 2 Kgs. 11 : 18.   [3] Esth. 4 : 8.
[4] 2 Sam. 17 : 11.   [5] Gen. 13 : 9.   [6] Ps. 30 : 5.
[7] 1 Sam. 2 : 10.   [8] Gen. 19 : 28.   [9] Judg. 19 : 2.
[10] Ex. 21 : 19.   [11] Gen. 13 : 17.   [12] Ezra 3 : 11.
[13] Ex. 40 : 17.

c. Naturally long â, in the great majority of instances, was rounded to ô (§ **30. 6**).

2. Naturally long î (י ָ, sometimes ָ), is found:

a. As the contraction of *iy* (§§ **81. 82.**).

b. In certain nominal forms of which it is characteristic (§ **91.**).

c. In certain nominal forms in which it is compensative (§ **92.**).

d. In certain ל״ה forms, before consonant-additions (§ **82.**).

e. In Hif'îl forms, in which ē would naturally have been expected.

f. In certain forms of middle-vowel verbs.

3. Naturally long û (ו, sometimes ֻ) is found:

a. As characteristic of certain middle-vowel Ḳăl forms (§ **86.**).

b. As the contraction of *uw*, whenever the combination *uw* would be final; in certain פ״ן Hŏf'ăl forms (§ **80.**); and in certain middle-vowel and ע״ע Hŏf'ăl forms, which seem to follow the analogy of פ״ן forms.

c. As characteristic of certain nominal forms, including the Ḳăl passive participle.

4. *a.* בֵּין (1 : 4); בֵּית[1]; עֵינַיִם (3 : 6).

   b. תֵּיטִיב (4 : 7) = têṭîv *from* תֵּיטִיב; הֵינִיקָה (21 : 7) *from* הֵינִיקָה.

   c. עָשָׂה (6 : 14) = ʿăśê *from* עָשִׂי; מִקְוֵה (1 : 10) = mĭḳwê *from* מִקְוִי.

   d. צִוִּיתִי (3 : 11)]; הַרְאָת[4]; צִוִּיתִי[3]; [*cf.* צִוִּיתִי[2]; הִכֵּיתִי].

   e. דְּמֵי (3 : 7); עֵינִי (1 : 16); שְׁנֵי; פְּנֵי (1 : 2) = pᵉnê *from* פָּנַי (4 : 10).

   f. מֵישָׁר (7 *from* מֵישָׁר; מֵיטָב; אֵיתָן[6] *from* אֵיתָן[5] *from* מֵיטָב.

5. *a.* תְּפוּצֶינָה[12]; תִּצְלֶינָה[11]; תְּסֻבֶּינָה[10]; תְּבְכֶּינָה[9]; תַּעֲשֶׂינָה[8].

   b. [סוּסָיִהָ]; פָּנֶיךָ (4 : 6); אַפֶּיךָ (3 : 19); חַיֶּיךָ (3 : 14).

   c. הַשָּׂדֶה (2 : 5); עָשֹׂה (1 : 11); יַעֲשֶׂה (18 : 25).

---

[1] Gen. 12 : 15.　　　[2] Ex. 3 : 10.　　　[3] Deut. 3 : 21.　　　[4] Deut. 4 : 35.
[5] 1 Sam. 15 : 9.　　[6] Gen. 49 : 24.　　[7] Isa. 26 : 7.　　　[8] Deut. 1 : 44.
[9] Ruth 1 : 9.　　　[10] Gen. 37 : 7.　　[11] 1 Sam. 3 : 11.　　[12] Zech. 13 : 7.

4. Naturally long ê (written ‎יִ֫, yet sometimes ‎ֵ and ‎ֵה‎)
comes from the contraction of *ay* or *ai*, and is found:

a. In the inflection of ‎עִ"י Segolates (§ **109.**).

b. In the Hif'il forms of verbs originally ‎פִ"י.

c. In the Imperative (2 m. sg.) of verbs ‎לִ"ה (§ **82.**); and in
the construct state of nouns ending in ‎הֶ֫ (*ê*) (§ **111.**).

d. In ‎לִ"ה perfects before consonant additions (§ **82.**).

e. In the plural construct ending of masc. nouns, ‎לִ"ה (§ **109.**).

f. In the penult of a few nominal formations.

Note.—The ê of *d* very frequently yields to î, especially in *active
perfects.*

5. Besides ê, there is another naturally long *e*-sound, which likewise arises out of *ay.* It is written ‎יֵ and ‎הֵ and may, for the sake
of distinction, be transliterated as *ê.* It is found:

a. In ‎לִ"ה Imperfects and Imv's before the fem. plur. termination ‎נָה (§ **82.**); and, after the analogy of these forms, also as a
separating vowel in similar middle-vowel and ‎עִ"ע forms.

b. In the forms of plural nouns before the pronominal suffixes ‎ךָ
and ‎הָ (§ **109.**).

c. In the absolute forms of nouns from ‎לִ"ה roots and in the
Ḳăl Impf. and the Participles of ‎לִ"ה verbs.

6. *a.* ‎אָכֹל (2 : 16) = 'ăχôl *for* 'ăχâl; ‎יֵצֵא (2 : 10) = yôṣē', *for* yâṣē';

‎רֹמֵשׂ (1 : 26) = rômēś *for* râmēś; ‎סֹבֵב (2 : 13) = sôvēv *for*
sâvēv.

b. ‎יֹאמֶר (1 : 3) = yô'měr *for* yâ'měr; [‎יִקֹּל = yĭḳḳôl *for* yĭḳḳâl].

c. ‎אֱלֹהִים (1:1) = 'ĕlôhîm; ‎דּוֹר (6 : 9); ‎עוֹלָם (3 : 22); ‎שָׁלוֹם
(26 : 31).

d. ‎יְעוֹפֵף (1 : 20) = yᵉʻôfēf; ‎יִתְבֹּשָׁשׁוּ (2 : 25) = yĭθbôšăšû.

e. ‎הֲקִמֹתִי (6 : 18); ‎הֲשִׁיבֹתִיךָ (28 : 15); ‎סַבֹּתִי¹; ‎קַלּוֹת²

7. *a.* ‎יוֹם (1 : 5); ‎תּוֹךְ (1 : 6) = θôχ [*cf.* ‎תָּוֶךְ].

b. ‎תֹּסֵף (4 : 2) = tôsěf; ‎הוֹלִידוּ (5 : 4); ‎נוֹרָא³

---

¹ 1 Sam. 22 : 22.   ² Nahum 1 : 14.   ³ Isa. 18 : 2.

c. תּוֹלְדוֹת (2:4); מוֹעֵד (1:14).

d. לְמִינוֹ (1:11); בּוֹ (1:11); זַרְעוֹ (1:11); אָהֳלֹה (12:8).

8. בְּעָנָן (9:13, 14, 16); הֶעָרִים (19:25, 29); תֵּרָאֶה (1:9);

[1].מְבֹרָךְ

6. Naturally long ô, for the most part written defectively, is in many cases only the rounding of a naturally long â (§ 30. 1). This is the case:

a. In the forms of the Infinitive Absolute (§ 67. 1. b), and in the Ḳal Active Participle (§ 68. 1. a).

b. In the Ḳal Imperfect of verbs פ״א (§ 79.), and in the Nïf'äl of middle-vowel verbs (§ 86.).

c. In a large number of nominal formations (§§ 91. 92.).

d. In so-called Pôlēl (or Pô'ēl), and Hïθpôlēl (or Hïθpô'ēl) forms.

e. In the separating vowel used before consonant terminations in the Perfects of ע״ע and middle-vowel verbs (§§ 85. 86.).

7. There is, however, a second naturally long ô, which is the result of the contraction of au or aw. This is found:

a. In a large number of monosyllabic nouns from middle-vowel stems.

b. In the Nïf'äl and Hïf'îl of verbs originally פ״ו (§ 80. 3. b).

c. In many פ״ו nominal formations (§§ 98.).

d. In the contraction of âhû = ô (seldom written ה).

8. Vowels strengthened in compensation for the loss of a consonant are unchangeable, like naturally long vowels.

Note 1.—Naturally long vowels are usually written fully (§ 6. 4. N. 2), and are thus distinguished from tone-long vowels. There are many cases, however, in which the distinction can be determined only from a knowledge of the grammatical form in which the vowel stands.

Note 2.—Naturally long vowels are unchangeable. The exceptions to this rule are so few as scarcely to deserve notice.

---

[1] Num. 22 : 6.

31. Tone-Long Vowels

1. a. אָדָם (1:26); אֶחָד (1:5); אָכַלְתָּ (3:11); יִצְמָח (2:5);
   תָּוֶךְ (15:10).

   b. בָּרָא (1:1); חַיָּה (1:28); בְּהֵמָה (1:26); יַבָּשָׁה (1:9);
   מֵוֶת[1] (1:1); הָאָרֶץ (1:1); הִשְׁקָה (2:6); יִקְרָא (1:5).

   c. רָקִיעַ (1:6) for רְקִיע; בָּרָא (1:1) for בַּרָא;
   יִקְרָא (2:23); תִּפָּקַחְנָה (3:7); מָקוֹם (1:9) for מַקוֹם;
   וָבֹהוּ (1:2); תָּשׁוּב (3:19).

   d. תִּפָּקַחְנָה (3:7); בָּנֶיהָ[2]; צִוִּיתִיךָ (3:11); אָכַלְתָּ (3:11);
   לַיְלָה (1:5); צָפֹנָה (13:14).

A short vowel (–, ֽ, ֻ), when it would stand in close proximity
to the tone, frequently becomes long, ă becoming å, ĭ becoming ē,
ŭ becoming ō. These vowels are called, from their origin, *tone*-long.

1. Tone-long å, instead of an original ă, is found:

   a. In a closed *tone*-syllable,
      (1) in the absolute state of nouns;
      (2) in pause (§ 38.);
      (3) in a few Seğolates from middle-vowel roots;

   b. In an open *tone*-syllable,
      (1) in the more recent feminine ending הָ (from ăθ)
          (§ 106. 2. c);
      (2) in ל"ה and ל"א verbal forms (§§ 82. 83. 1);
      (3) in some Seğolate nouns;

   c. In an open *pretone*-syllable; *always*, except as indicated in
§ 32. 2.

   d. In an open *posttone*-syllable,
      (1) in the case of the pronominal ending תָ, and frequently
          the suffixes הָ and ךָ;
      (2) in the feminine plural termination נָה, and the locative
          ending, הָ (*directive*) (§ 105.).

---

[1] Deut. 19:6.   [2] Ruth 1:8.

2. *a.* זָקֵן; לָבֵשׁ; וַיִּבֶשׁ; רֹמֶשׂ (1:26); הָלֵךְ (2:14); סֹבֵב
יֵצֵא (4:16); תֵּן (4:42); תֵּת (4:12); יִתֵּן (1:17); (2:11);
שֵׁב (20:15); יַקְדֵּשׁ (2:3); יַבְדֵּל (1:4); יִשְׁכֵּן (3:24);
יִתְחַבֵּא (3:8); מִתְהַלֵּךְ (3:8); זָקֵן (19:4); עָקֵב (3:15);
מָגֵן (15:1); עָרֵל (17:14); שָׁלֵם (15:16); עֵץ (2:16); שֵׁם
(2:11); אֵת (1:1); כֵּן (1:7); בֵּן (4:25); עֵשָׂו (1:11);
עֵזֶר (2:18); סֵפֶר (5:1); יֵצֶר (6:5); עֵדֶן (2:8).

b. בְּהֵמָה (1:24); נְקֵבָה (1:27); תַּרְדֵּמָה (2:21); לֵבָב (Dt.
28:28); שֵׁנִי (1:8); יֵצֵא (4:16); וַיֵּשֶׁב (4:16) *for* יֵשֶׁב;
יֵדַע (4:17) *for* יֵדַע.

3. *a.* מְשֹׁל (1:18); יִשְׁבַּת (2:2); יַסְגֵּר (2:21); קָטֹנְתִּי (32:11);
יָכֹלְתִּי (1:30). אָדֹם (25:30); עָמֹק (30:8); כֹּל[1] (1:30).

b. שֹׁהַם (1:5); בֹּקֶר (1:2); חֹשֶׁךְ (1:2); בֹהוּ (1:2); תֹהוּ
(2:12).

c. יְבָרֶךְ[4]; מְבָרֵךְ[3]; gō-rᵉšû[2]; גֹּרְשׁוּ

2. Tone-long ◌ֵ, instead of short ◌ִ or ◌ַ, is found:

　　a. In a closed *tone*-syllable; always, except in a few monosyllabic
particles. Worthy of notice is its occurrence,

　　　　(1) in the Ḳăl Perfect of many stative verbs (§ 61. 2), and in
the Ḳăl Active Participle (§ 68. 1. *a*);

　　　　(2) in the Ḳăl Imperfect and Imperative of נָתַן (§ 78.), and
of verbs originally פ״ן (§ 80.);

　　　　(3) in Nĭfʿăl, Pĭʿēl, Hĭfʿĭl and Hĭθpăʿēl forms in which the ĭ,
whence ē comes, was originally ă (§ 59. 1);

　　　　(4) in many monosyllabic and dissyllabic nominal formations;

　　　　(5) in *i*-class Segōlates (§ 89.).

　　b. In an open *pretone* (or *ante-pretone*) syllable, always instead
of ĭ, as,

　　　　(1) in nominal formations;

---

[1] Lev. 13 : 3.　　　[2] Ex. 12 : 39.　　　[3] Num. 22 : 6.　　　[4] 2 Sam. 7 : 29.

(2) in the preformative of the Ḳăl Impf. of פ"ן verbs (§ 80. 2. *a*).

3. Tone-long ‑ (ō), instead of ‑, is found:

    a. In a closed *tone*-syllable. Worthy of notice is its occurrence,

        (1) in the Ḳăl Infinitive Construct, Imperative, and Imperfect (§ 66. R. 2);

        (2) in the Ḳăl Perfect of a few stative verbs (§ 64. 3);

        (3) in a few nominal forms (§ 90. 1. *c*);

    b. In an open *tone*-syllable, in *u*-class Seğolates.

    c. In an open *pretone*-syllable.

Note 1.—Tone-long vowels are correctly written defectively; in the later language the incorrect *full* writing is frequent.

Note 2.—The tone-long vowel, arising from the rejection of Dăğĕš-fŏrtē from a following laryngeal, is unchangeable.

32. Reduced Vowels

1. *a.* מְ־אוֹר (1 : 16) *from* גְּ־דֹל; מְאֹרֹת (1 : 16) *from* גְּ־דָל; גְּ־דֹלִים (1 : 16) *from* עָ־וֹן עָ־וֹנִי.

    b. עֲ־זַבְתֶּם[2] *for* עֲ־זַבְתֶּם; עֲ־שִׂיתֶם *for* עֲ־שִׂיתֶם[1].

    c. גְּ־אַלְתִּיךְ[3] *for* גְּ־אַלְתִּיךְ; הָ־רֵגוּ (4 : 25) *for* הָ־דָרְגוּ.

2. *a.* תֵּלְדִי; יִשְׁרְצוּ (1 : 20) *for* יִשְׁרְצוּ; הָיְתָה (1 : 2) *for* הָיְתָה; נָתְנָה (3 : 12) *for* נָתְנָה; תֵּלְדִי (3 : 16) *for*.

    b. דְּמֵי (1 : 16); שְׁנֵי (1 : 2); פְּנֵי; רְקִיעַ (1 : 20) *from* רְקִיעַ (4 : 10).

    c. יָדֵעַ; יֹדְעֵי (3 : 5) *from* צָעַק; צְעָקִים (4 : 10) *from*.

    d. גְּחָנְךָ (3 : 14); קֹלֶךָ (3 : 10); אֲכָלְכֶם (3 : 5); אֲכָלֵךְ (2 : 17); זַרְעֵךְ (3 : 15).

Remark.—בְּ originally בַּ; לְ orig. לַ; כְּ orig. כַּ; וְ orig. וַ.

3. *a.* אֲדָמָה (2 : 6); אֲשֶׁר (1 : 7); אֱלֹהִים (1 : 1); אֲרוּרָה (3 : 17); נָעֳמִי[4].

---

[1] Ruth 1 : 8.   [2] Ruth 2 : 16.   [3] Ruth 3 : 13.   [4] Ruth 1 : 2.

³בְּסָעְרָה ; ²תְּאַלְּצֵהוּ ; ¹שְׁבֲּלֵי ; לְקָחָה for (2 : 23)   *b.* לָקְחָה

⁴וַיִּקְרַב־ ; (27 : 26)   וְשָׁקָה ; (1 : 18)   וְלְהַבְדִּיל ; (2 : 12);   *c.* וְזָהָב

A short vowel, or a tone-long vowel, gives way to Šᵉwâ, either simple or compound, when it would stand in an open syllable at a distance from the tone. The change may be called reduction (§ 36. 3). Reduced vowels are found:

1. In what would be the *antepretone*-syllable,

   a. In the inflection of nouns (§ 36. 2. *b*).

   b. Before the grave termination in the inflection of verbs (§ 71.).

   c. In many verbal forms to which a pronominal suffix is attached.

2. In what would be the *pretone*-syllable,

   a. In the inflection of verbs, before הָ_, וֹ and יִ_ (§ 36. 2).

   b. In the formation of the construct state of nouns (sg. and pl.).

   c. In the nominal inflection of participial forms.

   d. Before the suffixes ךָ, כֶם and כֶן, when attached to nouns and to certain verbal forms.

   Remark.—In many particles which originally had _, there is found _, but before the tone the original ă often becomes _ (§§ 47. 5; 49. 4).

3. The simple Šᵉwâ (§ 9. 1) may represent the vowel-sound of any class. But the compound Šᵉwâ (§ 9. 2) has three distinct forms, one for each class, and is found:

   a. Chiefly under laryngeals (§ 42. 3). But sometimes also,

   b. Under a letter which is, or should be, doubled.

   c. Under a letter preceded by the prefix וֹ.

   Note 1.—The Šᵉwâ under a laryngeal, if vocal, *must* be compound Šᵉwâ; since a simple Šᵉwâ standing under a laryngeal is *always* silent.

   Note 2.—The Ḥâṭēf Sᵉġôl never appears anywhere but under laryngeals.

   Note 3.—Simple Šᵉwâ is always vocal (1) at the beginning of a word, (2) under a consonant with dâ̆ğēš-fŏrtē, (3) after another Šᵉwâ, except in the case of a final consonant.

---

¹ Zech. 4 : 12.   ² Judg. 16 : 16.   ³ 2 Kgs. 2 : 1.   ⁴ Ps. 55 : 22.

33. The A-Class Vowels

In accordance with the foregoing statements (§§ 29–32.) it is seen that the A-class vowels include:

1. The pure short —— (ă).

2. The attenuated —— (ĭ), arising in unaccented closed, and especially sharpened, syllables.

3. The short —— (ĕ) which is deflected from ă, either with or without the tone.

4. The naturally long —— (â), which has come from contraction or from compensative lengthening, or from a lengthening characteristic of nominal forms.

5. The naturally long —— (ô), which has come by rounding from a naturally long â.

6. The tone-long —— (å), which has arisen from an original ă through the influence of the tone.

7. The simple —— (ᵉ), which is a reduction of ——, through the influence of the tone.

8. The compound —— (ᵃ), which occurs instead of —— according to the usage mentioned in § 32. 3. a. d.

9. The naturally long ׳—— (ê) which is probably diphthongal in character.

34. The I-Class Vowels

In accordance with the foregoing statements (§§ 29–32.) it is seen that the I-class vowels include:

1. The pure short —— (ĭ), now found chiefly in unaccented closed, and especially sharpened, syllables.

2. The deflected —— (ĕ), found in unaccented closed syllables.

3. The naturally long ׳—— (î), from iy, see â, § 33. 3.

4. The naturally long ׳—— (ê), which is diphthongal in its character, coming, as it always does, from the contraction of ai or ay.

5. The tone-long —— (ē), which has come from an original ——, through the influence of the tone.

6. The simple —— (ᵉ), cf. § 33. 7.

7. The compound —— (ᵉ), occurring instead of —— chiefly under laryngeals.

35. *The U-Class Vowels*

In accordance with the foregoing statements (§§ 29–32.), it is seen that the U-class vowels include:

1. The pure short ◌ֻ (ŭ), now found chiefly in sharpened syllables.
2. The deflected ◌ֻ (ŏ), found chiefly in unaccented closed syllables.
3. The naturally long וּ (û), from *uw;* and see â, § 33. 4.
4. The naturally long וֹ (ô), which is diphthongal in its character, coming, as it always does, from the contraction of *au* or *aw.* [On the ô rounded from â, see § 33. 5.]
5. The tone-long ◌ֹ (ō), which has arisen from an original ◌ֻ, through the influence of the tone.
6. The simple ◌ֻ (ᵒ), see § 33. 7.
7. The compound ◌ֳ (ᵒ), occurring instead of ◌ֻ chiefly under laryngeals.

36. *Changes of Vowels*

1. *a.* אֶרֶץ (1 : 24); דָּבָר *from* דְּבַר; צְדָקָה *from* צַדְקַת (16 : 2); סֵפֶר *from* סְפַר; אֶרֶץ *from*.

b. הֶרֶג (4 : 25) *from* הָרְגוּ; דָּבָר *from* דְּבַר (15 : 1) דְּבָרִים; קָטֵל *from* שָׁמַיִם; שָׁמַיִם (1 : 1) *from* הָקֵם; הָקֵם, but הֻקְטַל *from* קָטֵל.

c. שֵׁרְצוּ (1 : 21) *for* שָׁרְצוּ; מָשְׁלוּ *for* מָשְׁלוּ.

d. בְּרָאתִי (6 : 7); קָרָאת (17 : 19) קָרָאתָ (1 : 5); יִקְרָא (1 : 1); בָּרָא.

e. לָמַיִם (3 : 11); יִצְמַח (2 : 5); שָׁמַיִם (1 : 17); אַתָּה (1 : 6).

2 *a.* שֶׁרֶץ *but* שָׁרְצוּ (1 : 21); תֹּאכַל *but* תֹּאכְלוּ (2 : 16) (3 : 1); תֵּלֶד *but* תֵּלְדִי (1 : 20); יִשְׁרְצוּ; תֹּאכְלוּ (3 : 16); יַהֲרָגֵנִי *but* יַהַרְגֻהוּ (4 : 8); (יַהֲרֹג *for* יַהֲרֹג) but (4 : 14).

b. גָּדַל *but* גְּדֹל (1 : 20); רָקִיעַ *but* רְקִיעַ (1 : 2); פְּנֵי *but* פָּנִים; בָּשָׂר *but* מָאוֹר *but* מְאֹרֹת (1 : 16); גְּדֹלִים (1 : 16); בְּשָׂרִי (2 : 23).

---

[1] Deut. 22 : 4.

In the formation of stems and the inflection of words, the following vowel-changes occur:

1. Tone-long vowels are found,

a. Usually when in nouns an original short vowel comes under the tone, either in open or closed syllables.

b. When a short vowel would stand in an open syllable before the tone. This is characteristic of nominal formations.

c. When in verbs an originally ante-pretonic short vowel becomes pretonic, in an open syllable.

d. When a following weak consonant becomes quiescent.

e. When an originally short vowel comes to stand in pause.

Under such circumstances, ă is usually *rounded* to å; ĭ is *lowered* to ē, and ŭ to ō (see §§ **33–35.**).

Note.—*Cf.* German *ălle*, but English *åll*.

2. *Reduction* is the process by which a vowel is minimized or compressed to its smallest proportions. *Cf. heaven*, pronounced *hev'n*, but Anglo-Saxon *heofon; even*, pronounced *ev'n*, but Anglo-Saxon *efen* and *ebhan;* also the initial *a* in *America* when pronounced quickly. This process takes place,

a. When an ultimate ─. (ă), ─. (ĭ), or ─. (ŭ) in the inflection of *verbs* loses the tone; as when personal terminations consisting of a vowel, or pronominal suffixes connected by a vowel, are added.

b. When a penultimate vowel, in the inflection of *nouns*, no longer stands immediately before the tone, as in the formation of the construct state, when terminations of gender and number are appended, and when pronominal suffixes are added.

Note 1.—Herein consists the great difference between verbal and nominal inflection, that in verbal, the ultimate vowel, in nominal, the penultimate vowel is changed.

Note 2.—In some *verbal* forms, the vowel of whose ultima is unchangeable, the penultimate vowel is reduced.

Note 3.—In some *nominal* forms, the vowel of whose penultima is unchangeable, the ultimate vowel is reduced.

Note 4.—Only vowels standing in an open syllable may be reduced. Naturally long vowels are never reduced.

3. a. ‏הַבְדִּיל‎ but ‏הַבְדִּיל‎ ;יֵשׁ' originally (2:2) ‏יִשְׁבֹּת‎ (1:18).

   b. ‏[קְטֵל‎ but ‏וְיַקְטֵל]‎ ;קֹדֶשׁ but יְקַדֵּשׁ (2:3); בַּת but‏¹ בָּתִּי‎.²

   c. (24:30) ‏דִּבְרֵי‎ for ‏דִּמְכֶם‎ ;דְּמְכֶם for (9:5) ‏יְלַדְתִּיךָ‎;³ דִּבְרֵי.

4. a. ‏חָפְצוּ‎;⁴ אָכְלָה for הַקְטֵל for (1:29) ‏אָכְלָה‎ [וְהַקְטֵל.

   b. ‏יַעֲטֵל]‎ for נַעֲטֵל ;נַעֲטֵל for הֶעֱטִיל ;הֶעֱטִיל for [וְהַעֲטִיל.

   c. ‏אֶרֶץ‎ (1:24); ‏עֶרֶב‎ (1:5); ‏רֶמֶשׂ‎ (1:24); ‏רֶחֶם‎ (20:18).

5. ‏אֵת‎ (with), ‏אֶת⁻‎ (4:1); ‏אִתְּךָ‎ (6:18); יָקֶם = יַקֶּם ; יַנְקֶם = יָקֶם‎
   (4:15).

6. a. ‏לְמִינָה‎ (1:24) for לְמִינָהּ.

   b. ‏וִיהִי‎ = wĭy-hĭy; תְּהֹן (1:2) for תֹּהוּ = θōhǔw. וִיהִי for (1:6) ‏וִיהִי‎.

   c. ‏בֵּין‎ = bǎy(ĭ)n; לְמִינוֹ (1:11) for לְמִינֵהוּ; בֵּין (1:4) for ‏בּוֹ‎;
      ‏בְּהֹן‎ (1:11) for בָּהֶן, etc., etc.

   d. ‏קָם‎ (from ‏קַם‎); ‏נָקוֹם‎ (from ‏נַקַּם‎); ‏גָּדוֹל‎ (from ‏גַּדֵּל‎)
      (הַקְטִיל from) הַקְטֵל.

7. ‏קוֹטֵל‎ קָטַל; גָּדוֹל from גַּדֵּל; שׁוֹפְטֵי from ‏שָׁפְטֵי‎.

8. a. ‏בִּרְקִיעַ‎ (1:14); ‏לִמְאֹרֹת‎ (1:15); ‏בְּדִנֵת‎ (1:26).

   ‏בְּחֻרִי‎;⁵ כִּדְמוּתֵנוּ (1:26); לֵאמֹר for (1:22) ‏לֵאמֹר‎ ;לַעֲבֹד (2:5);

   b. ‏יַהֲרְגֵהוּ‎ [וַיַּהֲרְגֵהוּ] for (4:8) נַעֲטְלָה for נֶעֶטְלָה.

9. a. ‏עֶרֶב‎ (1:5); ‏זֶרַע‎ (1:11); ‏פַּעַם‎ (2:23); ‏בֵּית‎ (19:4); ‏בְּהֹן‎
   (1:2).

   b. ‏מְרַחֶפֶת‎ (1:2) for מְרַחֶפֶת; מֶמְשֶׁלֶת (1:16) for ‏מֶמְשָׁלֹת‎.

   c. ‏וַיַּעַשׂ‎ (1:22) for יֵרֶב; וַיַּעַשׂ for (1:7) ‏יֵבֶן‎ (2:22)
      ‏יֵבֶן‎ for.

---

¹ Ex. 2:1.　　² Ruth 2:8.　　³ Ps. 2:7.　　⁴ Ps. 1:2.
⁵ Ezek. 20:5.

3. *Attenuation* is a thinning of — (ă) to — (ĭ). It is the same change as that seen in *sang, sing; tango, attingo;* and in *master* which becomes *mister*, when used as a proclitic title (*cf.* Oxford Dictionary, s. v. *Mr.*). It takes place,

a. In closed syllables containing preformatives: as in the Ķăl Imperfect, the Nĭf'ăl and Hĭf'îl Perfects.

b. In sharpened syllables: as in the Pĭ'ēl Perfect, and various nominal formations.

c. In closed syllables which have lost the tone, especially in the construct plural of nouns and before grave suffixes.

4. *Deflection* involves a change of quality in vowels, whereby ă becomes ĕ, ĭ becomes ĕ, and ŭ becomes ŏ. The same change is seen in the Greek and Latin forms, *mihi* and *meus, bulbus* and $\beta o\lambda\beta\acute{o}s$, *nummus* and $\nu\acute{o}\mu os$. It often takes place,

a. When they would stand in an unaccented closed syllable.

b. When they would stand before a laryngeal with Šᵉwâ.

c. When ă stands as the original vowel of a Seğolate form.

5. Original short vowels usually stand unchanged in sharpened syllables.

6. *Lengthening* (or contraction) takes place,

a. When two similar vowels, generally by the dropping of a consonant, come together.

b. When a vowel and a semi-vowel come together; then $i+y=\hat{\imath}$, $u+w=\hat{u}$.

c. When ă or å is followed by ĭ or y, or by ŭ or w; then $a+i$ or $y=\hat{e}$, $a+u$ or $w=\hat{o}$.

d. As characteristic of certain verbal and nominal forms.

7. *Rounding* is a process applied not only in producing å from ă, but also in changing the vowel â to ô. The same change is seen in the Anglo-Saxon *hām, hame,* or *haam* becoming *home; stān,* becoming *stone.*

8. A vocal Šᵉwâ must always be followed by a full vowel, rather than by another Šᵉwâ. Hence:

a. At the beginning of a word, an original short vowel, that ordinarily is reduced to Šᵉwâ, will remain without reduction if followed by a Šᵉwâ, yielding only to such attenuation or deflection as may be necessary; ă is commonly attenuated to ĭ, but if the Š⁺wâ is compound, the short vowel is assimilated to it.

b. In the middle of a word, where a compound Š⁺wâ stands as helping-vowel under a laryngeal, when inflectional change brings a vocal Š⁺wâ immediately after the compound Š⁺wâ, the latter in every case gives place to the corresponding short vowel (or a deflection of it) as helping-vowel.

9. When two vowelless consonants would come together at the end of a word, a helping-vowel is usually inserted between them to aid in pronunciation. The helping-vowel practically constitutes a new syllable, but the nature of the vowel treatment in many cases shows that the new syllable was not fully recognized—(*cf.* § **27.**). This helping-vowel is generally ĕ, but with a laryngeal it is usually ă, with ׳__ it is ĭ, and with ן__ it is generally ŭ. The most common instances of this are:

a. The large class of nouns called Seğolates (§ **89.**).

b. A class of feminine formations resembling Seğolates.

c. Certain short verbal forms (§ **78. 1**).

Note.—The use of a helping-vowel is common in carelessly spoken English; *e. g., elm* becomes *ellum; prism=prisum; film= fillum; Henry=Henery; athletic=atheletic,* etc.

37. *Tables of Vowel-Changes*

The following tables summarize the various possible vowel-changes:

TABLE I

$i+i$ or $i+y$	= î
$a+y$	= ay
$a+i$ or $a+y$	= ê
$a+y$	= ê
$a+a$	= ô
$a+a$	= â
$a+w$	= aw
$a+u$ or $a+w$	= ô
$u+u$ or $u+w$	= û

TABLE II

ă
- ĭ — original *a* attenuated to ĭ which then is treated like an original ....ĭ
- ă — original *a* retained as ....ă
- å — original *a* rounded to ....å
- ĕ — original *a* deflected to ....ĕ
- ˘ε — original *a* reduced to ....ᵉ
- a — original *a* reduced to ....ᵃ

ī
- ĕ — original *i* deflected to ....ĕ
- ĭ — original *i* retained as ....ĭ
- ē — original *i* lowered to ....ē
- ˘ε — original *i* reduced to ....ᵉ
- ε — original *i* reduced to ....ᵉ

ŭ
- ŏ — original *u* deflected to ....ŏ
- ŭ — original *u* retained as ....ŭ
- ō — original *u* lowered to ....ō
- ˘ε — original *u* reduced to ....ᵉ
- ε — original *u* reduced to ....°

38. Pause

1. אִשְׁתֶּ֑ךָ (3:17); בַּעֲבוּרֶ֑ךָ (7:11); נִפְתָּ֑חוּ (2:25); יִתְבֹּשָׁ֑שׁוּ (3:17).

2. זֶ֑רַע (2:5); יִצְמָ֑ח (3:11); אָכַ֑לְתָּ (1:5); לָ֑יְלָה (1:2); הַמָּ֑יִם (1:29) *for* זֶ֫רַע (=זָרַ֑ע); הֶ֑בֶל (4:2) *for* הֶ֫בֶל (=הַ֑בֶל).

3. אָנֹ֑כִי (3:10) *for* אָנֹ֫כִי; אַתָּ֑ה (3:11) *for* אַתָּ֫ה.

4. תָּמֻ֑ות (2:17); *but* וַיָּ֫מָת (11:28); *and* וַיָּ֑מָת (5:5, 8, 11, 14, 17, etc.).

The pause at the end of a verse or clause, indicated by the more powerful accents (§ **23**. 3), causes certain changes:

1. Šᵉwâ yields to its original vowel, and this, if short, undergoes the customary tonal change and is accented.

Note.—The Š͏ᵉwâ standing before the suffix ָך, yields to its original—̱, which becomes ê (§ **30.** 5).

2. A short vowel becomes tone-long.   The —̱ in Seḡolates in pause becomes —̄.

3. The tone is frequently shifted from the ultima to the penult.

4. The tone which, in short forms, is on the penult is given to the ultima.

VII. Euphony of Consonants

39. Assimilation

1. מִקֶּדֶם; מִן־כָּל־ for (2:2) מִכָּל־; מִן־תַּחַת for (1:7) מִתַּחַת (2:8).

יִנָּטַע for (2:8) יִנָּבַח; יִנָּפַח for (2:7) יִפַּח; יִנָּתֵן for (1:17) יִתֵּן.

2. אֶחְדְּתָ for (2:21) אֶחָת (35:2); הִטֶּהָרוּ; מִתְדַּבֵּר for מְדַבֵּר [1]

3. אֶיצֹק for [2] אֶצֹק (18:4); יִקַּח; יִלְקַח for (2:15) יִקַּח.

4. לִנְפֹּל (6:7); נִחַמְתִּי; מִן־הָאָרֶץ (2:6); שְׁכַנְתִּי [3]; — **Remark.**

Assimilation of the final consonant of a closed syllable to the initial consonant of the following syllable takes place:

1. In the case of the weak נ, of the preposition מִן (§ **48. 1**), and of the first radical of verbs פּ"ן (§ **78.**).

Note.—This is a very common thing in English, *e. g. irresistible* for *inresistible*, *illegible* for *inlegible.*

2. In the case of ת of הִתְ (§ **58. 7. N.**) and rarely of ד.

Note.—*Cf. attract* for *adtract; attest* for *adtest; annotate* for *adnotate; appropriate* for *adpropriate.*

3. In the case of ל in לָקַח *to take* (§ **78. R. 2**) and י in a few פּ"י verbs (§ **81.**).

Remark.—The letter נ is *not* assimilated when it stands (1) in an accented syllable, or (2) before a laryngeal (except ח), or (3) after the preposition ל.

Note.—Assimilation is indicated by a Dågěš-fŏrtē in the following consonant, which, however, is rejected from final consonants (§ **14. 1**).

40. Rejection

1. *a.* (נ)שֵׂאת (19:9); (נ)גֹשׁ־ (4:11); (ל)קַחַת (4:12); (נ)תֵת (4:7).

b. (י)לֶדֶת (4:2); (י)דַע (20:7); (י)דַעַת (2:9); (י)דֵעַ (11:31); (י)לֶכֶת.

---

[1] Num. 7:89.   [2] Isa. 44:3.   [3] Ex. 25:8.   [4] Num. 14:3.

c. נַחְנוּ (42:11) *for* אֲנַחְנוּ; אָכַל [1] *probably for* מַאֲכָל.

2. יְהַבְדֵּל (1:7) *for* יַבְדֵּל; לְהָאוֹר (1:5) *for* לָאוֹר.

3. הָיִי (2:10) *for* הָיָה (3:3); תְּמוּתוּן (42:20) *but* תָּמוּתוּ.

The consonants most liable to rejection are the laryngeals א and ה, the dentals ל and נ, and the vowel-letters ו and י. These are often rejected:

1. From the beginning of a word when there is no vowel beneath to sustain them,

　　a. In the case of נ of verbs פ״נ (§ 78.) and of ל in לְקַח in the Ḳăl Imv. and Infinitive Construct.

　　b. In the case of ו or י of verbs פ״ו in the same forms.

　　c. In a few isolated cases.

2. From the middle of a word when preceded only by a Sʰᵉwâ.

3. From the end of a word, by ordinary attrition, as in the case of ן of the plural ending וּן; and of a final י in verbs ל״ה (§ 82.).

　　Note 1.—On the rejection of א and ה, see also § 43.

　　Note 2.—On the rejection of ו and י, see also § 44.

41.　Addition, Transposition, Commutation

1. אֶתְנַן [6]; אֶשְׂכָּל [5]; אַזְכָּרָה [4]; אֶזְרוֹעַ [3] *and* זְרוֹעַ [2].

2. נְתִשְׁחֲוֶה *for* נִשְׁתַּחֲוֶה [8]; הִתְשַׁמֵּר *for* הִשְׁתַּמֵּר [7].

3. *a.* הִתְצַיֵּד *for* הִצְטַיֵּד [10]; הִתְצַדֵּק *for* הִצְטַדֵּק [9].

　　b. עָשׂוּ [12] *for* עָשׂוּי; וְצַר *for* קַיָּם [11] *for* קוּם; וְצַר (2:8) *for* יָצַר.

1. The *addition* of a letter sometimes takes place at the beginning of a word to avoid harshness in pronunciation, as in the case of א, called prosthetic, when used in the formation of nouns.

2. The *transposition* of letters, of frequent occurrence in the province of the lexicon, occurs in the grammar only in the case of ת of the Hiθpăʻēl of verbs when it would stand before a sibilant fricative.

---

[1] Ex. 3 : 2.　　　[2] Ex. 6 : 6.　　　[3] Jer. 32 : 21.　　　[4] Lev. 2 : 2.
[5] Gen. 14 : 13.　　[6] Deut. 23 : 19.　　[7] Mic. 6 : 16.　　　[8] Gen. 22 : 5.
[9] Gen. 44 : 16.　　[10] Josh. 9 : 12.　　[11] Ruth 4 : 7.　　　[12] Ex. 3 : 16.

3. The *commutation* of letters, of frequent occurrence in the province of the lexicon, occurs in the grammar in the case of

a. ת and ט in the Hiθpăʻēl stem.

b. ו and י in פ"ו, middle-vowel and ל"ה forms (see § 44. 1. *a—d*).

42. The Peculiarities of Laryngeals

1. *a.* הָרָקִיעַ (1:7); הָאֲדָמָה (1:25); הָעוֹף (1:22); וַתֵּרָאֶה (1:9).

   b. מְרַחֶפֶת (1:2); הַהוּא (2:12); הַחַיָּה (1:21); הַחֹשֶׁךְ (1:4); וּפָעַל.

2. *a.* נַעֲשֶׂה (1:26); לַעֲבֹד (2:5); יַעֲלֶה (2:6); וַיִּרָא (1:4); יַעֲזֹב־ (2:24).

   b. יִפַּח (2:7); יִטַּע (2:8); יִצְמַח (2:9); יֵדַע (4:25); [קְטַח].

   c. נֶחְמָד (2:9); יֶחְזַק (41:56); תֶּחְדַּל; הֶעֱבַדְתַּנִי.

   d. רְקִיעַ (1:29); מַזְרִיעַ (1:11); רָקִיעַ (1:6); רוּחַ (1:2); (1:15).

3. *a.* שְׁאָלָה from šăʼălă; אֱלֹהִים (1:1) from ʼĭlâh; חֱלִי from hŏlĭ.

   b. עֲבֹד (2:5); עֲשׂוֹת (2:4); אֱמֹר (1:22); הֱיוֹת (2:18); *cf.* וְהָיָה (12:2).

   נַעֲשֶׂה (1:26); יַעֲלֶה (2:6); אֶעֱשֶׂה (2:18); פָּעֳלֶךָ; [הֶעֳטַל].

Remarks.— יַהַרְגֻהוּ (2:9); נֶחְמָד (2:24); יַעֲזֹב־ but (2:2) יִשְׁבֹּת; וְהַעֲמַדְתָּ but (4:8); הֶעֱמִיד and הֶעֱמַדְתָּ for יַהַרְגֻהוּ.

The laryngeals, in the order of their strength beginning with the weakest, are א, ע, ה, ח. ר shares some of their characteristics. They have the following peculiarities:

1. They refuse to be doubled (*i. e.*, to receive Dăğēš-fŏrtē). But here a distinction must be made between,

   a. א and ר, which entirely reject the doubling, and require a strengthening of the preceding vowel (§ 75. 1. *a*); and

---

¹ Deut. 23 : 23.   ² Isa. 43 : 24.   ³ Ex. 3 : 22.   ⁴ Deut. 28 : 61.

⁵ Ruth 2 : 12.   ⁶ Num. 5 : 18, 30.   ⁷ Ps. 31 : 9.   ⁸ Num. 3 : 6; 8 : 13

b. ע, ה, and ח, of which ע sometimes, ה and ח nearly always, receive a so-called Dåğeš-fŏrtē *implied*, and allow a preceding vowel to remain short.

2. They take, particularly before them, the *a*-vowels; hence,

a. The vowel — (ă) is chosen instead of — (ĭ) or — (ĕ), especially when ă was the original vowel.

b. The vowel — (ă) is chosen instead of — (ē) or — (ō), especially when ă was a collateral form.

c. The vowel — (ĕ), arising by deflection from ă, is chosen for the sake of dissimilarity.

d. The vowel — steals in between a heterogeneous long vowel and a final laryngeal as an aid in pronunciation. This — is called Păθăḥ-*furtive;* it is a mere transition-sound and does not make a syllable. It disappears when the laryngeal ceases to be final.

Note 1.—The letter ר (1) does not receive Dåğeš-fŏrtē, and (2) often shows a preference for —, and is consequently frequently classed for convenience with the laryngeals.

Note 2.—A final א is not a consonant, nor is final ה, unless it contain Măppîḳ (§ **16.** 1). *Point placed in final ה when used as a consonant + not as vowel*

3. They have a decided preference for compound Šᵉwâ. Hence there is found under laryngeals,

a. A compound Šᵉwâ, rather than a simple Šᵉwâ, in the place of an original vowel; and in this case the compound Šᵉwâ of the class to which the original vowel belonged, is used.

b. An *inserted* compound Šᵉwâ for facilitating the pronunciation; and here,

> (1) an initial laryngeal takes —, except in the case of א, and of ה and ח in the verbs הָיָה and חָיָה, which prefer —;
>
> (2) a medial laryngeal takes that Šᵉwâ which corresponds to the preceding vowel.

Remark 1.—Thus where in *strong* forms there is found a silent Šᵉwâ, in *laryngeal* forms there is usually found a compound Šᵉwâ as a helping-vowel, which does not affect the syllabification.

Remark 2.—Under the strong laryngeals, especially ה, the use of the compound Šᵉwâ for the facilitation of pronunciation is not so general.

Remark 3.—When a compound Šᵉwâ would stand before a simple Šᵉwâ, the former always gives way to a vowel (§ 36.).

Remark 4.—The combination ⸗ ⸗ often yields to ⸗ ⸗, when removed to a distance from the tone.

43. The Weakness of א and ה

1. *a.* בָּרָא (1:1); יִקְרָא (1:5); תּוֹצֵא (1:24).

b. רְאָשִׁים (2:10) *for* רָאשִׁים; רֵאשִׁית (1:1) *for* רֵאשִׁית; לֵאמֹר (1:22) *for* לֵאמֹר; לִקְרֹאת (15:10) *for* לִקְרַאת; יַאֲמֶר (1:3) *for* יֹאמֶר; כֵּאֱלֹהִים (3:5) *for* כֵּאלֹהִים.

Remarks.—יְרֵשִׁית; וָאֹכֵל (3:12) *for* אֹכֵל; חֶטְא[1]; וַיִּרָא (1:4); רֵאשִׁית *for* רֵאשִׁית.

2. *a.* בַּיּוֹם; לְהַחֲשֵׁךְ (1:5) *for* לַחֲשֵׁךְ; לְהָאוֹר (1:5) *for* לָאוֹר (1:18).

b. תְּהֵרָאֶה (1:9) *for* תֵּרָאֶה; יְהַבְדֵּל (1:7) *for* יַבְדֵּל.

c. אֹתוֹ (2:3) בְּהוֹ (1:11) *for* בּוֹ; לְמִינָהוּ (1:11) *for* לְמִינוֹ; אֹתָהוּ *for* אֹתוֹ.

The letters א and ה, being exceedingly weak, not only occasion change, but likewise suffer change:

1. א loses its consonantal power and is said *to quiesce* or *to be silent*,

a. Always, when it stands at the end of a word; here belong all forms of a ל״א character.

b. Often, when it stands in the middle of a word; then,

(1) a preceding vowelless consonant receives its vowel;

(2) or, it loses its compound Šᵉwâ after a preceding vowel. The Šᵉwâ disappears as soon as א quiesces and the preceding short vowel is strengthened in compensation for the loss of the א.

Remark 1.—A final א, preceded by a simple Šᵉwâ is otiose.

---

[1] Deut. 15 : 9.　　　[2] Deut. 11 : 12.

Remark 2.—A quiescent א is frequently elided from the middle of a word.

2. The consonant ה at the end of a word is always distinguished from the vowel-letter ה by the presence of a Măppîḳ (§ 16. 1). But on account of its weakness it is often entirely lost, *a dot in ה when used as consonant*

a. In the case of the article after an inseparable preposition (§ 47. 4).

b. In Hĭf'îl, Hŏf'ăl and Hĭθpă'ēl verbal forms after a preformative of gender or person.

c. From between two vowels, which then contract.

Note.—The ה of ל"ה verbs and nouns (§ 82.) is *always* a vowel-letter and has no connection with the ה here considered.

44. The Weakness of ו and י

1. *a.* יֶלֶד (4:23) *for* וֶלֶד (*cf.* וָלָד 11:30); יָשַׁב [*cf.* יֵשֶׁב (4:16)] *for* וְשֶׁב.

b. קֶים[1]; יִתְיַלְּדוּ[2] *but cf.* הִתְוַדֵּע (45:1).

c. יִרְבְּין; עָשׂוֹתָ *for* עָשִׂיתָ *for* עָשׂוּי[3].

d. יוֹצֵר (2:7) *for* יִיצֵר; יוֹשָׁן (2:21) *for* יִישָׁן.

2. *a.* דַּעַת (3:22) *for* וְדַע; צֵא (8:16) *for* וְצֵא; יֵצֵא (4:16) *for* יוֹצֵא.

b. הָיָה (2:10)=hâyå; יֵעָלֶה (2:6)=yǎ'ălê.

הִשְׁקָה (2:6)=hĭšḳå; יִהְיֶה (1:29)=yĭhyê.

The semi-vowels, or vowel-consonants, ו and י, occasion a very large number of changes:

1. *Commutation of ו into י takes place,*

a. Almost always at the beginning of a word, the exceptions being very few.

b. Frequently in the Pĭ'ēl of middle-vowel verbs, and generally in פ"ן verbs after הִת of the Hĭθpă'ēl.

---

[1] Ruth 4 : 7.   [2] Num. 1 : 18.   [3] Ex. 3 : 16.   [4] Deut. 8 : 13.

c. Whenever it is retained as the third radical in verbs ל״ה,
both when final and when medial (§ **82.** 3).

d. When it would follow *i* in a closed syllable, as in the Ḳǎl Imperfect of verbs פ״ן which have a פ״י treatment (§ **80.**).

2. *Elision takes place,*

a. Of an initial ן when supported only by Šᵉwâ, as in certain
פ״ן Inf's Construct and Imv's (§ **80.**); and also when in the Ḳǎl
Impf. the ן, following ĭ, does not go over to י, according to 1. *d* above.

b. Of a final ן and י in verbs called ל״ה, the original vowel following them having been previously lost; in this case the vowel preceding, nearly always ǎ, is rounded to â in Perfects, and becomes ê in
Imperfects and Participles (see for details, § **82.**).

3. *a.* נוֹדֵע (41:21); תּוֹצֵא (1:11) *for* תַּוְצֵא; תֵּיטִיב (4:7) *for*
תֵּיטִיב.

אַפֶּיךָ (3:19). חַיֶּיךָ (3:14) *for* ḥǎy-yǎy-kâ; תַּעֲשֶׂינָה¹;

b. עֹשֶׂה (6:14) = ᵃśê *for* עֲשֹׂי; פְּנֵי (1:2) = pᵉnê *for* פְּנָי.

c. יִיצֶר (2:7) יוֹשֵׁן=יִישֵׁן *for* יִישֵׁן (2:21); הוּסַד; הוֹסַד² *for* הוּסַד;
for יִיצֶר.

4. *a.* וּנְקֵבָה (1:27); לִמְקְוֵה (1:10); וּמִלְאוּ (1:22); וּבֵין (1:4);

b. (יִשְׁתַּחֲוֶה) יִשְׁתַּחֲוֻ³ *for* יִשְׁתַּחֲוֻ (18:2); יִשְׁתַּחוּ *for* תְּהוּ (1:2); תְּהוּ.

c. פָּנָיו (4:5); אַפֵּיהוּ *for* אַפָּין (2:7); -תִּיהוּ; וּשְׁמַעְתָּיו⁴ *for* וּשְׁמַעְתָּיו.

5. *a.* יֵלֵךְ (4:26); יָדַע (4:1); יֵלֶד (4:18); יִיצֶר (2:8); יָקֻוּ (1:9);
וּבֹהוּ (1:2).

b. עָשֹׂוּ⁵; גֹּוּי⁶; see also the cases under 4. *c*, above.

c. שָׁלָוְתִּי⁷; חַוָּה (3:20); יֵלֶד (4:18).

3. *Contraction takes place,*

a. Of vowelless ן or י with a preceding ǎ, as

   (1) in the פ״ן Nif'ǎl and Hif'il (§ **80.**), and the פ״י Hif'il
       (§ **81.** 2);

---

¹ Deut. 1 : 44.   ² Ezra 3 : 11.
³ In these cases a helping — is inserted (§ **30.** *m*).   ⁴ Deut. 1 : 17.
⁵ Ex. 3 : 16.   ⁶ Deut. 4 : 7.   ⁷ Job 3 : 26.

(2) before נָה in לְּ"ה Imperfects and Imv's, and before הָ

and הָ in plural of nouns (§ 30. 5); here *ay* gives יִ_ (*ê*).

b. Of final ו or י with a preceding *a,* in forms that are closely tied to the following word, as

(1) in the Imperative of verbs לְ"ה (§ 82. 1. *f*);

(2) in the Construct plural ending יִ_ (= *ay*)(§ 108. 3. *b*).

c. Of ו or י with a preceding *u* or *i* respectively, when a consonant follows, as in the פ"ן Hŏph'ăl (§ 80. 3. *c*), and in the Ḳăl Impf. of פ"ו and פ"י verbs.

4. *Vocalization of* ו *to* וּ *takes place,*

a. At the beginning of a word in the case of the conjunction וּ (§ 49. 2).

b. At the end of a word, whenever ו would be preceded by a consonant, as

(1) in the case of לְ"ה (or לְ"ן) Seǧolates (§ 89. 2. *c*);

(2) in certain short forms of the imperfect. But

c. The reverse takes place, viz., change of וּ to ו, especially in the case of the suffix הֶן, when it is attached

(1) to verbal forms ending in a vowel, and

(2) to the plural ending used before suffixes, viz., יִ_, of which, however, the י is lost (being only orthographically retained), and the ă rounded to å (§ 108.) as an assimilation to the ו.

5. *The consonantal force of* ו *or* י *is retained,*

a. When as radicals they stand at the beginning of syllables.

b. When a heterogeneous vowel, except ă, precedes.

c. When they would receive Dåǧēš-fŏrtē (§ 86.), and in a few exceptional cases.

PART SECOND—ETYMOLOGY

VIII. Inseparable Particles

45. *The Article*

1. הַשָּׁמַיִם (1:1); הַמַּיִם (1:2); הַיַּבָּשָׁה (1:9); הַיּוֹם (1:14); הַלַּיְלָה (1:14).

2. הַחֹשֶׁךְ (1:4); הַחַיָּה (1:21); הַהוּא (2:12); הַהֹלֵךְ (2:14).

3. הָאָרֶץ (1:1); הָרָקִיעַ (1:7); הָעוֹף (1:22).

4. ⁴הֶעָוֹן; ³הֶהָרִים; ²הֶחָזָק; הֶחָג¹

Remark 1.—הַיְאֹרָה; ⁶הַיְאֹרָה *for* הַמְיַלֶּדֶת; ⁵הַמְיַלֶּדֶת *for*

Remark 2.—⁸הָעָם; הָהָר *for* ⁷הָהָר; הָאָרֶץ; הָאָרֶץ (1:1) *for* הָעָם *for*

Remark 3.—לָאוֹר (1:5) *for* הָאוֹר + לְ; לַחֹשֶׁךְ (1:5) *for* הַחֹשֶׁךְ + לְ.

1. The usual form of the Article is הַ with a Dåḡēš-fŏrtē in the following letter . . . . הַ•

2. Before the strong laryngeals ה and ח which may be doubled by implication (§ 42. 1. *b*), it is . . . . הַ

3. Before the weak laryngeal א and before ר, and generally before ע, which cannot be doubled (§ 42. 1. *a*), ־ is rounded to ־ָ . . . . הָ

4. Before חָ, and before an unaccented הָ, עָ, the ־ is deflected to ־ֶ (ĕ) for the sake of dissimilarity . . . . הֶ

Remark 1.—The Dåḡēš-fŏrtē of the Article may of course be omitted from vowelless consonants (§ **14. 2**).

Remark 2.—The words for *earth, mountain, people* irregularly change their vowel after the Article.

Remark 3.—The ה of the Article is elided after the prepositions בְּ, כְּ, לְ (§ **43. 2.** *a*) and the vowel is given to the preposition.

¹ 1 Kgs. 8:65.   ² Num. 13:18.   ³ Gen. 7:19.   ⁴ 1 Sam. 25:24.
⁵ Ex. 1:19.   ⁶ Ex. 1:22.   ⁷ Ex. 3:12.   ⁸ Gen. 14:16.

46. Hē Interrogative

1. אָכָלְתָּ‎ …. הֲמִן־הָעֵץ‎ (3:11); הֲשֹׁמֵר אָחִי אָנֹכִי‎ (4:9).

2. אִשָּׁה‎[1] הַאֵלֵךְ וְקָרָאתִי לָךְ‎ (30:15); הַמְעַט קַחְתֵּךְ אֶת־אִישִׁי‎

3. הֶאָמַר‎[2]; הֲהָיְתָה‎[3]; הַלְּבֶן מֵאָה שָׁנָה יִוָּלֵד‎ (17:17).

In direct, and likewise indirect, interrogation, a particle is used called Hē Interrogative:

1. It is usually written with Hâṭēf Pǎθǎḥ .... הֲ
2. Before vowelless consonants, and laryngeals, it is written הַ
3. Before laryngeals with ◌ָ, it is written (§ 29. 4. e) .... הֶ

while rarely, especially with letters which have simple Šᵉwâ, it is written with Dâğēš-fŏrtē separative (§ 15. 4) .... הַּ‎·

Note.—Frequently no sign of interrogation appears; then the context must be depended upon to reveal the interrogative character of the statement.

47. The Inseparable Prepositions

1. בְּרֵאשִׁית‎ (1:14); לְהַבְדִּיל‎ (1:11); לְמֵינוֹ‎ (1:6); בְּתוֹךְ‎ (1:1);

2. כִּדְמוּתֵנוּ‎ (1:18); לִמְשֹׁל‎ (1:15); לִמְאוֹרֹת‎ (1:14); בִּרְקִיעַ‎ (1:26).

3. לַעֲשׂוֹת‎ (2:3); לַעֲבֹד‎ (2:5); לֵאמֹר‎ for לֵאמֹר‎ (1:22); בְּחִרִי‎[4];

4. לָאוֹר‎ (1:5); לַחֹשֶׁךְ‎ (1:5); לָרְקִיעַ‎ (1:7); לַיַּבָּשָׁה‎ (1:10); בַּיּוֹם‎ (1:18).

5. לַמָּיִם‎ (1:6); לָכֶם‎ (1:29); לָדַעַת‎ (3:22).

Remark 1.—לַאדֹנָי‎ (18:30, 32); כֵּאלֹהִים‎ (3:5); לֵאלֹהִים‎ (17:7, 8).

Remark 2.—לַיהוָֹה‎ (4:3) for לַאדֹנָי‎; proper writing לַיהוָֹה‎.

Three prepositions, לְ, כְּ, בְּ‎, are always prefixed to the words

---

[1] Ex. 2:7.　　　[2] Job 34:31.　　　[3] Joel 1:2.　　　[4] Ex. 11:8.

which they govern. Their vowel was, originally, ◌ֲ; but now they are found written:

1. Ordinarily, with simple Š°wâ reduced from ă . . . . ◌ְ

2. Before consonants having simple Š°wâ, with ĭ attenuated from ă . . . . ◌ִ

3. Before laryngeals having compound Š°wâ, with the corresponding short vowel . . . . ◌ֲ, ◌ֱ, ◌ֳ (ŏ)

4. Before the Article, with the vowel of the Article . . . . ◌ַ or ◌ָ (å)

5. Before a tone-syllable, sometimes with tone-long . . . . ◌ָ (å)

Remark 1.—The א of אֲדֹנָי LORD and אֱלֹהִים GOD loses its consonantal force after the prepositions (§ 43. 1. *b*).

Remark 2.—The word יְהוָה, which is written יְהוָֹה, *i. e.*, with the vowels of אֲדֹנָי, rather than יֱהוִֹה as it should be written, appears with the preposition as לַיהוָֹה (to be pronounced לַאדֹנָי).

Note 1.—The original ◌ֲ of the prepositions is usually reduced to ◌ְ, or rounded to ◌ָ (å); it is retained before laryngeals with ◌ֲ, but assimilated to ◌ֲ before ◌ְ, and to ◌ָ (ŏ) before ◌ֲ.

Note 2.—For prepositions with pronominal suffixes, see § 51. 3, 4.

48.　*The Preposition* מִן

1. מִקֶּדֶם (2:8); מִן־תַּחַת (1:7); מִתַּחַת *for* מִן־תַּחַת (2:6); מִן־הָאָרֶץ *for* מִן־קֶדֶם.

2. מִן־אִישׁ *for* מֵאִישׁ (2:23); מִן־עַל; מֵעַל (1:7) *for* מִן־עַל (6:14); מִחוּץ.

The preposition מִן *from*, is really the construct state of an ancient noun and is written separately, chiefly before the Article; elsewhere it is *prefixed* and appears:

1. Usually with its נ assimilated (§ 39. 1) . . . . מִ

2. Before ה, rarely with Dåğēš-fŏrtē implied (§ 42. 1. *b*) . . . . מִ

but before other laryngeals, with ◌ִ lowered (§ 36. 1) . . . . מֵ

Note.—On the form of מִן before pronominal suffixes, see § 51. 5.

49. Wâw Conjunctive

1. וְאֵת (1:1); וְהָאָרֶץ (1:2); וְלַחֹשֶׁךְ (1:5); וְשָׁנִים (1:14); וְשָׁמַיִם (2:4).

2. וּלְמִקְוֵה (1:10); וּבְעוֹף (1:26); וּמָלְאוּ (1:22); וּבֵין (1:4); וּנְקֵבָה (1:27).

3. וַאֲנִי (6:17); וַעֲשִׂיתֶם[1]; וֶהְיֵה; וְהָיָה for (12:2); וַעֲשֵׂה (24:12).

4. וּבְהוּ (1:2); וְרֶמֶשׂ (1:24); וְרַע (2:9); וְנָד (4:12).

The conjunction *and*, originally וְ, is now found written:

—1. Ordinarily with simple Šᵉwâ (§ 32. 2. R.) . . . .   וְ

— 2. Before בּ, מ, פ (§ 44. 4), and vowelless consonants . . . . .   וּ

3. Before laryngeals having compound Šᵉwâ, with the corresponding short vowel . . . . ־ֱ, ־ֲ, ־ֳ (ŏ)

— 4. Before a tone-syllable, sometimes with tone-long ־ָ (§ 31. 1. *c*) . . . . (å)

Note 1.—וְ with יְהִי gives וִיהִי (1:6).

Note 2.—On וַ‧, the strengthened form of וְ, which is called Wâw Conversive and is used with the Imperfect, see § 70.

_____

[1] Deut. 4 : 6, 16, 23, 25.

IX. Pronouns

50. *The Personal Pronoun*

1. The following are the forms of the Personal Pronoun:

He	הוּא	*They* (m.)	הֵמָּה, הֵם
She	הִיא	*They* (f.)	הֵנָּה, הֵן
Thou (m.)	אַתָּה	*Ye* (m.)	אַתֶּם
Thou (f.)	אַתְּ	*Ye* (f.)	אַתֵּנָה, אַתֵּן
I	אֲנִי, אָנֹכִי	*We*	נַחְנוּ, אֲנַחְנוּ

2. The following are pausal forms:

אֲנַחְנוּ ; אָתָּה *and* אָתָּה ; אָנִי, אָנֹכִי

3. The following remarks on the forms of the Pronouns are to be noted:

a. הִיא *she* is written הוּא in the Pentateuch, except eleven times.

b. אַתָּה *thou* (m.) is written five times defectively אַתְ.

c. אַתְּ *thou* (f.) was originally אַתִּי or אַתִּין; seven times Kᵉθîv has אַתִּי, which would be pronounced ăttî.

d. אֲנִי *I* (c.) is more common than the longer form אָנֹכִי.

e. הֵנָּה *they* (f.) is more common than הֵן, the latter occurring only with prefixes.

f. אַתֵּן *ye* (f.) occurs but once,[1] אַתֵּנָה, but four times.[2]

g. אֲנַחְנוּ *we* is the usual form, נַחְנוּ occurring but six times,[3] and a form אֲנוּ but once.[4]

Note 1.—The הָ— which appears in several of the forms was perhaps originally demonstrative, but has lost its force.

Note 2.—The following comparative table of the personal Pronouns in the more important Semitic languages will be of interest:

---

[1] Ezek. 34 : 31.   [2] Gen. 31 : 6; Ezek. 13 : 11, 20; 34 : 17.
[3] Gen. 42 : 11; Ex. 16 : 7, 8; Num. 32 : 32; 2 Sam. 17 : 12; Lam. 3 : 42.
[4] Jer. 42 : 6 (Kᵉθîv).

Arabic.	Assyrian.	Aramaic.	Hebrew.
huwă	šû	הוּא	הוּא
hiyă	šî	הִיא	הִיא
anta	atta	{ אנתה / אַנְתְּ or אַתְּ / אנתי }	אַתָּה
anti	atti		אַתְּ
ană	anāku	אֲנָא	אָנֹכִי
hum	šûnu	הִמּוֹ, אֲנוּן, הִמּוֹן	הֵמָּה, הֵם
hunna	šîna	אִנִּין, אֲנוּן	הֵנָּה, הֵן
antum	attuna	אַתּוּן, אַנְתּוּן	אַתֶּם
antunna	attina	אַתֵּין	אַתֵּנָה, אַתֵּן
naḥnu	anīni	אֲנַחְנָא	נַחְנוּ, אֲנַחְנוּ

Note 3.—We may note here also the expression פְּלֹנִי אַלְמֹנִי, equivalent to *a certain one*, and used as an indefinite pronoun.[1]

51. *Pronominal Suffixes*

Tabular View

1. Separate Forms.	2. With אֵת.	3. With בְּ and לְ	4. With כְּ.	5. With מִן.
		Singular		
3 m. הוּ	אֹתוֹ	בּוֹ	כָּמוֹהוּ	מִמֶּנּוּ
3 f. הָ	אֹתָהּ	בָּהּ	כָּמוֹהָ	מִמֶּנָּה
2 m. ךְ	אֹתְךָ, אֹתָךְ	בְּךָ, בָּךְ	כָּמוֹךָ	מִמְּךָ
				מִמֶּךָ
2 f. ךְ	אֹתָךְ	בָּךְ	—	מִמֵּךְ
1 c. נִי or ־ִי	אֹתִי	בִּי	כָּמוֹנִי	מִמֶּנִּי
		Plural		
3 m. הֶם or הָם	אֹתָם, אֶתְהֶם ם	בָּם, בָּהֶם	כָּמוֹהֶם, כָּהֶם	מֵהֶם
3 f. הֶן or ן	אֶתְהֶן, אֹתָן	כָּהֶן	כָּהֵנָּה	מֵהֶן
				מֵהֵנָּה
2 m. כֶם	אֶתְכֶם	בָּכֶם	כָּמוֹכֶם, כָּכֶם	מִכֶּם
2 f. כֶן	—	בָּכֶן	—	מִכֶּן
1 c. נוּ	אֹתָנוּ	בָּנוּ	כָּמוֹנוּ	מִמֶּנּוּ

---

[1] *Cf.* Ruth 4 : 1; 2 Kgs. 6 : 8.

When a pronoun is to be governed by a verb, a noun or a preposition, a shortened form must be used:

1. The "separate forms," given above, are the fragments of the pronouns which are thus used. They are attached directly to nominal and verbal forms ending in a vowel, but a so-called connecting-vowel is employed with forms ending in a consonant.

a. The suffixes כֶם, כֶן, הֶם and הֶן always receive the accent and are termed *heavy;* all others are *light.*

b. יָ is used with nouns; נִי with verbs.

c. הֶם and הֶן are used with nouns in both singular and plural, but chiefly with the plural; ם and ן are used with verbs and singular nouns.

Note.—On the union of verbs with suffixes, see § **71.**; on the union of nouns with suffixes, see §§ **108, 109.**

2. When for any reason it is impossible, or undesirable, to attach the suffix directly to a governing verb, it may be written in connection with אֵת, the sign of the definite accusative, which, however, except before כֶם, assumes the form אֹת or אֹות ('ôθ).

3. The prepositions בְּ and לְ restore and round their original ─ before the suffixes (except יָ and ךְ); this vowel

a. Contracts with הֶן and forms וֹ (ô), the ה falling out and å contracting with û; with ךְ the final å is dropped, the ă of the preposition is rounded to å, and ה is preserved as a consonant with măppîḳ, the resulting form being הָ֫; but elsewhere,

b. It appears as å either before or under the tone.

Note.—While either בָּם or בָּהֶם may be used, only לָהֶם is found.

4. Between the preposition כְּ and the suffixes, there is generally found an inserted syllable מוֹ. This syllable is found in poetry also after בְּ and לְ (but not when suffixes are added).

5. The preposition מִן before most of the suffixes takes a special form; in some cases,

a. The final ן is assimilated: מִמֶּנִּי *for* מִמֶּנִּי; מִמְּךָ *for* מִמֶּנְךָ; מִמֶּנּוּ *(from us) for* מִמֶּנְנוּ.

b. The consonant of the suffix is assimilated backwards and represented in נ: מִמֶּנּוּ (*from him*) *for* מִמֶּנְהוּ; מִמֶּנָּה *for* מִמֶּנְהָ.

Note 1.—The ־ֶ in מִמֶּנּוּ, etc., is deflected from ־ִ (§ 29. 4).

Note 2.—Many variant forms, besides those given, are found, especially in poetry.

52. The Demonstrative Pronoun

1. זֶה *this* (m.)	{ זֹאת *this* (f.)	(אֵל) אֵלֶּה *these* (m. or f.)
	{ זוֹ, זֹה *this* (f.)	{ הֵמָּה or הֵם *those* (m.)
2. הוּא *that* (m.)	הִיא *that* (f.)	{ הֵנָּה or הֵן *those* (f.)

1. *a.* זֶה; *cf.* זוֹ rounded from זַי.

b. זֹאת = zô'θ, for zâ'θ (§ 30. 6), *i. e.*, זַי with feminine ending ת, *cf.* the shorter forms זוֹ, זֹה.

c. אֵלֶּה has Dåğēš-förtē *firmative;* אֵל occurs only eight times, and then always in the Pentateuch and with the article.

2. The personal pronouns of the third person are used as remote demonstratives.

3. The forms הַלָּזֶה (*masc.*), הַלָּזוּ (*fem.*), and הַלָּז (*masc.* and *fem.*), *this*, represent a stronger demonstrative, appearing only in the singular. They are not commonly used,—the first occurring twice,[1] the second, once,[2] the third seven times.[3]

53. The Relative Particle

1. אֲשֶׁר *who, which, that.*

2. ־שֶׁ, sometimes ־שַׁ.

3. זוּ.

1. The more frequent relative was originally a noun in the construct state meaning *place:*

a. It is indeclinable.

b. It is really a mere sign of relation, indicating the presence of some kind of a subordinate clause, the precise nature of which is indicated by other words, or by the general context.

---

[1] Gen. 24 : 65; 37 : 19.   [2] Ezek. 36 : 35.
[3] Judg. 6 : 20; 1 Sam. 14 : 1; 17 : 26; 2 Kgs. 4 : 25; 23 : 17; Dan. 8 : 16; Zech. 2 : 8.

2. ·שֶׁ, or ·שַׁ is in no way connected with אֲשֶׁר, but is a distinct pronoun. It is found:

    a. Exclusively in the Song of Songs, and frequently in Ecclesiastes.

    b. Occasionally in other books, as Judges, 2 Kings, 1 Chronicles, Job, and the later Psalms.

3. זוּ is in reality a demonstrative (*cf.* זֶה); but its chief use is as a relative (*cf.* the similar usage of the English *that*, Greek ὅς, etc.). It is indeclinable.

54. *The Interrogative Pronoun*

1. מִי *who?*   מָה *what?*

2. *a.* מַה־יִּקְרָא (2:19); מַה־זֹּאת (3:13); מַה־שְּׁמוֹ (Ex. 3:13).

  b. מַה־הִיא[1]; מַה־הוּא; מֶה חָטָאתִי (31:36).

  c. מָה הִנֵּה[3]; מָה רְאִיתֶם[4]; *also* מָה־אֵלֶּה (21:29).

  d. מֶה־חָדֵל[5]; מֶה־חָטָאתִי (20:9); מֶה עָשִׂיתָ (4:10).

1. מִי refers to persons; מָה, to things.

2. מָה is variously pointed, according to the character of the consonant which follows:

    a. Before consonants which can be doubled, it is . . . . ·מַה

    b. Before strong laryngeals (ה and ח), it is . . . . מַה

    c. Before weak laryngeals (א, ע, and ר) it is . . . . מָה

    d. Before laryngeals with ָ , it is . . . . מֶה

Note 1.—The Dăgēš-fŏrtē following מָה is compensative (§15.1), arising from the assimilation of ה which was a consonant.

Note 2.—The forms מֶה and מָה are sometimes found before other letters than laryngeals.

Note 3.—In the majority of cases מָה is connected with the following word by Măḳḳēf, and with זֶה often forms a single word, מַזֶּה.

Note 4.—By means of אִי (*where?*) prefixed to the demonstrative זֶה or זֹאת, another interrogative is formed.[6]

---

[1] Num. 16:11.   [2] Num. 13:18.   [3] Zech. 1:9.   [4] Judg. 9:48.
[5] Ps. 39:5.   [6] *Cf.* Jer. 5:7; Eccles. 11:6; 1 Kgs. 13:12.

X. The Verb

55. Roots

1. בְּרָא (1:1); מִתְהַלֵּךְ (3:8) *from* בָּדַל; מַבְדִּיל (1:6) *from* בָּדַל;

הַמְטִיר; הֵלֵךְ; הֲקִימֹתִי (9:17) *from* קָם; שָׁבַת (2:3); הֵלֵךְ;

מָטָר (2:5) *from* תִּפָּקַחְנָה; (3:7) *from* פָּקַח.

2. בְּרָא (1:1) *he created;* שָׁבַת (2:3) *he rested;* לָקַח (2:22)
   he took.

   הָלַךְ (3:8) *he walked;* שָׁמַע (3:17) *he heard;* פָּקַח (3:7) *he*
   opened.

3. מוּת (3:4) *to die,* מֵת *he died;* שִׂים (2:8) *to put,* שָׂם *he put.*

All words are derived from so-called roots; concerning these it may
be noted:

1. While there are a very few roots of *four* letters, most Hebrew
roots consist of three or two letters, called *radicals.*

2. The root is generally pronounced with the vowels of the third
person singular masculine of the Perfect tense (§ **57.** 3. N. 1), this
being the simplest of all verbal forms.

3. Biliteral roots of the middle-vowel classes are commonly pronounced with the vowel of the infinitive construct.

Note 1.—The root is not in itself a word; it exists solely in the
mind of the philologist. בְּרָא is a root, but the word is בָּרָא.

Note 2.—Many of the roots now appearing to be triliteral, were
once biliterals; their triliteral forms are a later development.

Note 3.—For many words there has as yet been found no root.

56. Classes of Verbs

1. *a.* קָדַשׁ (1:4); בָּדַל (1:18); מָשַׁל (2:24); דָּבַק (2:3); שָׁבַת
   (2:3).

b. עֹזֵב (2:24); הָרַג (4:8); רָחַף (1:2); זָרַע (1:11); שָׁלַח
(3:22).

c. נָתַן (1:17); יָצַר (2:7); בָּרָא (1:1); בָּנָה (Lam. 3:5).

2. *a.* סבב (2:11); חלל (4:26); חָנַן (33:5); גָּלְלוּ (29:3).

b. מוּת (3:4); בִּין[1]; קוּם (13:17); יָשִׂים (30:42).

Verbal roots vary in inflection according to the number and nature
of the consonants of which they are composed. They are therefore
classified as:

1. *Triliteral,* when composed of three consonants. These again
subdivide into three classes:

a. Strong verbs, *i. e.,* those containing no consonant which will
in any way affect the vowels usually employed in a given inflection.

b. Laryngeal verbs, *i. e.,* those containing one or more laryngeals,
which involve certain variations in vocalization from the so-called
strong verb.

c. Weak verbs, *i. e.,* those containing one or more consonants
which may suffer assimilation (נ__), contraction and elision (ו__ and
י__), or quiescence (א__). Such changes in the consonants, of
course, affect the vowels seriously.

2. *Biliteral,* when composed of two consonants. These subdivide
into two classes:

a. The so-called *'áyin-doubled* (ע״ע) verbs, in which the consonantal element of the root is emphasized in inflection.

b. The *middle-vowel* verbs, in which the vowel-element is emphasized.

57. Inflection

1. *a.* בָּרָא (1:1) *from* ברא; שָׁב (18:33) *from* שׁב; סֹב (Deut.
2:3) *from* סב.

b. וַיְקַדֵּשׁ (2:3) *from* קדשׁ; לָקַח (3:23) *from* לקח; יָלַד (4:26) *from* ילד; סוֹבֵב (2:13) *from* סב.

---
[1] Prov. 23 : 1.

הוּחַל; מַטַר *from* (2:5) הִמְטִיר; פקה *from* (3:5) וְנִפְקְחוּ *c.*
יָשַׁב *from* (Jer. 6:8) נוֹשְׁבָה; חָלַל *from* (4:26).

2. יֵשֵׁב (2:2) *he will rest;* שָׁמַעְתִּי (3:10) *I heard;* שָׁרְצוּ
(1:21) *they swarmed;* אָכַלְתָּ (3:11) *hast thou eaten?*
יָבֹא (4:3); (17:12) יָמוּל; *they were opened* (3:7) וַתִּפָּקַחְנָה.

3. יַהַרְגֵנוּ (4:8) *he will kill him;* תֹּאכְלֶנָּה (3:17) *thou shalt eat it.*

The inflection of a verb includes three things:

1. The formation of verb-stems, of which there are,

    a. The simple verb-stem, generally identical with the root.

    b. Verb-stems formed by strengthening the simple root in various ways, especially by doubling or repetition of one or more radicals.

    c. Verb-stems formed by the use of *prefixes.*

2. The addition to the verb-stem of affixes and prefixes for the indication of tense or mood, person, number, gender.

3. The various changes of the verbal forms, which take place when pronominal suffixes are attached as objects.

Note 1.—The Hebrew verb has for each stem (1) a Perfect tense, which indicates finished or completed action, (2) an Imperfect, which indicates unfinished action, (3) an Imperative (except in Passive stems), (4) two Infinitives, and (5) a Participle.

Note 2.—The Perfect and Imperfect, which may be called tenses, are inflected to distinguish number, person, and *gender.*

Note 3.—The Imperative is used only in the second person, masculine and feminine, singular and plural.

58. The Verb-Stems

1. בָּלַל (11:9). יָשַׁב¹; לָקַח (3:22); בָּרָא (1:1); שָׁ־בַת (2:3).

2. נִשְׁמַר *watch* נִכְקַל]; נִכְבַּד²; נָבְנָה⁴; נָבֹן (41:32); נָסַב³; נָשַׁב [one's self; נִשְׁפַּט *go to law one with another.*

---

¹ Jer. 30 : 18.   ² 2 Sam. 6 : 20.   ³ Num. 34 : 4.   ⁴ 1 Kgs. 6 : 7.

3. [קָטַל]; דִּבֶּר (12:4); מִלֵּא¹; כִּלָּה (18:33); בֵּרַךְ (24:1); שֵׁרֵשׁ uproot; שָׁרֵשׁ root; לִמֵּד teach; לָמֵד learn.

4. [קָטַל]; פֻּקַד²; קֹרָא³; מְבֹרָךְ⁴; לֻקַּח he was taken; לָקַח he took.

5. [הִקְטִיל]; הִפְקִיד (39:5); הֶחֱזִיק⁵; הֵקִים⁶; הֵסֵב⁷.

6. [הָקְטַל]; הֻפְקַד⁸; הֻגַּד⁹; הָמְלַךְ¹⁰; הֻשְׁלַךְ¹¹.

7. [הִתְקַטֵּל]; הִתְהַלֵּךְ (6:9); יִתְעַצֵּב (6:6); אֶשְׁתַּמֵּר¹².

הִטַּהֲרוּ¹⁴ for נִצְטַדָּק (44:16) נִתְצַדָּק; יִדַּכְּאוּ for יִתְדַּכְּאוּ¹³ הִטַּהֲרוּ for הִתְטַהֲרוּ.

There are in common use seven verb-stems, each representing a different aspect or development of the primary meaning of the verb.

1. The simple verb-stem is called *Ḳăl* (קַל), i. e., *light*, since it presents the verb in its simplest form, not encumbered with the additions characteristic of the other stems.

2. *a.* The Passive of the Ḳăl stem is called *Nǐf'ăl*.

Note.—In all stems other than the Ḳăl, the stem name is formed from the paradigm-verb used by the Arabic and the Jewish grammarians, viz., פָּעַל; thus the name of this stem = נִפְעַל.

b. The formal characteristic of this stem is the prefixed נ.

c. The meaning of the stem is usually passive, but it occurs also with its original *reflexive* force, and sometimes as *reciprocal*.

3. *a.* The intensive active stem is called *Pǐ'ēl* (triliteral) or *Pôlēl* (biliteral).

b. The formal characteristic of this stem is the doubling or repetition of the second radical of the root.

c. The stem is used as an intensive of the Ḳăl, and expresses various shades of meaning such as (1) intensity, (2) repetition, (3)

---

¹ Ex. 35 : 35. ² Ex. 38 : 21. ³ Isa. 48 : 8. ⁴ Num. 22 : 6.
⁵ Judg. 7 : 8. ⁶ Josh. 4 : 9. ⁷ 2 Kgs. 16 : 18. ⁸ Jer. 6 : 6.
⁹ Dan. 9 : 1. ¹⁰ Josh. 9 : 24. ¹¹ Dan. 8 : 11. ¹² Ps. 18 : 24.
¹³ Job 5 : 4. ¹⁴ Ezr. 6 : 20.

causation, and (4) a privative idea, in the case of Pï'ēls from nominal forms.

4. *a.* The intensive passive stem is called *Pŭ'ăl* (triliteral) or *Pôlăl* (biliteral).

b. The formal characteristic of this root is the doubling or repetition of the second radical, with ŭ or ô under the first radical.

c. The regular usage of this stem is as a passive of the Pï'ēl; but sometimes it serves as passive of the Ķăl.

5. *a.* The active causative stem is called *Hĭf'ĭl.*

b. The formal characteristic of this stem is the prefix ‗הַ, which undergoes modification in inflection.

c. This stem serves as a causative of the Ķăl.

6. *a.* The passive causative stem is called *Hŏf'ăl.*

b. The formal characteristic is the prefix ‗הָ, which undergoes change in inflection.

c. The usage of this stem is as a passive of the Hĭf'ĭl.

7. *a.* The intensive reflexive stem is called *Hĭθpă'ēl.*

b. The formal characteristic of this stem is the prefix ‗הִת, joined to the Pï'ēl stem.

c. This stem is used primarily as a reflexive of the Pï'ēl stem; but it occurs also with (1) a reciprocal, (2) a passive force, and (3) the force of the indirect Greek middle.

Note.—The ת of the prefix is always *transposed* when it would stand before ס, שׂ or שׁ; it is transposed and partly *assimilated*, becoming ט, when before צ; and it is completely assimilated before ד, ט or ת.

XI. The Triliteral Verb

A. THE STRONG VERB

59. General View of the Triliteral Verb-Stems

TABLE

	Original Form.	Form appearing in the Perfect.	Name.	Force.	Characteristics.
1.	קְטֹל	קָטַל	Ḳăl	Simple Root meaning	None
2.	נִקְטֹל	נִקְטַל	Nïf'ăl	Reflexive, Reciprocal, Passive	נ
3.	קַטֵּל	קִטֵּל	Pï'ēl	Intensive Active	Dăǧēš-förtē in 2d radical
4.	קֻטַּל	קֻטַּל	Pŭ'ăl	Intensive Passive	Dăǧēš-förtē and ֻ
5.	הַקְטֵל	הִקְטִיל	Hïf'ïl	Causative Active	הַ (הֶ)
6.	הַקְטֵל	הָקְטַל	Hŏf'ăl	Causative Passive	הָ (הֻ)
7.	הִתְקַטֵּל	הִתְקַטֵּל	Hïθpă'ēl	Reflexive, Reciprocal	הִת and Dăǧēš-förtē

REMARKS

1. An original penultimate — is attenuated to —, in Nïf'ăl, Pï'ēl, and Hïf'ïl.

2. An ultimate — is lowered to —, in some Pï'ēl, Hïf'ïl and Hïθpă'ēl forms.

3. An ultimate — is anomalously lengthened to ◌ִי, in some Hïf'ïl forms.

4. An original penultimate — is deflected to — (ŏ) in the Hŏf'ăl.

NOTES[1]

1. Only 6 verbs out of about 1400 have all seven stems, viz.: בָּקַע,
גָּלָה, חָלָה, יָדַע, יָלַד, פָּקַד.

2. 379 verbs are found in Ḳăl only; 40 in Nĭf'ăl only; 68 in Pĭ'ēl
only; 11 in Pŭ'ăl only; 58 in Hĭf'îl only; 6 in Hŏf'ăl only; 19 in
Hĭθpä'ēl only.

3. In all, 1090 verbs have a Ḳăl stem; 433, a Nĭf'ăl stem; 405, a
Pĭ'ēl stem; 188, a Pŭ'ăl stem; 503, a Hĭf'îl stem; 104, a Hŏf'ăl stem;
177, a Hĭθpä'ēl stem.

60. The Ḳăl Perfect (Active)
TABULAR VIEW

1. *He killed*   קָטַל   the simple verb-stem.

2. *She killed*   קָטַל = קָטְלָה with הָ (originally תְ_),
                                  the usual feminine sign.

3. *Thou* (m.) *killedst* קָטַל = קָטַלְתָּ with תָּ; cf. the pronoun
                                  אַתָּה *thou* (m.).

4. *Thou* (f.) *killedst* קָטַל = קָטַלְתְּ with תְּ; cf. the pronoun אַתְּ
                                  thou (f.).

5. *I killed*   קָטַל = קָטַלְתִּי with תִּי, the affix of 1st
                                  person in all Perfects.

6. *They killed*   קָטַל = קָטְלוּ with וּ, the usual plural sign
                                  with verbs.

7. *Ye* (m.) *killed*   קָטַל = קְטַלְתֶּם with תֶּם; cf. the pronoun
                                  אַתֶּם *ye* (m.).

8. *Ye* (f.) *killed*   קָטַל = קְטַלְתֶּן with תֶּן; cf. the pronoun
                                  אַתֶּן *ye* (f.).

9. *We killed*   קָטַל = קָטַלְנוּ with נוּ; cf. the pronoun
                                  אֲנַחְנוּ, אָנוּ *we.*

---

[1] Young's *Introduction to Hebrew*, pp. 16, 17.

REMARKS

1. The pronominal elements used in the inflection of the Perfect are always *af*-fixed to the stem.

2. The inflection of the verb exhibits distinctions for number, person and *gender*. Special forms for the feminine occur in the 2d and 3d person sing., and in the 2d person plur.

3. *a.* The original vowels of the Ḳăl Perfect are ă—ă (קְטַל). In the form קָטַל, the ă under the tone remains unchanged, while the ă in the open syllable before the tone is rounded to â. The same vowel change takes place in forms 3, 4, 5 and 9.

b. In forms 2 and 6, the vowel-terminations ה_ (=*she*) and ‍ו (=*they*) draw the preceding consonant away from the ultimate vowel (ă) of the stem; the change of this vowel to Šᵉwâ follows (§ 36. 2) and the ă of the preceding syl. being now immediately before the tone-syl. is rounded to â.

c. The heavy terminations תֶּם (=*ye* (m.)) and תֶּן (=*ye* (f.)) carry the tone; the ă in the final syl. of the stem is retained unchanged in the closed unaccented syllable; while the ă of the open antepenult is reduced to Šᵉwâ (§ 36. 2. N. 2).

61.　*The Ḳăl Perfect* (*Stative*)

[For the full inflection, see Paradigm B.]

TABULAR VIEW

	3 m. sg.	3 f. sg.	3 c. pl.	2 m. pl.	1 c. pl.
Middle **A**	קָטַל	קָטְלָה	קָטְלוּ	קְטַלְתֶּם	קָטַלְנוּ
Middle **E**	קָטֵל	קָטְלָה	קָטְלוּ	קְטַלְתֶּם	קָטַלְנוּ
Middle **O**	קָטֹל	קָטְלָה	קָטְלוּ	קְטַלְתֶּם	קָטַלְנוּ

1. דָּבַק (2:24); שָׁרְצוּ (1:21); שְׁמַעְתֶּם (42:22); שָׁמַעְתִּי (3:10).

2. זָקֵן (18:12); זָקַנְתִּי (18:13); כָּבֵד (12:10); כָּבְדָה (18:20); אֲהֵבוֹ; יָבֵשׁוּ²; אָהֵב (37:3), *but* אָהַב (27:9); כָּבְדָה¹ (44:20).

---

¹ Judg. 20 : 34.　　　² Joel 1 : 12.

3. שָׁכֹלְתִּי (32:11); קָטֹנְתִּי (30:8); יָכֹלְתִּי; יִכְלוּ¹ (32:26); יָכֹל
(43:14).

Certain verbs expressive of physical or mental states of being are
called *stative* verbs. They show some characteristic forms in inflection.

1. Stative verbs with —̣ under the second radical of the Ḳăl stem
are inflected in the manner described in the preceding section (§ **60.**).

2. Verbs with —̱ (lowered from —̣) under the second radical, do
not differ from those with —̣ in the inflection of the Perfect, except
that the —̣ appears

    a. in the Perfect 3 masc. sing., and

    b. when restored in pause (§ **38. 1**), or before the tone.

3. Verbs with —̇ (lowered from —̇) under the second radical retain the ō whenever the tone would rest upon it, and in pause.

62. *The Remaining Perfects*

[For the full inflection, see Paradigm B.]

TABULAR VIEW OF IMPORTANT FORMS

	3 m. sg.	3 f. sg.	3 c. pl.	2 m. pl.	1 c. pl.
Nĭfʿăl	נִקְטַל	נִקְטְלָה	נִקְטְלוּ	נִקְטַלְתֶּם	נִקְטַלְנוּ
Pŭʿăl	קֻטַּל	קֻטְּלָה	קֻטְּלוּ	קֻטַּלְתֶּם	קֻטַּלְנוּ
Hŏfʿăl	הָקְטַל	הָקְטְלָה	הָקְטְלוּ	הָקְטַלְתֶּם	הָקְטַלְנוּ
Pĭʿēl	² קִטֵּל	קִטְּלָה	קִטְּלוּ	קִטַּלְתֶּם	קִטַּלְנוּ
Hĭθpăʿēl	הִתְקַטֵּל	הִתְקַטְּלָה	הִתְקַטְּלוּ	הִתְקַטַּלְתֶּם	הִתְקַטַּלְנוּ
Hĭfʿîl	הִקְטִיל	הִקְטִילָה	הִקְטִילוּ	הִקְטַלְתֶּם	הִקְטַלְנוּ

1. *a.* נִשְׁמָר³; נִסְתְּרָה⁴; נִפְקְחוּ (3:5); נִשְׁמַרְתֶּם⁵; נִדְבַּרְנוּ⁶.

   b. יָלַד⁷ (4:26); יָלְדָה (24:15); יָלְדוּ (6:1); יְלַדְתֶּם⁷; יָלַדְתִּי⁸.

---

¹ Ex. 8 : 14.   ² Or קֻטַּל.   ³ 2 Sam. 20 : 10.   ⁴ Num. 5 : 13.

⁵ Deut. 2 : 4.   ⁶ Mal. 3 : 13.   ⁷ Jer. 22 : 26.   ⁸ Jer. 20 : 14.

c. הֻפְקַד[1]; הֻכְרַת[2]; הֻשְׁלְכוּ[3]; הֻשְׁלַכְתָּ[4]; הֻשְׁבַּרְתִּי[5].

2. a. דֻּבַּר (44:2); דֻּבְּרָה (39:19); דֻּבְּרוּ (45:15); דֻּבַּרְתֶּם[6].

b. הִתְקַדָּשׁ[7]; הִתְקַדְּשׁוּ[8]; הִתְקַדַּשְׁתֶּם[9]; וְהִתְגַּדִּלְתִּי[10].

c. הֻמְטִיר[13]; הֻכְרִיתָה[11]; הֻצְדִּיקוּ[12]; הֻדְבַּקְתִּי (2:5); הֻמְלַכְתָּ[14].

Of the remaining Perfects, it will be noticed that

1. Three follow entirely the inflection of the Ḳăl Perfect, viz.,

   a. The Nĭf'ăl (נִקְטַל *from* נִקְטַל).

   b. The Pŭ'ăl (קֻטַּל).

   c. The Hŏf'ăl (הָקְטַל, also sometimes הֻקְטַל).

2. Three present slight variations from the inflection of the Ḳăl, viz.,

   a. The Pĭ'ēl (קִטֵּל *and* קִטַּל, *from* קִטֵּל), in which — appears in the ultima before terminations beginning with a consonant.

   b. The Hĭθpă'ēl (הִתְקַטֵּל *and* הִתְקַטַּל), in which, also, ă appears, but sometimes ĭ is retained.

   c. The Hĭf'ĭl (הִקְטִיל, anomalous for הִקְטַל, *from* הַקְטֵל), in which,

     (1) before the vowel-terminations הָ— and ‬, the anomalous î is retained and *accented;* while

     (2) before terminations beginning with a consonant, — everywhere appears.

63. The Ḳăl Imperfect (Active)

TABULAR VIEW

1. *He will kill*	יִקְטֹל, for יַקְטֹל (with יַ).	
2. *She will kill*	תִּקְטֹל, for תַּ תַּקְטֹל the usual sign of the feminine, here prefixed.	

---

[1] Lev. 5 : 23.   [2] Joel 1 : 9.   [3] Jer. 22 : 28.   [4] Isa. 14 : 19.
[5] Jer. 8 : 21.   [6] Ex. 12 : 32.   [7] Isa. 30 : 29.   [8] Num. 11 : 18.
[9] Lev. 11 : 44.   [10] Ezek. 38 : 23.   [11] Lev. 26 : 22.   [12] Deut. 25 : 1.
[13] Jer. 13 : 11.   [14] 1 Kgs. 3 : 7.

3. *Thou* (m.) *wilt kill*   תִּקְטֹל, for תַּ_קְטֹל, תַ being a pronom. root of 2d pers., *cf.* אַתָּה *thou* (m.).

4. *Thou* (f.) *wilt kill*   תִּקְטְלִי, for תַּקְטֹל (with תַ as above), and יִ__ (*cf.* הִיא *she*) used as a sign of fem.; *cf.* אַתִּי[1] *thou* (f.).

5. *I shall kill*   אֶקְטֹל, for אַקְטֹל, with אַ; *cf.* אָנֹכִי *I*.

6. *They* (m.) *will kill*   יִקְטְלוּ, for יַקְטֹל (with יִ, see above), and וּ, the usual plur. ending of verbs.

7. *They* (f.) *will kill*   תִּקְטֹלְנָה, for תַּקְטֹל (with תַ as above), and נָה; *cf.* הֵנָּה *they* (f.).

8. *Ye* (m.) *will kill*   תִּקְטְלוּ, for תַּקְטֹל (with תַ as above), and וּ, the usual plur. ending of verbs.

9. *Ye* (f.) *will kill*   תִּקְטֹלְנָה, for תַּקְטֹל (with תַ as above), and נָה; *cf.* אַתֵּנָה *ye* (f.).

10. *We shall kill*   נִקְטֹל, for נַקְטֹל, with נַ, a pronominal root; *cf.* נַחְנוּ *we*.

REMARKS

1. The pronominal elements employed in the inflection of the Imperfect are not so clearly recognized as in the Perfect; they are

a. Pre-fixes: יִ, תַ, תַּ, תַּ, אַ, יַ, תַּ, תַּ, נַ, in all of which ⸗ is attenuated to ⸗, but under א is deflected to ⸗ (ĕ).

b. Af-fixes: —, —, —, יִ_, —; וּ, נָה וּ, נָה —

---

[1] אַתִּי is found in Kᵉthîv seven times for אַתְּ *thou* (f.).

2. *a.* The stem of the Imperfect is קְטֹל, whence comes קְטֹל
through the influence of the tone. *Cf.* Arabic *yaḳtul.*

The original form of the Impf. stem was *ḳuṭul,* and the same stem
forms the basis of the Imperative and Infinitive Construct forms.
When the preformative of the Impf. was added, it naturally drew to
itself a secondary tone, and so the ŭ of the following syllable was
easily lost (*cf. business,* pronounced *biz-ness*). It reappears in certain forms of the Infinitive Construct and Imperative.

b. The ō is often written fully (וֹ); but this must be regarded
as an error, since it is a tone-long vowel.

c. When יִקְטֹל and similar forms are connected by Măḳḳēf
with a following word, thus losing the tone, the original ŭ is not
lowered to ō, but deflected to ŏ (ֳ).

3. The vowel-terminations יִ_ (seldom יִן_) and וּ (seldom וּן)
draw the preceding consonant away from the ultimate vowel, which
then necessarily passes into Šᵉwâ (§ 36. 2. *a*).

4. The termination נָה (seldom ןָ) does not receive the tone.

64.　*The Ḳăl Imperfect* (*Stative*)
[For full inflection, see Paradigm B.]
TABULAR VIEW OF IMPORTANT FORMS

	3 m. sg.	2 f. sg.	3 m. pl.	3 f. pl.
Impf. with ō	יִקְטֹל	תִּקְטְלִי	יִקְטְלוּ	תִּקְטֹלְנָה
Impf. with ă	יִקְטַל	תִּקְטְלִי	יִקְטְלוּ	תִּקְטַלְנָה
Impf. with ē	יִקְטֵל	תִּקְטְלִי	יִקְטְלוּ	תִּקְטֵלְנָה

1. יִשְׁבֹּת (2:2); יִסְגֹּר (2:21); יִשְׁרְצוּ (1:20); יִתְפְּרוּ (3:7);
יִגְבְּרוּ (7:18).

2. יִשְׁכַּב (30:15) *from* שָׁכַב; יִגְדַּל (21:8) *from* גָּדַל; יִגְבְּרוּ
יִשְׁלַח (2:8); יִמַּע (2:5); יִצְמַח (27:45); אֶשְׁכַּל (7:18);
תִּגְּעוּ (3:3); (3:22).

3. יִתֵּן (1:17); תִּתֵּן (3:6); תֵּלֵךְ (3:14); יֵצֵא (4:16).

1. Stative verbs with middle A, with some exceptions, have in the Imperfect the form יִקְטֹל (orig. yăk-ṭŭl), the inflection of which is given in § 63.

2. Verbs middle E and verbs middle O, with some verbs middle A, have in the Imperfect a stem with ă instead of ō; this ă is treated like the ō.

Remark.—The Imperfect stem קְטַל, instead of קְטֹל, is used also in verbs, whether active or stative, which have a laryngeal for the second or third radical.

3. Some verbs whose first radical is נ, and the verb נָתַן *to give*, have for the Imperfect stem the form קְטֵל, *i. e.*, ē instead of ō or ă. No strong verb has this stem.

Note 1.—There were three Perfect stems, קָטַל, קָטֵל, and קָטֹל; and so there are three Imperfect stems, יִקְטֹל, יִקְטַל, and יִקְטֵל, the ă in each case being original, while the ē and ō have come from ĭ and ŭ respectively.

Note 2.—It will be seen later that the stem-vowel of the Imperative varies with that of the Imperfect.

65. *The Remaining Imperfects*

[For full inflection, see Paradigm B.]

TABULAR VIEW OF IMPORTANT FORMS

	3 m. sg.	2 f. sg.	1 c. sg.	3 f. pl.
Nĭf'ăl	יִקָּטֵל	תִּקָּטְלִי	אֶקָּטֵל	תִּקָּטַלְנָה (טֵל)
Pĭ'ēl	יְקַטֵּל	תְּקַטְּלִי	אֲקַטֵּל	תְּקַטֵּלְנָה (טֵל)
Hĭθpă'ēl	יִתְקַטֵּל	תִּתְקַטְּלִי	אֶתְקַטֵּל	תִּתְקַטֵּלְנָה (טֵל)
Pŭ'ăl	יְקֻטַּל	תְּקֻטְּלִי	אֲקֻטַּל	תְּקֻטַּלְנָה
Hŏf'ăl	יָקְטַל	תָּקְטְלִי	אָקְטַל	תָּקְטַלְנָה
Hĭf'îl	יַקְטִיל (יַקְטֵל)	תַּקְטִילִי	אַקְטִיל	תַּקְטֵלְנָה

1. יִפְרֹד (2:10); אֶסְתַּר (4:14); תִּשְׁחֵת (6:11); יִסְכְּרוּ (8:2).

2. יְקַדֵּשׁ (2:3); יְדַבֵּר (8:15); תְּדַבֵּר (31:24).

3. [2]יִתְעַצֵּב (6:6) יִתְלַקְּטוּ; תִּשְׁתַּפֵּכְנָה.

4. [7]תִּשְׁלָכִי; [6]תָּקְטָר; [5]יֻסְפַּר; [4]תְּלֻקְּטוּ; [3]יְכֻפַּר.

5. יֻשְׁכַּן (1:4); יַבְדֵּל [7]תַּשְׁבִּיתוּ; [8]תִּשְׁחִיתוּן; (3:21); יַלְבֵּשׁ
(3:24); תֻּשְׁלַךְ (21:15).

1. *a.* The *stem* of the Nĭf'äl Imperfect differs from that of the
Nĭf'äl Perfect in two particulars:
    (1) the first radical has a vowel,
    (2) the original form of the Imperfect was *yănăḳăṭĭl*. Emphasis
        upon the preformative caused the elision of the second ă,
        with the consequent assimilation of the n to the following
        ḳ and its representation by dåǧ. fŏrtē and attenuation of
        the preformative ă to ĭ.

Note.—The vowel of the ultima, generally ⊤, is sometimes ⊤;
cf. the interchange of these vowels in the Pĭ'ēl, and Hĭθpä'ēl.

   b. In the *inflection* of the Nĭf'äl Imperfect, there is to be noted,
    (1) the use of either ⊤ or ⊤ before נֶה;
    (2) the occurrence of ⊤ sometimes instead of ⊤ under the
        pref. אֶ.[10]

2. *a.* The *stem* of the Pĭ'ēl Imperfect is identical with that of the
corresponding Perfect, except that the original penultimate ⊤ is now
retained.

   b. In the *inflection* of the Pĭ'ēl Imperfect, there is to be noted,
    (1) the use of Šᵉwâ under the preformatives, just as also in
        the Pŭ'äl (compound Šᵉwâ under the laryngeal אֶ); this
        reduction of the preformative vowel in Pĭ'ēl and Pŭ'äl is
        due to strong stress on the following syllable.
    (2) the use of either ⊤ or ⊤ (prevailingly the former) before
        נֶה.

3. *a.* The *stem* of the Hĭθpä'ēl Imperfect is the same as that of the
corresponding Perfect, except that ה does not appear in the preformative syllable.

---

[1] Judg. 11 : 3.   [2] Lam. 4 : 1.   [3] Isa. 27 : 9.   [4] Isa. 27 : 12.
[5] Ps. 88 : 12.   [6] Lev. 6 : 15.   [7] Ezek. 16 : 5.   [8] Deut. 4 : 16.
[9] Ex. 12 : 15.
[10] Always so in the punctuation system of the Babylonian Jews.

b. In the *inflection* of the Hĭθpă‛ēl Imperfect, there is likewise to be noted the use of either ⸗ or ⸗ (prevailingly the former) before נָה.

4. The stem and inflection of the Pŭ‛ăl and Hŏf‛ăl present no new peculiarities.

5. *a.* The *stem* of the Hĭf‛ĭl Imperfect is identical with that of the corresponding Perfect, except that (1) under the preformatives the original ⸗ is retained, and (2) the causative הֵ is elided, as also in the Hŏf‛ăl Imperfect.

b. In the *inflection* of the Hĭf‛ĭl Imperfect, there is to be noted,

(1) the form יַקְטֵל, used as a Jussive (§ **69**.), and with Wâw Conversive (§ **70**.), the ⸗ of which is regularly lowered from ⸗;

(2) the retention and accentuation of the stem-vowel י⸗ before the vowel-additions י⸗, ‍ו;

(3) the occurrence of ‍_, rather than י‍_, before נָה.

Note 1.—The following table will be found serviceable:

1. Name of stem,   Ḳăl, Nĭf., Pĭ., Pŭ., Hĭf., Hŏf., Hĭθpă.
2. Preformative with vowel, יִ   יִ   יְ   יְ   יַ   יָ   יִתְ
3. First radical with vowel, ק   קָ   קַ   קֻ   ק   ק   ק

Note 2.—The various elements used as preformatives and afformatives appear from the following table, the asterisks representing radicals:

3 m.	*He will*	‍י***	*They will*	‍ו***
3 f.	*She will*	‍ת***	*They will*	‍תָּנָה***
2 m.	*Thou wilt*	‍ת***	*Ye will*	‍תְּ***
2 f.	*Thou wilt*	‍תִּי***	*Ye will*	‍תְּנָה***
1 c.	*I shall*	‍א***	*We shall*	‍נ***

66. The Imperatives
TABULAR VIEW

	Impf.	Imv. 2 m. sg.	Imv. 2 f. sg.	Imv. 2 m. pl.	Imv. 2 f. pl.
Ḳăl with ō	יִקְטֹל	קְטֹל	קִטְלִי	קִטְלוּ	קְטֹלְנָה
Ḳăl with ă	יִקְטַל	קְטַל	קִטְלִי	קִטְלוּ	קְטַלְנָה
Nĭf‛ăl	יִקָּטֵל	הִקָּטֵל	הִקָּטְלִי	הִקָּטְלוּ	הִקָּטַלְנָה

Pĭ'ēl	קַטֵּלְנָה קַטְּלוּ קַטְּלִי קַטֵּל יְקַטֵּל
Hĭf'îl	הַקְטֵלְנָה הַקְטִילוּ הַקְטִילִי הַקְטֵל יַקְטִיל
Hĭθpă'ēl	הִתְקַטֵּלְנָה הִתְקַטְּלוּ הִתְקַטְּלִי הִתְקַטֵּל יִתְקַטֵּל

1. a. שְׁכַב[4], (30:15) יִשְׁכַּב; כְּתֹב[3], יִכְתֹּב[2], זְכֹר[1]; (8:1) יִזְכֹּר.

   b. (20:8) יַשְׁכֵּם, תַּשְׁכִּים[8], הַשְׁלֵךְ[7], יַשְׁלֵךְ[6], יַשְׁלִיךְ[5]; הַשְׁכֵּם[9].

   c. תִּתְחַתֵּן[11], הַשְׁלֵךְ[7], יַשְׁלִיךְ[5], (24:6) תִּשָּׁמֶר[10], הִשָּׁמֶר; הִתְחַתֵּן[12].

2. a. חֶשְׂפִּי[13] (1:22); כִּבְשֻׁ(הָ)[13] (1:28); מִלְאוּ.

   b. הַקְשִׁיבָה[16], הַקְשֵׁב[15], הַשְׁלִיכִי[14]; (37:22) הַשְׁלִיכוּ, הַשְׁלֵךְ[17].

1. The *stem* of the Imperative is the same in every case as that of the Imperfect; it will be noted that, like the Imperfect,

   a. The Ḳăl has two forms, one (active) with ō, and one (stative) with ă.

   b. The Hĭf'îl corresponds in form to the Jussive Imperfect in ē (§ 69.), rather than to the usual Imperfect, which has î. Both forms are naturally more quickly spoken than the Indicative.

   c. The initial ה which is always absent from a preformative in the Impf., appears in the Imperative of the Nĭf'ăl, Hĭf'îl, and Hĭθpă'ēl.

   Note.—The pure passives Pŭ'ăl and Hŏf'ăl have no Imperative.

2. In the *inflection* of the Imperatives, it will be seen that

   a. Before vowel-additions, the vowel of the stem disappears (except in the Hĭf'îl); and the short ĭ under the first radical of the Ḳăl fem. sg., and masc. pl., stands in a closed syllable, the transliteration being ḳĭṭ-lî, ḳĭṭlû.

   Note.—Occasional forms like מָלְכִי[17], מָשְׁכוּ[18], and certain forms with pronominal suffixes (§ 71. 3. b) show that the original Imv.

[1] Deut. 9 : 7. [2] Ex. 24 : 4. [3] Ex. 17 : 14. [4] 2 Sam. 13 : 5.
[5] Isa. 2 : 20. [6] Ex. 7 : 10. [7] Ex. 7 : 9. [8] Judg. 9 : 33.
[9] Ex. 8 : 16. [10] Judg. 13 : 13. [11] Deut. 7 : 3. [12] 1 Sam. 18 : 22.
[13] Isa. 47 : 2. [14] Jer. 7 : 29. [15] Job 33 : 31. [16] Ps. 5 : 3.
[17] Ezek. 32 : 20. [18] Judg. 9 : 10, 12 (Ḳᵉrê).

stem was probably vocalized קְטֵל. Hence the ĭ of fem. sg. and
masc. pl. is perhaps thinned from ŭ.

b. The Hĭf'ĭl Imv. has ē as its stem-vowel in the masc. sg., and
fem. pl., but î in the fem. sg. and masc. pl.

Note 1.—The stem of the Imperative receives no preformatives,
and its afformatives are those of the Imperfect.

Note 2.—On the Imperative with הָ‎ (cohortative) see § 69.

67. *The Infinitives*
TABULAR VIEW

Ḳăl.	Nĭf'ăl.	Pĭ'ēl.	Pŭ'ăl.	Hĭθpă'ēl.	Hĭf'ĭl.	Hŏf'ăl.
קָטוֹל {נִקְטֹל / הִקָּטֵל}	{קַטֵּל / קַטֹּל}	קֻטַּל	הִתְקַטֵּל	הַקְטֵל	הָקְטֵל
קְטֹל	הִקָּטֵל	קַטֵּל		הִתְקַטֵּל	הַקְטִיל	

1. ⁴הָשְׁכֵּם; ¹שָׁמוֹר‎ ²הִנָּתֹן; נִכְסֹף (31:30); ³דַּבֵּר; גְּנֹב (40:15);
    ⁵הַבְדֵּל.

2. *a.* ⁶הִכָּרֵת; מְשֹׁל (1:18); שָׁמֹר (3:24); *but* שְׁכַב (34:7);
    ⁸הִתְכַּבֵּד; הַבְדִּיל (1:18); ⁷בַּקֵּשׁ (17:22); דַּבֵּר.

    b. ¹¹מָשְׁחָה; ¹⁰רָחְצָה; ⁹קָרְבָה.

Each stem has two Infinitives, called Absolute and Construct;
but no example is found of a Pŭ'ăl or Hŏf'ăl Infinitive Construct.

1. The Infinitive *Absolute* has the form of a noun, and is not based
upon either the Perfect or Imperfect stem.

    a. In the penult, an original ă becomes å in the Ḳăl and in one
form of the Nĭf'ăl, ĭ in the other Nĭf'ăl, and remains unchanged in the
Pĭ'ēl, Hĭθpă'ēl and Hĭf'ĭl; while original ŭ appears in the Pŭ'ăl and is
deflected to ŏ in the Hŏf'ăl.

¹ Deut. 5 : 12.	² Jer. 32 : 4.	³ Ex. 4 : 14.	⁴ 1 Sam. 17 : 16.
⁵ Isa. 56 : 3.	⁶ Num. 15 : 31.	⁷ 1 Sam. 10 : 2.	⁸ Nah. 3 : 15.
⁹ Ex. 36 : 2.	¹⁰ Ex. 30 : 18.	¹¹ Ex. 29 : 29.	

b. In the ultima:

   (1) ô (=â) in the Ḳăl, Nĭf'ăl, Pŭ'ăl, and sometimes in Pĭ'ēl.

   (2) ē in the Hĭf'îl, Hŏf'ăl, Hĭθpă'ēl and usually in Pĭ'ēl.

Remark. 1.—The Nĭf'ăl Infinitive Absolute has two forms, one (נִקְטֹל) following the analogy of the Perfect; the other (הִקָּטֹל), following the analogy of the stem appearing in the Inf. Construct and Imperative.

Remark 2.—The ô in the Inf. Abs., arising always from â, is seldom written fully. Old noun forms in Arabic likewise show long vowels written defectively.

2. *a.* The Infinitive *Construct* has, in each case, the form of the stem found in the Imperfect and Imperative.

Remark.—Stative verbs, which have ă in the Imperfect and Imperative, have, nevertheless, ō in the Infinitive Construct. The cases of an Infinitive Construct with ă are very few.

b. The Ḳăl Inf. Construct not infrequently takes a form with ָה_. This form is found especially with the preposition לְ.

Note 1.—The ultimate vowel of the various Infinitives Construct is changeable, while that of the Infinitives Absolute is unchangeable.

Note 2.—Only to the Infinitives Construct may prepositions be prefixed, or suffixes added.

68. The Participles

TABULAR VIEW

Ḳăl Active.	Ḳăl Stative.		Ḳăl Passive.	Nĭf'ăl.
קֹטֵל	קָטֵל		קָטוּל	נִקְטָל

	Pĭ'ēl.	Pŭ'ăl.	Hĭf'îl.	Hŏf'ăl.	Hĭθpă'ēl.
Impf.	יְקַטֵּל	יְקֻטַּל	יַקְטִיל	יָקְטַל	יִתְקַטֵּל
Part.	מְקַטֵּל	מְקֻטָּל	מַקְטִיל	מָקְטָל	מִתְקַטֵּל

1. *a.* רְמֹשׁ (1:26); חֹלֵם (41:1); הֹלֵךְ (2:14); עֹבֵד (4:2); נֹתֵן (9:12).

b. זָקֵן (18:11); כָּבֵד (13:2); שָׁלֵם (33:18); גָּדֵל[1] (26:13).

c. בָּרוּךְ (9:26); כָּתוּב[1]; דְּרוּשָׁה[2]; שָׁבוּר[3].

2. נִסְתָּר; נִשְׁבָּר[5]; נִפְרָד[6]; נִשְׁפָּט[7].

3. מְדַבֵּר (27:6); מְבַקֵּשׁ (37:16); מְקַדֵּשׁ[8]; מִתְהַלֵּךְ (3:8);
מַבְדִּיל (1:6); מַשְׁחִית (6:13); מַמְטִיר (7:4); מֹשְׁלֵךְ[9].

1. The Ḳăl stem has two participles; the remaining stems, one each:

    a. The Ḳăl *active* is קֹטֵל (sometimes קוֹטֵל) = ḳôṭēl *for* ḳâṭĭl; the ô being obscured from an original â, the ē lowered from ĭ.

    b. The Ḳăl *stative* participle has the form of the Perfect 3 masc. sg., קָטֵל (=ḳâṭēl); it is not so uniformly used, however, as is the Ḳăl *active.*

    c. In the Ḳăl *passive* participle, viz., קָטוּל (=ḳâṭûl *for* ḳăṭûl); the û is unchangeable, but the â, rounded from ă, is changeable.

2. The Nĭf'ăl Participle is the same as the Nĭf'ăl Perfect, with the vowel of the ultima rounded, since the Participle is a nominal form (§ 36.).

3. The remaining Participles are made by prefixing מ to that form of their respective stems which is used in the Imperfect:—

    a. This מ has ־ָ under it in the Pĭ'ēl and Pŭ'ăl, while in the other stems it takes the place of the initial ה of the stem.

    b. The ultimate vowel, if not long in the stem, is changed under the tone, the participle being a nominal form.

Note 1.—The מ is probably related to the pronouns מִי and מָה.

Note 2.—For feminine forms of the participle, see § 115.

69. Special Forms of the Imperfect and Imperative

1. אַהַרְגֶנָּה (27:41) *I will kill;* אֲגַדֶּלָה (12:2) *I will make great;*
אֲדַבֵּרָה[10] *I will* (= must) *speak;* נִלְבְּנָה (11:3) *Let us make*

---

1 Deut. 28:61.   2 Isa. 62:12.   3 Lev. 22:22.   4 Ps. 19:7.
5 Isa. 61:1.   6 Judg. 4:11.   7 Jer. 2:35.   8 Ezek. 48:11.
9 2 Sam. 20:21.   10 2 Sam. 14:15.

brick; נִשְׂרְפָה (11:3) *Let us burn;* נִכְרְתָה (31:44) *Let us cut* (a covenant); נַזְכִּירָה.[1]

2. יַפְקֵד; תַּסְתֵּר[3]; יִכָרֵת[2]; (41:34). *cf.* יַקְטִיל, יַקְטֵל.

3. זָכְרָה[4] *Think;* הַלְצָה[5] *Oh save;* הַקְשִׁיבָה[6] *Attend.*

Remark.—אִמָּלְטָה־נָא; שִׁמְעוּ־נָא[7]; הִפָּרֶד־נָא (13:9); (19:20).

Some special forms of the Imperfect and Imperative deserve notice:

1. The *Cohortative* Imperfect:

a. This is characterized by the ending הָ ֫, before which a preceding vowel, unless unchangeable, becomes Šᵉwâ. It is found, with few exceptions, only in the first person singular and plural.

b. Its special signification is that of *desire, determination,* and, in the plural, *exhortation.*

2. The *Jussive* Imperfect:

a. This is, wherever possible, a shorter form than the regular Imperfect. It is found chiefly in the 2d and 3d persons; and in *strong* verbs only in the Hîf‘îl stem (viz., with ־ instead of ־י); but in *all* stems of verbs ל״ה (§ 82.) and ע״ו (§ 86.). The wâw-conversive form of the Imperfect is also that of the Jussive (*cf.* § 70.).

b. Its special signification is that of *wish, command;* with a negative, *dissuasion, prohibition.*

3. The *Cohortative* Imperative; this, like the Cohortative Imperfect, is characterized by the ending הָ ֫, and is often more emphatic than the ordinary form. The Hif. Imv. changes ־ to ־י before הָ ֫.

Remarks.—The modal idea in each of these three forms is intensified or enlivened by the particle נָא, which is frequently found in connection with them.

Note 1.—The regular Imperfect and Imperative forms may without change convey the ideas characteristic of the forms here discussed.

---

[1] Ct. 1:4.   [2] Mal. 2:12.   [3] Ps. 27:9.   [4] Neh. 5:19.
[5] Ps. 6:5.   [6] Ps. 5:3.   [7] Judg. 13:14.

Note 2.—The shorter form of the Imperative corresponding to
the Jussive is confined to ל״ה verbs, *e. g.*, גַּל for גַּלֵּה.

70.   *The Perfect and Imperfect with Wâw Conversive*

1. *a.* ‥‥וַיֹּאמֶר (3)‥‥וְהָאָרֶץ הָיְתָה (2)‥‥בְּרֵאשִׁית בָּרָא (1:1)

‥‥וְלַחשֶׁךְ קָרָא‥‥וַיִּקְרָא (5)‥‥וַיַּבְדֵּל‥‥וַיַּרְא (4)‥‥וַיְהִי

‥‥וַיְהִי‥‥וַיַּבְדֵּל‥‥וַיַּעַשׂ (7)‥‥וַיֹּאמֶר (6)‥‥וַיְהִי‥‥וַיְהִי

‥‥וַיְהִי‥‥וַיֹּאמֶר (9)‥‥‥וַיְהִי‥‥וַיְהִי‥‥וַיִּקְרָא (8)

וַיַּרְא‥‥וּלְמִקְוֵה הַמַּיִם קָרָא‥‥וַיִּקְרָא (10)

b. ‥‥וַיֹּאמֶר אֱלֹהִים] יְהִי מְאֹרֹת בִּרְקִיעַ הַשָּׁמַיִם (1:14)

‥‥וְהָיוּ לְמְאוֹרֹת‥‥וְהָיוּ לְאֹתֹת

(3:22) פֶּן יִשְׁלַח יָדוֹ וְלָקַח גַּם מֵעֵץ הַחַיִּים וְאָכַל וָחַי
לְעֹלָם:

2. *a.* וַיִּשְׁבֹּת (2:2); וַיַּבְדֵּל (1:4); וַיִּסְגֹּר (2:21); (2:3)
וַיְבָרֶךְ (1:22).

b. וַדְָּבַק (2:24); וְלָקַח (3:22); וְאָכַל (3:22); (24:14)
וְאָכַלְתָּ (3:18).

3. *a.* וַיַּהַרְגֵהוּ (4:8); וַיַּבְדֵּל (1:7); וַיִּרְדְּפֵם (14:15); וַיְבָרֶךְ
וַיַּחְשְׁבֶהָ (15:6). ;(1:22)

וַיִּבֶתֶר (15:10); וַיִּשְׁקְפוּ (18:16); וַיְדַבֵּר (17:3); וַיִּשְׁבֹּת
(2:2).

Remark.—וַיִּלְבַּשׁ, *but* וַיַּלְבִּשֵׁם (3:21).

b. ¹ וְאָמַרְתִּי (3:13); וְאָסַפְתָּ (3:16); וְשָׁלַחְתִּי (3:20); וְנָתַתִּי
(3:21); וְגָאַלְתִּי (6:6).

The use of the Perfect and Imperfect with the so-called Wâw
Conversive² is one of the most marked peculiarities of the language.

_____

¹ These cases are cited from Exodus.
² The form is usually called Wâw Consecutive; but this name claims too much for
the form; the older term *Conversive*, while not ideal, is less objectionable.

Only what relates to the forms of the conjunction, and to the verbal forms to which the conjunction is joined, will here be noticed.

1. The facts in the case, briefly stated, are as follows:

a. In continued narrations of the past, the first verb is in the Perfect, while those that follow, *unless they are separated from the conjunction by intervening words,* are in the Imperfect and connected with the preceding Perfect by means of Wåw Conversive.

b. In the narration of actions which are to occur in the future, or which can only be conditionally realized, or which are indefinite so far as their character or occurrence is concerned, the first verb is in the Imperfect (or Participle, or Imperative), while those that follow, *unless they are separated from the conjunction by intervening words,* are in the Perfect and connected with the preceding verb by means of Wåw Conversive.

Note.—This more common usage is very often modified in various ways; but a consideration of these questions belongs to Syntax, and cannot be taken up here.

2. The form of the conjunction, however, is not the same in both cases:

a. With the *Imperfect,* the conjunction is וַ, but

    (1) the following consonant regularly has Dåĝēš-fŏrtē;

    (2) the Dåĝēš-fŏrtē may be omitted from a consonant which has only Šᵉwâ under it (§ **14.** 2), and

    (3) before א, in the first person, the Dåĝēš-fŏrtē being omitted, the preceding ־ַ becomes ־ָ.

b. With the *Perfect,* the conjunction is the same as the ordinary Wåw Conjunctive, with its various pointings (§ **49.**).

3. With reference to the verbal form employed,

    a. In the case of the *Imperfect,* there is used,

        (1) in the first person, a lengthened form exactly similar to that of the Cohortative (§ **69.**)[1]—a usage which is rare and late;

---

[1] *Cf.* וָאֶשְׁלְחָה (32 : 6); וַנַּחְלְקָה (41 : 11); וַנְּפַתְּחָה (43 : 21); וָאֶתְּנָה (Num. 8 : 19); *also* Ez. 7 : 27–9 : 6, in which there are seventeen cases.

(2) in the second and third persons, a short form like that of the Jussive (§ **69.**) and found in many weak and bi-literal verbs and in the Hif'il of strong verbs.

(3) a form with accent on the penult, and the consequent vowel changes; but the penult cannot carry the accent unless it is an open syllable, and the final syllable has a changeable vowel. This form cannot occur in the strong verb.

(4) the ordinary verbal form unchanged.

Remark.—With Wâw Conversive the Hif'il, therefore, has ē instead of î; but this î is usually restored, though written defectively, before suffixes.

    b. In the case of the *Perfect*, the usual verbal form is employed; but, *whenever possible*, this form is marked by a change of accent, the tone passing from the penult to the ultima.

    Note.—As a matter of fact, the cases in which there is no change of tone are as numerous as those in which there does occur change. These cases are grouped by Driver[1] as follows: (1) in those forms of the Perfect (3 sg., 2 fem. sg., 3 com. pl., 2 masc. pl., 2 fem. pl.) which are already *Milră*; (2) when the Perfect is immediately followed by a mono-syllable, or dissyllable accented on the penult; (3) when the Perfect is *in pause;* (4) in the 1 pl. of all conjugations, and in 3 fem. sg. and 3 pl. of the Hif'il; (5) in the Ḳal of verbs ל״א and ל״ה; (6) frequently in those forms of ע״ע and Middle-Vowel Ḳals and Nif'âls which end in ו and ה ָ.

71. The Verb with Suffixes

[See Paradigm C at end of book.]

1. *a.* [־קְטַלַת for קְטָלָה]; אֲכָלַתְהוּ (37:20); סְמָכְתַּנִי[2];

יְלָדַתְנִי[5]; [־קְטַלְתְּ for קְטַלְתִּי]; מְצָאַתְנוּ[4]; שְׁטָפַתְנִי[3];

צְמָתַּנִי[8]; [קְטַלְתֶּם for קְטַלְתּוּ]; נְתַתִּיהוּ[7]; הִכְרַעְתָּנִי[6];

הֶעֱלִיתֻנוּ[9]; נְטַשְׁתַּנִי (31:28); זְכַרְתָּנִי (40:14).

---
[1] *Use of the Tenses in Hebrew,*[3] § 110.
[2] Isa. 63 : 5.   [3] Ps. 69 : 3.   [5] Jer. 15 : 10.
[6] Judg. 11 : 35.   [7] Ezek. 16 : 19.   [4] Num. 20 : 14.   [8] Zech. 7 : 5.   [9] Num. 20 : 5.

b. דְּפָקוּם; גְּמָלוּךְ (50:17) for גְּמָלוּךְ; [קְטָלוּךְ for קְטָלוּ.
(33:13) for דְּפָקוּם.

Remarks.—אִשְּׁרוּנִי (30:13); שְׁכֵחוּנִי[1]; אֲהֵבוּ (44:20); הִשְׁבִּיעֲךָ; אֲכַבֶּדְךָ[2] (50:6).

c. גְּמָלוּךְ (50:17). שְׁפָטוּ־ם; דְּרָשֻׁנְ־הוּ[4]; [קְטָלוּ־ךָ].

אֲהֵבְךָ[6]; נְתָנָ־ם; נְתָנָ־הוּ for (31:7) נְתָנוֹ; [קְטָל־הוּ];
שְׁאָלֵךְ (32:18). שְׁלָחֲךָ[8]; רִחֲמָךְ[9]; עֲבָדְךָ.

אֲכַלְתֶּם[11]; אֲחַזְתֶם[10]; see above, 1. a; [קְטַלְתֶּךָ, קְטַלְתָּנוּ].

Remark.—יְדַעְתִּיו (18:19) for הֲרַגְנוּ (4:25) for הֲרַגְנֻהוּ; יְדָעָה (24:16) for יְדָעָהּ; יִלַּדְתּוּ for יְלָדַתְהוּ[12] יְדַעְתִּיהוּ;
אֲחֻזָתָהּ[13] for אֲחֻזָתָה.

When the object of a verb is a pronoun, it is often expressed by the union of אֵת and the pronominal suffix. More often, however, the pronominal suffix is joined directly to the verbal form. This occasions certain changes of termination and of stem. When a suffix is added to a verbal form, the form becomes subject, so far as the influence of the tone is concerned, to the laws controlling the vocalization of nouns.

1. In the case of the *Perfect with suffixes*, it is to be noted,

　a. In reference to *termination-changes*, that the older endings are in many cases retained, as

　(1) the older תָ_, for the later הָ_ (3 sg. fem.);

　(2) the older תִּי, for the later תְּ (2 sg. fem.);

　(3) the older תּוּן, for the later תֶּם (2 pl. masc.), perhaps after the analogy of ן in the 3d plural.

　Remark.—תָ occurs for תָּ (2 m. sg.), often before נִי.

---

[1] Jer. 2 : 32.　　[2] Num. 22 : 17.　　[3] Deut. 25 : 1.　　[4] 1 Chron. 13 : 3.
[5] Josh. 10 : 19.　　[6] Deut. 15 : 16.　　[7] Deut. 15 : 12.　　[8] 1 Sam. 20 : 22.
[9] Deut. 13 : 18.　　[10] Ps. 48 : 7.　　[11] Hos. 2 : 14.　　[12] Ruth 4 : 15.
[13] Jer. 49 : 24.

b. In reference to *stem-changes*, that, in the Ḳăl,

    (1) the first syllable, being no longer pretonic when a suffix is appended, reduces its original ă in the open syllable to Šᵉwâ; while

    (2) the ă of the second syllable, which has been reduced before personal terminations beginning with a vowel, is retained, and, in the open syllable before the tone, rounded to å.

Remark 1.—The ◌֖ of verbs Middle E appears before suffixes.

Remark 2.—The Pǐʿēl and Hǐθpǎʿēl take ◌֖ in the last syllable before ךָ, כֶם, כֶן, but elsewhere the vowel is rejected; while the ultimate î of the Hǐfʿîl suffers no change.

c. In reference to the *union of termination and suffix*, that

    (1) to a verbal form ending in a vowel, the suffix is attached directly;

    (2) to a verbal form ending, in ordinary usage, with a consonant, the suffix is attached by means of a so-called connecting-vowel which is generally å, but before ךָ, כֶם, and כֶן, is Šᵉwâ, and before ךְ is ē.

    (3) to the 3 sg. fem. termination תָ, suffixes forming a syllable are attached without a connecting-vowel; other suffixes have a connecting-vowel, viz., ĕ before ךָ, but ă before ם; the accent, peculiarly, in every case stays on the feminine ending תָ.

Note.—Certain changes are quite frequent: (1) הֻן to וּ; (2) יְהוּ to יוּ; (3) תְהוּ to תוּ; (4) הָ to הָ; (5) תְהָ to תָהּ. In the *third* and *fifth* of these cases, the dăǧ. is, perhaps, in compensation for the ה. In the fifth, the ה of the present form is merely a vowel-letter. In the *fourth* case, the final vowel was dropped, and the Măppîḳ in ה shows it to be a genuine consonant, rather than a vowel-letter.

2. *a.* תּוֹכִיחֵךְ[1]; תַחְשְׁבֵנִי; וּתְקַטְלֶנָה| *for* תְּקַטְלוּ[2].

---

[1] Job. 19 : 15.   [2] Jer. 2 : 19.

b. [וְיִקְטְלֵנִי]; ¹יִשְׁפְּטֵנִי; ²אֶזְכְּרְכִי; יִפְגָּשֶׁךָ (32:18); ³אֶזְכְּרֵךְ;
⁴יִזְכְּרֶהָ

⁶תִּשְׁכָּחֵנִי (40:23); ⁵יִשְׁכָּחֵהוּ; יִלְבָּשֵׁנִי; [וְיִקְטְלֵנִי]

⁸אֲחַמְּרֵךְ; ⁷תְּלַמְּדֵם (3:23); יְשַׁלְּחֵהוּ; [וַיִּקְטְלֵךְ]; [יְקְטְלֵנִי]

⁹אַשְׁמִידֵם (37:20); נַשְׁלִכֵהוּ (3:21); יַלְבִּשֵׁם; [וַיַּקְטִילֵנִי]

c. ¹²תַּשְׁלִיכֵהוּ; ¹¹תַּכְלִימוּהָ; ¹⁰יַסְגִּירוּ־נִי; see examples
under b.

¹³תִּזְכְּרֶנּוּ (9:5); אֶדְרְשֶׁנּוּ; [וְיִקְטְלֶנּוּ]

3. a. ¹⁴אֲמַרְכֶם; אֲכָלְכֶם (3:5); אֲכָלְךָ (2:17); [קְטָלְךָ]; but
בְּבָרְחֲךָ (35:1).

¹⁶עָבְדֵנוּ; ¹⁵אֲמָרָם; שְׁמָרָהּ (2:15); עָבְדָהּ (2:15); [קְטָלָהּ]

Remarks.—[קְטָלֵךְ]; ¹⁷לְבַקֶּשְׁךָ; ¹⁸דְּבֶרְכֶם; ¹⁹דַּבְּרִי;
²⁰לְבַקְשֵׁנִי

b. ²⁴עֶזְרֵנוּ; ²³שְׁמָרֵם; ²²שְׁמָרֵנִי; ²¹זָכְרֵנִי; [קְטָלֵנִי]

²⁷עֲבָדָהוּ; ²⁶תִּפְשֹׂם; ²⁵עֲזָרוּנִי; [קְטָלוּהָ]

²⁸הַשְׁמִיעֵנִי; שְׁמָעֵוֹנִי (23:11); שְׁמָעֵנִי (23:8); [קְטָלֵנִי]
²⁹הַשְׁלִיכֵהוּ

2. In the case of the *Imperfect with suffixes*, it is to be noted,

a. In reference to *termination-changes*, that נָה (2 and 3 pl.
fem.) always yields to ן. Note the analogy to the 3d. pers. plur.
in ן, as also appears in the 2d. pers. plur. masc. (see above).

---

¹ 1 Sam. 24:16.   ² Ps. 137:6.   ³ Ps. 42:7.   ⁴ 1 Sam. 1:19.
⁵ Job 29:14.   ⁶ Ps. 13:2.   ⁷ Deut. 5:31.   ⁸ Ps. 57:10.
⁹ Deut. 9:14.   ¹⁰ 1 Sam. 23:11.   ¹¹ Ruth 2:15.   ¹² Ex. 1:22.
¹³ Ps. 8:5.   ¹⁴ Jer. 23:38.   ¹⁵ Ps. 42:11.   ¹⁶ Ex. 14:5.
¹⁷ 1 Kgs. 18:10.   ¹⁸ Ex. 12:31.   ¹⁹ Ex. 19:9.   ²⁰ 1 Sam. 27:1.
²¹ Judg. 16:28.   ²² Ps. 16:1.   ²³ Prov. 4:21.   ²⁴ Josh. 10:6.
²⁵ Josh. 10:4.   ²⁶ 1 Kgs. 20:18.   ²⁷ 1 Sam. 7:3.   ²⁸ Ps. 143:8.
²⁹ Ex. 4:3.

b. In reference to *stem-changes*, that before suffixes,

    (1) the ŭ (lowered to ō) of Ḳăl forms ending in a consonant usually becomes ⲻ, but ŏ before הָ, כֶם, כֶן, the Šᵉwâ preceding the suffix being vocal;

    (2) the ă of Ḳăl forms ending in a consonant is retained and rounded to å;

    (3) the final vowel of Pĭ'ēl forms ending in a consonant is ordinarily reduced to ⲻ, but is deflected to ĕ before הָ, כֶם, כֶן; while the î of Hĭf'îl forms remains.

c. In reference to the *union of termination and suffix*, that

    (1) to verbal forms ending in a vowel the suffix is attached directly; while

    (2) to verbal forms ending in a consonant, the suffix is attached by means of a connecting-vowel, which is generally ē, but ⲻ before הָ, כֶם, כֶן; and ĕ, sometimes å, before הָ;

    (3) in pausal and emphatic forms, suffixes are often attached to a verbal form ending in *an*, which under the tone becomes ĕn, of which the נ is generally assimilated.

Note 1.—This syllable, ordinarily treated as a union-syllable and called *Nûn Epenthetic* or *Demonstrative*, is found also before suffixes in old Aramaic. It is probably an old form of the verb.

Note 2.—In the endings נּוּ (3 m. sg.) and נָּה (3 f. sg.), the Dåḡēš-fŏrtē in נ perhaps is in compensation for the ה from הוּ and הָ respectively.

3. In the case of *Infs. and Imvs. with suffixes*, it is to be noted that,

    a. The Ḳăl *Infinitive* (construct) takes

        (1) before הָ, כֶם, כֶן, generally, the form קָטְל (ŏ); but

        (2) before other suffixes the form קָטְל, the ŏ, in both cases, standing in a closed syllable.

        (3) as connecting-vowels, those used in the inflection of nouns.

Remark 1.—The Pĭ'ēl Infinitive takes ⲻ before הָ, כֶם, כֶן.

Remark 2.—The Infinitive may take either the *verbal* suffix, נִי, or the *nominal* suffix ִי.

b. The Ḳăl *Imperative*, taking the connecting-vowel of the Impf.,

(1) in the 2 masc. sg., follows the analogy of the Infinitive;

(2) in the 2 masc. pl., suffers no change;

(3) in the 2 fem. pl., has the form קְטֹלְנָה instead of קְטֹלְנָה,

just as in the corresponding form of the Imperf. with suffixes.

Remark 1.—The Imperative in ă retains and rounds the ă, as does the Imperfect.

Remark 2.—In the Hĭf'îl, the form הַקְטִיל is used instead of הַקְטֵל.

Note.—The Participles, before suffixes, undergo the same vowel changes as regular nouns of the same formation, and may take either the nominal or the verbal suffixes.

72. General View of the Strong Verb

Mood or Tense.	1. Ḳăl.	2. Nĭf'ăl.	3. Pĭ'ēl.	4. Hĭθpă'ēl.	5. Pŭ'ăl.	6. Hĭf'îl.	7. Hŏf'ăl.
Perfect (3 m. sg.)	קָטַל	נִקְטַל	קִטֵּל²	הִתְקַטֵּל³	קֻטַּל	הִקְטִיל	הָקְטַל
Imperfect (3 m. sg.)	יִקְטֹל	יִקָּטֵל	יְקַטֵּל	יִתְקַטֵּל	יְקֻטַּל	יַקְטִיל	יָקְטַל⁴
Imperative	קְטֹל	הִקָּטֵל	קַטֵּל	הִתְקַטֵּל	——	הַקְטֵל	——
Infinitive Absolute	קָטוֹל	{ נִקְטֹל קַטֵּל / הִקָּטֹל קַטֹּל }	הִתְקַטֵּל	קַטֹּל	הַקְטֵל	הָקְטֵל
Infinitive Construct	קְטֹל	הִקָּטֵל	קַטֵּל	הִתְקַטֵּל		הַקְטִיל	
Participle Active	קֹטֵל		מְקַטֵּל	מִתְקַטֵּל		מַקְטִיל	
Participle Passive	קָטוּל	נִקְטָל			מְקֻטָּל		מָקְטָל

---

¹ *Cf.* also the Middle E and Middle O forms, קָטֵל, קָטֹל.

² *Cf.* also the form with original ⸚ in the ultima, קִטַּל.

³ *Cf.* also the form with original ⸚ in the ultima, הִתְקַטַּל.

⁴ *Cf.* also the forms with ⸚ and ⸚, יִקְטֹל, יַקְטֵל.

⁵ *Cf.* also the form used as a Jussive, and with Wâw Conversive, יַקְטֵל.

REMARKS

1. The Ḳăl is the simple verb-stem (§ 58.).

2. The Nĭf'ăl has in every form the letter נ; this letter, however, is assimilated and represented by Dåḡēš-fŏrtē in the Imperfect, Imperative, and Infinitives (§ 58.).

3. The Pĭ'ēl has everywhere (1) the vowel ־ under the first radical (except in the Perfect), and (2) a Dåḡēš-fŏrtē characteristic in the second radical (§ 58.).

4. The Hĭθpă'ēl is the same as the Pĭ'ēl (except in the Perfect) with the syllable הִתְ prefixed (§ 58. 7).

5. The Pŭ'ăl has everywhere (1) the vowel ־ֻ under the first radical, and (2) a Dåḡēš-fŏrtē characteristic in the second radical (§ 58. 4).

6. The Hĭf'ĭl has in all forms (except the Perfect) the vowel ־ under the *preformative* (§ 58. 5).

7. The Hŏf'ăl has in all forms the vowel ŏ (or ŭ) under the *preformative* (§ 58. 6).

B. THE LARYNGEAL VERB

73. Classes of Laryngeal Verbs

1. עָזַב (2:24); הָפַךְ (3:24); אָבַל‎[1] חָדַל (18:11); עָצַר (20:18).

2. נִבְהַל‎[5] שָׁאַל‎[4] בְּעֵרָה‎[3] שָׁחַט‎[2] (1:2); רָחַף

3. שָׁמַע (3:8); שָׁלַח (3:22); בָּטַח‎[6] בָּקַע (7:11); פָּתַח (42:27); גָּבַהּ‎[7]

Remark.—וַיְבָרֶךְ (1:28); תֶּרְמְסֶנָה‎[8] קְרַבְתִּי‎[9]

A Laryngeal Verb is one the root of which contains one or more laryngeal radicals. They fall into three classes, viz.:

1. Pē ('פ) Laryngeal, of which the first radical is a laryngeal (§ 74.).

2. 'Ăyĭn ('ע) Laryngeal, of which the second radical is a laryngeal (§ 75.).

---

[1] Isa. 24 : 7.　　　[2] Jer. 39 : 6.　　　[3] Num. 11 : 3.　　　[4] Judg. 5 : 25.
[5] 1 Sam. 28 : 21.　　[6] Ps. 28 : 7.　　　[7] Isa. 55 : 9.　　　[8] Isa. 28 : 3.
[9] Isa. 46 : 13.

3. Lāmĕd ('ל) Laryngeal, of which the third radical is a laryngeal (§ 76.).

Remark.—Verbs with ר as first or second radical show some of the characteristics of laryngeal verbs, especially in the refusal of ר to take Dåḡēš-fŏrtē.

Note.—The terms Pē Laryngeal, etc., are based upon the order of the radicals in the old paradigm-verb, פָּעַל, the first radical being designated by פ, the second by ע, and the third by ל.

74. Verbs 'פ Laryngeal

[For full inflection, see Paradigm D]

TABULAR VIEW

	Ḳăl with ō in Impf.	Ḳăl with ă in Impf.	Nif'ăl.	Hif'il.	Hŏf'ăl.
Perf.	עָטַל	עָטַל	נֶעֱטַל	הֶעֱטִיל	הָעֳטַל
Impf.	יַעְטֹל	יֶעֱטַל	יֵעָטֵל	יַעֲטִיל	יָעֳטַל
Imv.	עֲטֹל	עֲטַל	הֵעָטֵל	הַעֲטִיל	—
Inf. abs.	עָטוֹל	עָטוֹל	{ נַעֲטֹל / הֵעָטֵל }	הַעֲטֵל	הָעֳטֵל
Inf. const.	עֲטֹל	עֲטַל	הֵעָטֵל	הַעֲטִיל	—
Part act.	עֹטֵל	עֹטֵל		מַעֲטִיל	
Part. pass.	עָטוּל	עָטוּל	נֶעֱטָל		מָעֳטָל

1. יַהֲפֹךְ[וַיַּעֲטֹל]; וַתֵּרֶא (1:9); אֶהֱבָא (3:10); יֹאכַל (6:21); ¹

2. a. יַעֲשׂוּ[וַיַּעֲטֹל]; יַעֲלֶה (2:6); תַּעֲבֹד־ (4:12); יַעֲזֹב־ (2:24); (3:7).

b. תֶּחְדַּל[נֶעֱטַל נַעֲטֹל]; הֶעֱטִיל[וְהֶחֱזַק] יֶחֱזַק (41:56); נֶהְפַּךְ־²; ³ הֶעֱבִיר (47:21); but יֶחְיֶה־ יִחְיֶה (1:29); יֶחֱיֶה (31:32); וְהֶחֱזִיק⁴; יֶאֱסֹף (29:22).

---

¹ Ex. 14 : 5.　　² Ex. 7 : 15.　　³ Ruth 1 : 18.　　⁴ Deut. 22 : 25.

3. *a.* עֲשׂוֹת (2:4); עֲבֹד (2:5); אֲכָלְךָ (2:17); אֲרוּרָה (3:17);

לֵאמֹר *whence* אָמֹר (6:14); עֲשֵׂה (4:25); הֲרָגֹו (1:22);

אֶסֹף (47:24); אֲכֹל.[1]

b. נֶחְמָד (2:9); [הֶעְטַל]; אֶעֱשֶׂה (2:18); נַעֲשֶׂה (1:26);

תֶּחְדַּל[2]; נֶהְפָּךְ[3]; יַחְגֹּר[4]; יַחְשְׁבָהָ (15:6).

c. יַהַרְגֻהוּ (4:8); יַעַבְדוּךָ (27:29); יַעַבְרוּ (37:28); נֶהְפְּכוּ.[5]

d. יַאַסֹף[8]; וְהַעֲמַדְתָּ[7]; *but* הֶעֱמַדְתָּ[6], *but* יֶאְסֹף (29:22) יֵאָסֵף.

Verbs, whose first radical is a laryngeal, exhibit the following peculiarities (§ 42. 1–3):

1. *The laryngeal refuses to be doubled;* hence the Dåğeš-förtē, representing נ, in the Nïf'ăl Impf., Imv., and Infs., is rejected, and the
preceding -̱- becomes -̱- (even before ה).

2. *The laryngeal prefers before it the a-class vowels;* hence

a. In the Ķăl Impf. with ō, and in the Ķăl Impf. of verbs that
are also ל״ה (§ 82.), the original ă of the preformative is retained;
while

b. In the Ķăl Impf. with -̱-, in the Nïf'ăl Perf. and Part., and in
the Hïf'ïl Perf., the original preformative vowel is deflected to ĕ, for
the sake of euphony.

Remark 1.—A few cases occur of forms like יַעֲטֹל or יֶעְטַל.

Remark 2.—In הָיָה and חָיָה the preformative vowel is regularly attenuated to ĭ as in the strong verb.

Remark 3.—In the Hïf. Pf. 3d sg. masc. and fem. and 3d pl.,
the ĕ of the preformative is due to the influence of the other six forms
in which ă is the stem-vowel and the preformative vowel undergoes
deflection on its account.

3. *The laryngeal prefers compound to simple Šᵉwâ;* hence

a. When the first radical is initial and, according to the inflection of the strong verb, would have a simple Šᵉwâ, it takes instead
-̱-, or, particularly in the case of א, -̱-.

---

[1] Num. 21 : 16.   [2] Ruth 1 : 18.   [3] Ex. 7 : 15.   [4] Lev. 8 : 7.
[5] Ex. 7 : 17.   [6] Ps. 31 : 9.   [7] Num. 3 : 6.   [8] Ex. 4 : 29.

b. When the first radical is medial, it may either, according to
the inflection of the strong verb, have under it a silent Šᵉwâ or, in
order to facilitate the pronunciation, it may receive a compound
Šᵉwâ as a helping-vowel, which always corresponds to the preceding
vowel; thus, ־֖ ־֗, ־֖ ־֗, ־֖ ־֗ (ŏ).

c. When, in inflection, a compound Šᵉwâ would come to stand
before a simple Šᵉwâ, as when vowel-additions are made to a word,
the compound Šᵉwâ gives way to its corresponding short vowel.

d. The combination ־֖ ־֗ very frequently becomes ־֖ ־֗, when,
in inflection, the tone is removed to a greater distance.

Note.—The ה and ח of הָיָה and חָיָה have a silent Šᵉwâ
according to *b* (above), when medial and vowelless; but a compound
Šᵉwâ (־֖), when initial and without a full vowel.

75. *Verbs* 'ע *Laryngeal*

[For full inflection, see Paradigm E]

TABULAR VIEW

	Ḳăl.	Nifʻăl.	Pīʻēl (1).	Pŭʻăl (1).	Pīʻēl (2).	Pŭʻăl (2).	Hiθpăʻēl.
Perf.	קָאַל	נִקְאַל	קֵאַל	קָאַל	קָחַל	קֳחַל	הִתְקָאֵל
Impf.	יִקְאַל	יִקָּאֵל	יְקָאַל	יְקָאַל	יְקַחֵל	יְקֳחַל	יִתְקָאֵל
Imv.	קְאַל	הִקָּאֵל		קַחֵל			הִתְקָאֵל
Inf. abs.	קָאוֹל	נִקְאַל		קַחֵל			
Inf. const.	קְאַל	הִקָּאֵל		קַחֵל			הִתְקָאֵל
Part. act.	קֹאֵל		מְקָאֵל	מְקַחֵל			מִתְקָאֵל
Part. pass.	קָאוּל	נִקְאַל		מְקָאָל		מְקֳחָל	

1. *a.* כָּאַר¹; גְּאָלְנוּ²; מֵאַנְתֶּם³; *but also* שָׁאֲלוּ⁴; נָאַר⁵; נִאֵץ⁶;
בֵּרַךְ (28:6); גֵּרַשְׁתָּ (4:14); וַיְגָרֶשׁ (3:24); וַיְבָרֶךְ (1:22);
יְבֹרַךְ.⁷

---

¹ Deut. 1 : 5.　　² Mal. 1 : 7.　　³ Ex. 16 : 28.　　⁴ Ps. 109 : 10.
⁵ Lam. 2 : 7.　　⁶ Num. 16 : 30.　　⁷ 2 Sam. 7 : 29.

²רְחַץ; ¹נֻחֲמוּ; שַׁחֵת (6:17); נִחַמְתִּי (6:7); (1:2); b. מְרַחֶפֶת

מֵהֲרָתֶּם⁶; ¹כַּעֲסוּנִי; ⁴וּבַעַרְתָּ; ³הִטֶּהָרוּ

יְמַהֵר (18:6); (45:13).

2. a. (34:19); ⁷יִבְחַר; ⁸תִּגְאַל; ¹⁰גְּאַל; ⁹יְבַעֵר; שָׁאַל¹¹; אֵחַר⁷;
לָהַט¹².

b. ¹⁸טֶחֳנִי; ¹⁷שָׁאֲבִי; ¹⁶צַעֲקִי; ¹⁵נֻחֲמוּ; ¹⁴טַעֲנוּ; ¹³שֻׁחֲטוּ;
שְׁאָלִי¹⁹.

c. שָׁאַל²⁰; ²¹גְּאַל; ²²יִגְאַל; תִּשָּׁחֵת (6:11); יְבַעֵר⁶; יְמַהֵר
(18:6).

3. כַּעֲסוּנִי⁵; ²³נִבְהֲלוּ; cf. also the words cited under 2. b.

Verbs, whose second radical is a laryngeal, exhibit the following peculiarities (§ 42. 1–3):

1. *The laryngeal refuses to be doubled;* but

a. While in the case of א (generally), and of ר (always), the preceding vowel is changed (ă to å, ĭ to ē, ŭ to ō),

b. In the case of the stronger laryngeals, viz., ע (prevailingly), ה and ח (almost always), the preceding vowel is retained short, the doubling being implied (§ 42. 1. b).

Note 1.—Lowering of ŭ to ō in the Pŭ'ăl takes place frequently in verbs which retain the ĭ or ă of the Pĭ'ēl.

Note 2.—In a few verbs, especially those with א, the vowel is changed in some parts of the inflection, but in other parts retained.

Note 3.—The vowel which is strengthened on account of the rejection of Dǻḡēš-fŏrtē is unchangeable.

2. *The laryngeal prefers the a-class vowels;* this is seen

a. In the occurrence of ă, *after* the laryngeal, in the Ķăl Impf. and Imv., rather than ō, even in Active verbs; and sometimes in the Pĭ'ēl Perf., rather than ē.

¹ Isa. 40 : 1.   ² Prov. 30 : 12.   ³ Gen. 35 : 2.   ⁴ Deut. 13 : 6.
⁵ Deut. 32 : 21.   ⁶ 1 Kgs. 14 : 10.   ⁷ Gen. 13 : 11.   ⁸ Ruth 4 : 4.
⁹ Ex. 3 : 3.   ¹⁰ Ruth 4 : 6.   ¹¹ Deut. 4 : 32.   ¹² Mal. 3 : 19.
¹³ Ex. 12 : 21.   ¹⁴ Gen. 45 : 17.   ¹⁵ Isa. 40 : 1.   ¹⁶ Jer. 22 : 20.
¹⁷ Nah. 3 : 14.   ¹⁸ Isa. 47 : 2.   ¹⁹ Jer. 48 : 19.   ²⁰ Josh. 15 : 18.
²¹ Ruth 4 : 4.   ²² Lev. 25 : 30.   ²³ Ex. 15 : 15.

b. In the occurrence of ă, *before* the laryngeal, in the Ķăl Imv. fem. sg. and masc. plur. But it is to be noted that

c. In the Ķăl Inf. const., the usual ō remains; and likewise the ultimate ē in the Nĭf'ăl and Pĭ'ēl Imperfects.

Note.—As a matter of fact, the laryngeal exerts less influence on a following than on a preceding vowel.

3. *The laryngeal prefers compound to simple Šᵉwâ*; this is seen in the almost universal occurrence of ⸗ under the second radical instead of ⸗.

76. *Verbs* לֹ *Laryngeal*

[For full inflection, see Paradigm F]

TABULAR VIEW

	Ķăl.	Nĭf'ăl.	Pĭ'ēl.	Hĭf'ĭl.	Hĭθpă'ēl.
Perf.	קָטַח	נִקְטַח	קִטַּח	הִקְטִיחַ	הִתְקַטַּח
Impf.	יִקְטַח	יִקָּטַח	יְקַטַּח	יַקְטִיחַ	יִתְקַטַּח
Imv.	קְטַח	הִקָּטַח	קַטַּח	הַקְטַח	הִתְקַטַּח
Inf. abs.	קָטוֹחַ	נִקְטֹחַ	קַטֵּחַ	הַקְטֵחַ	——
Inf. const.	קְטֹחַ	הִקָּטַח	קַטַּח	הַקְטִיחַ	הִתְקַטַּח
Part. act.	קֹטֵחַ		מְקַטֵּחַ	מַקְטִיחַ	מִתְקַטֵּחַ
Part. pass.	קָטוּחַ	נִקְטָח			

1. *a.* יִצְמַח (2:5); יִפַּח (2:7); יִטַּע (2:8); יִשְׁלַח (3:22); שְׁלַח[1];

b. יוֹדַע (41:31); יִשְׁבַּע (31:53); הַלָּקַח[2]; שְׁלַח[3]; יִנְגַּע (12:17); יִשְׁלַח (8:7); שְׁלַח[4]; שְׁלֹחַ [Inf.] (8:10); יַצְמַח (2:9); הִתְוַדַּע[7]; יִתְנַגַּח[7]; הוֹדֵעַ[6]; הוֹשַׁע[5]; יִשָּׁבַע (50:25); (45:1); But *cf.*: וְזָרַע (1:29); יָדַע (3:5); מְזֻבָּח[8]; מִשְׁתַּגֵּעַ[9]; and הַמְלַח[14]; הַשְׁבַּע[13]; הַגְבֵּהַ[12]; פַּתֵּחַ[11]; שְׁלַח[10].

---

[1] Ex. 4 : 4.   [2] 1 Sam. 4 : 19.   [3] Ex. 9 : 7.   [4] Ex. 4 : 23.
[5] Jer. 31 : 7.   [6] Prov. 9 : 9.   [7] Dan. 11 : 40.   [8] 1 Kgs. 3 : 3.
[9] 1 Sam. 21 : 15.   [10] Deut. 22 : 7.   [11] Isa. 58 : 6.   [12] Isa. 7 : 11.
[13] Ex. 13 : 19.   [14] Ezek. 16 : 4.

c. מַזְרִיעַ (1:11); תַּצְמִיחַ (3:18); ¹זְרַע; ²פָּתוּחַ; ³פָּתֹחַ;

⁹יִשְׁמַע; ⁸יִזְרַע; ⁷לִשְׂמֹחַ; ⁶לִפְתֹּחַ; ⁵נִשְׁלוֹחַ; שָׁלֹחַ;

¹¹אֶשְׁלַח; ¹⁰בָּקַע.

[See also the cases cited above, in fourth and fifth lines under *b.*]

d. יָדַעַתְּ¹²; לָקַחַתְּ¹³; שָׁכַחַתְּ¹⁴; הִשְׁבַּעַתְּ¹⁵; הִמְלַחַתְּ.¹⁶

2. לָקַחְתָּ (3:19); יָדַעְתִּי (4:9); שָׁמַעְתִּי (3:10); תִּפְקַחְנָה (3:7);

נְשַׁלֵּחֲךָ (26:29); בְּשַׁלֵּחֲךָ¹⁹; שִׁלֵּחֲךָ¹⁸; שִׁלֵּחֲךָ¹⁷.

Verbs whose *third* radical is a laryngeal exhibit, according to § 42. 1–3, the following peculiarities:

1. *The laryngeal prefers the a-class vowels;* this is seen

a. In the occurrence of ă *before* the laryngeal, in the Ḳăl Impf. and Imv. (where ă was a collateral form), rather than ō, even in Active verbs.

b. In the retention of the original stem-vowel ă (§ 59.) in all forms where in the strong verb it becomes ē, except Infs. abs., and Participles.

c. In the insertion of a Păθăḥ-furtive (§ 42. 2. *d*) under a final laryngeal when the latter is preceded by a heterogeneous vowel, viz.:

(1) by a naturally long vowel, ִי‏, וֹ, or וּ, or

(2) by a vowel essential to the form, as ō in the Ḳăl Inf. construct; or

(3) by the tone-long ē, which is retained *in pause* and also in the Infs. abs. and Parts., because they are really nominal forms.

d. In the insertion of a helping-vowel, viz., Păθăḥ, under the laryngeal, in the 2 fem. sg. of the various Perfects.

2. *The laryngeal prefers compound to simple Šᵉwâ; but this preference is indicated only before pronominal suffixes; the simple Šᵉwâ*

---

¹ Ps. 97 : 11.   ² Num. 19 : 15.   ³ Deut. 15 : 8.   ⁴ Num. 22 : 37.
⁵ Esth. 3 : 13.   ⁶ Isa. 45 : 1.   ⁷ Ps. 106 : 5.   ⁸ Deut. 21 : 4.
⁹ 1 Sam. 1 : 13.   ¹⁰ Job 28 : 10.   ¹¹ Ex. 5 : 2.   ¹² 1 Kgs. 2 : 15.
¹³ Ezek. 22 : 12; *cf.* 1 Kgs. 14 : 3.   ¹⁴ Isa. 17 : 10; *cf.* Jer. 13 : 25.
¹⁵ Ezek. 27 : 33.   ¹⁶ Ezek. 16 : 4.   ¹⁷ Jer. 28 : 15.   ¹⁸ 1 Sam. 21 : 3.
¹⁹ Deut. 15 : 18.

being retained under the third radical wherever in ordinary inflection the strong verb would have it.

Note 1.—The Nif'ăl Inf. abs. is נִקְטֹחַ following the analogy of the Perfect stem, rather than that of the Imperfect (§ 67.).

Note 2.—The Pï'ēl Inf. abs. and Inf. const. are the same (cf. the 'ע laryngeal verb), except that the former, being treated as a noun, changes its ă through ĭ to — and takes Păθăḥ-furtive.

Note 3.—Verbs with הּ (i. e., ה with Măppîḳ) as their third radical are 'ל laryngeal, and are carefully to be distinguished from verbs with the vowel-letter ה (§ 82.).[1]

C. THE WEAK VERB

77. Classes of Weak Verbs

1. נָתַן (1:17); נָטַע (2:8); נָפַל (4:6); נָגַשׁ (33:7); נָכָה (32:12).

2. אָמַר (1:3); אָכַל (2:16); אָהַב (27:9); אָחַז (25:26); אָבָה (24:5); אָפָה (40:1).

3. יָשַׁב (4:16), for וְשֵׁב; יָצַר (2:8); יָבֵשׁ (8:14); יָלַד (4:18).

4. יָטַב (12:13); יָקַץ (9:24); יָנַק (21:7); יָשַׁר[2]; יָמַן (13:10).

5. עָשָׂה (35:7); גָּלָה (33:19); נָטָה (11:5); בָּנָה שָׁקָה (2:6); (1:11).

6. בָּרָא (1:1); קָרָא (1:5); מָצָא (2:20); מָלָא (1:28); נָשָׂא (4:7); טָמֵא (34:5).

Those verbs the roots of which contain one or more weak consonants are called Weak Verbs. The consonants in question are such as either easily contract, or quiesce, or suffer elision. The following classes of Weak Verbs are recognized:

1. Pē Nûn (פ"ן), in which the first radical is נ (§ 78.).

2. Pē 'Ålĕf (פ"א), in which the first radical is א, and is in some forms quiescent (§ 79.). There are six such verbs.

3. Pē Wåw (פ"ו), in which the first radical is ו and is sometimes contracted and sometimes elided (§ 80.).

---

[1] The following is a list of these verbs: גָּבַהּ be high; כָּמַהּ long for; מָהַהּ (in Hĭθpalpel) delay; נָגַהּ shine; תָּמַהּ be astonished.

[2] Jer. 18 : 4.

4. Pē Yôd (י״פ), in which the first radical is יִ__ and is contracted (§ 81.).

5. Lămĕd Hē (ל״ה), in which the last radical ו or י is often dropped. Many such forms close with the vowel-letter ה, whence the verb gets its name (§ 82.).

6. Lămĕd 'Ālĕf (ל״א), in which the last radical is א, which frequently quiesces (§ 83.).

Note 1.—The Weak Verbs were in all probability once Bi-literal Verbs, and should be treated in Chapter XII. They are kept here, however, for the sake of simplicity of presentation to students just entering upon the study of the language.

Note 2.—A single verb sometimes contains more than one weak radical and so combines characteristics of more than one class.

78. Verbs Pē Nûn (פ״ן)

[For full inflection, see Paradigm G, p. 201.]

TABULAR VIEW

	Ḳăl. Impf. w. ō.	Ḳăl. Impf. w. ă	Nĭf'ăl.	Hĭf'îl.	Hŏf'ăl.
Perf.	נָטַל	נָטַל	נִטַּל	הִטִּיל	הֻטַּל
Impf.	יִטֹּל	יִטַּל	יִנָּטֵל	יַטִּיל	יֻטַּל
Imv.	נְטֹל	טַל	הִנָּטֵל	הַטֵּל	——
Inf. abs.	נָטוֹל	נָטוֹל	נִטֹּל / הִנָּטֵל	הַטֵּל	הֻטֵּל
Inf. const.	נְטֹל	טֶלֶת	הִנָּטֵל	הַטִּיל	הֻטַּל
Part. act.	נֹטֵל	נֹטֵל		מַטִּיל	
Part. pass.	נָטוּל	נָטוּל	נִטָּל		מֻטָּל

1. a. גֶּשֶׁת[1]; גַּעַת[2]; טַעַת[3]; but cf. נְסֹעַ[4] (יִסַּע); נְגֹּעַ (20 : 6).

[1] Ex. 34 : 30.   [2] 2 Sam. 14 : 10.   [3] Eccl. 3 : 2.   [4] Num. 4 : 5.

b. גְּשׁ¹ וּ֫גְשׁוּ (45:4); וְשָׁקַה⁻ (27:26); שַׁל²; גַּע³.

Remark.—כִּנְבֵל⁴; לְנְדֹּר⁵; כִּנְפוֹל⁶; נְצֹר⁷; נְתֹץ; נִפְלוּ⁹.

2. *a.* נְצָבִים (6:7); נְחַ֫מְתִּי (3:3); תִּגְּעוּ (2:8); יִטַּע (2:7); יִפַּח
(18:2).

b. יָקֶם (4:15); וַיִּפֹּל (2:21); הִשִּׂיא (3:13); הַגֵּיד (3:11);
יֻגַּד (22:20).

Remark 1.—תִּנָּגְשׁוּ¹⁴ cf. יִנְהֲרוּ¹³; יִנְאַף¹²; יִנָּאֲמוּ¹¹; יִנָּחֵם¹⁰.

Remark 2.—לָקַה¹⁵ (2:22); יִקַּה (2:15); קַה (6:21); לָקַה
קַ֫חַת (4:11).

Remark 3.—נָתוֹן (14:21); תֵּן⁻ (1:17); יִתֵּן (1:29); נָתַ֫תִּי
(41:43); תֵּת (4:12).

Verbs whose first radical is נ exhibit the following peculiarities:

1. The *loss* of נ takes place (§ 40. 1) when initial and with only a
Šᵉwâ to sustain it:

   a. Generally in the Ḳăl Inf. Const. of verbs whose stem-vowel
in the Impf. and Imv. is ă; in this case the ending ת is taken on in
compensation and the form becomes a Seğolate.

   b. In the Ḳăl Imv. of verbs which have ă in the Imperfect.

   Remark.—The Ḳăl Infinitive and Imperative of verbs with ō
in the Imperfect do not often lose the initial נ.

2. The *assimilation* of נ takes place (§ 39. 1) when, having under
it a silent Šᵉwâ, it closes a preformative syllable,

   a. In the Ḳăl Imperfect, and Nîf‘ăl Perfect and Part.

   b. Throughout the Hîf‘îl and Hŏf‘ăl.

   Note 1.—The original preformative vowel ŭ appears in the
Hŏf‘ăl, on account of the sharpened syllable (§ 35. 1).

   Note 2.—Care must be taken not to confuse with verbs פ״ן,
(1) those verbs פ״ן which assimilate ן (§ 80.) or drop it (in Inf.
Const. and Imv. Ḳăl); (2) those so-called ע״ע forms which have a

---

¹ 2 Sam. 1 : 15.   ² Ex. 3 : 5.   ³ Ps. 144 : 5.   ⁴ Isa. 34 : 4.
⁵ Deut. 23 : 23.   ⁶ 2 Sam. 3 : 34.   ⁷ Ps. 34 : 14.   ⁸ Ps. 58 : 7.
⁹ Hos. 10 : 8.   ¹⁰ Isa. 5 : 29.   ¹¹ Jer. 23 : 31.   ¹² Lev. 20 : 10.
¹³ Jer. 51 : 44.   ¹⁴ Isa. 58 : 3.   ¹⁵ Deut. 31 : 26.

Dåğeš-fŏrtē (§ 85.); and (3) the Middle Vowel Nĭf'ăl Impf. which also has Dåğeš-fŏrtē.

Remark 1.—The נ remains *un*-assimilated in verbs 'ע laryngeal, and in a few isolated instances besides.

Remark 2.—The verb לָקַח *take* treats ל like נ in the Ḳăl and Hŏf'ăl, but in the Nĭf'ăl (נִלְקַח) the ל is retained.

Remark 3.—The verb נָתַן is peculiar (1) in its Inf. Const. תֵּת (= תֵּנְתְּ=תִּנְתְּ), which has as its stem-vowel ĭ, (2) in the appearance of the same vowel ĭ changed to ē, in the Imv. (תֵּן) and Imperf. (יִתֵּן), and (3) in the assimilation of the third radical in inflection.

79. Verbs Pē 'Ālĕf (פ"א)

[For full inflection, see Paradigm H, p. 202.]

1. וַיֹּאמֶר (1:3); תֹּאכֵל (2:16); נֹאכֵל (3:2); וַתֹּאמֶר (3:2); אֹכֵל (3:12).

2. תֹּאכֵל (2:16), *but* תֹּאכַל (3:6); נֹאכֵל (3:2), *but* יֹאכַל (3:6); וַיֹּאמֶר (1:3).

Remark.—אֲכָלְךָ (2:17); לֵאמֹר (1:22), *for* לְאֱמֹר; יֵאָכֵל (6:21); יֵאָמֵר (10:9).

Of the verbs having א for their first radical, there are six (see § 77.) which show certain peculiarities in the Ḳăl Imperfect:

1. The first radical א loses its consonantal character, and the vowel of the preformative, orig. ă, is ô (rounded from â, which was lengthened from ă in compensation for the quiescence of א).[1]

Note.—This א is retained orthographically, except in the first sing., where it is dropped after the preformative א (= I).

2. The Imperfect stem-vowel is ē (from ĭ) in pause; but elsewhere generally ă; when the accent recedes, it is ĕ.

Remark.—Outside of the Ḳăl Imperfect, these verbs are treated as verbs 'פ laryngeal (§ 74.).

Note.—A few verbs are treated sometimes as פ"א, sometimes as 'פ laryngeal.

---

[1] *Cf.* וַיֵּאָצֶל for וַיֶּאֱצַל (Num. 11 : 25).

80. Verbs Pē Wāw (פ"ו)

[For full inflection, see Paradigm I, p. 203.]

TABULAR VIEW

	Ḳăl. Impf. w. ē.	Ḳăl. Impf. w. ă.	Nĭf'ăl.	Hĭf'îl.	Hŏf'ăl.
Perf.	יָטַל	יָטַל	נוֹטַל	הוֹטִיל	הוּטַל
Impf.	יֵטֵל	יִיטַל	יִוָּטֵל	יוֹטִיל	יוּטַל
Imv.	טֵל	יְטַל	הִוָּטֵל	הוֹטֵל	—
Inf. abs.	יָטוֹל	יָטוֹל	—	הוֹטֵל	
Inf. const.	טֶלֶת	יְטֹל	הִוָּטֵל	הוֹטִיל	הוּטַל
Part. act.	יֹטֵל	יֹטֵל		מוֹטִיל	
Part. pass.	יָטוּל	יָטוּל	נוֹטָל		מוּטָל

---

1. יָדַע (4:1) for וָדַע; יָלַד (4:18) for וָלַד; יֵלֵד (4:26).

2. *a.* יֵצֵא (4:16); וַיֵּשֶׁב (4:16); וַתֵּלֶד (4:1).
   תֵּשֵׁב (24:55); תֵּלְדִי (3:16); אֵלֵד (18:13); יֵדַע (4:17);
   יֵדְעוּ (3:7).
   צֵא (8:16); לֵךְ (12:1); שֵׁב (20:15); דַּע (20:7); לֶדֶת (4:2);
   דַּעַת (3:22).

   b. ³תֵּירָאוּן (21:10); יִירַשׁ; ²יִירְאוּ; ¹אִישָׁן; יִישָׁן (2:21).

Remark 1.—⁶לֵדָה; ⁵דֵעָה (3:22); דַּעַת; ⁴רֶשֶׁת; לֶדֶת (4:2)
⁷יִרָא; ⁸בִּיבֵשׁ; ⁹לִיסֹד; יִבֵשֶׁת (8:7); ¹⁰יְכָלֶת.

Remark 2.—הָבָה (11:3); ⁹רְדָה (45:9); שְׁבָה (27:19); ¹¹לְכָה.

Remark 3.—תֵּלֵךְ (12:4); וַיֵּלֶךְ (26:16); לֵךְ (11:31); לֶכֶת (3:15).

3. *a.* יֻלַּד (4:18); יוּתַר (32:25); תּוֹרָשׁ (45:11); ¹²הוּסָרוּ;
   בְּהִוָּלֵד (21:5).

---
¹ Ps. 13 : 4. ² Gen. 20 : 8. ³ Deut. 1 : 29. ⁴ Lev. 20 : 24.
⁵ Ex. 2 : 4. ⁶ Isa. 37 : 3. ⁷ Josh. 22 : 25. ⁸ Isa. 27 : 11.
⁹ Isa. 51 : 16. ¹⁰ Deut. 9 : 28. ¹¹ Num. 22 : 6. ¹² Ps. 2 : 10.

b. וַיּוֹלֶד (5:4); הוֹלִידוּ (11:27); הוֹלִיד (21:3); נוֹלַד; יִנּוֹדַע[1]
(5:3).

c. יוּבַל[3]; תּוּבַלְנָה[2]; (39:1); הוּרַד

4. תְּצִיתוּ[8]; הִצִּית[7]; תִּצַּת[6]; (28:18); יִצַּק; יִצַּע[5]; יַצִּיעַ[4];

Verbs whose first radical was originally ו exhibit the following
peculiarities:

1. The original ו passes over into י (§ 44. 1. *a*) whenever it would
be initial, as in the Ḳăl, Pĭ̇ēl and Pŭ̇ăl Perfects and Inf. Abs., the
Ḳăl Part., and the strong form of the Ḳăl Inf. Const.; and frequently
also after the prefix הִת (§ 44. 1. *b*).

2. In the Ḳăl Imperfect, Imperative and Inf. Const., two treatments exist, according as the radical ו (or י) is rejected or retained:

   a. In those verbs which reject the radical ו,

   (1) the *Imperfect* has for its stem-vowel ē (from ĭ), or (before
   laryngeals) ă, while the preformative takes unchangeable
   ê in compensation for the loss of ו.

   (2) the *Imperative* has the same vowel as the Imperfect;

   (3) the *Infinitive construct*, taking on the ending ת in compensation (*cf.* verbs פ״ן, § 78. 1. *a*), assumes the form of
   an *a*-class Seğolate noun שֶׁלֶת (*for* שֶׁלְת, § 89.).

   b. In those verbs which retain the radical ו, the *Imperfect* has
for its stem-vowel ă, while the ו, changed to י, unites with the vowel
(ĭ) of the preformative and gives î.

   Note.—Only three verbs[9] retain ו (י) in the *Imperative*, and these
are verbs which have no third radical.

   Remark 1.—The Inf. Const. has most frequently the form
שֶׁלֶת (= שֶׁלְת), before suffixes שֶׁלְת; several cases, however,
occur of the form שֶׁלָה; the form יִטַּל is found a few times, while
יִטַּלֶת seldom occurs.

   Remark 2.—Seemingly for compensation, the Imperative often
assumes the cohortative ending ה_ (§ 69.).

---

[1] Ex. 2 : 14.   [2] Ps. 45 : 16.   [3] Isa. 18 : 7.   [4] Isa. 58 : 5.
[5] Isa. 14 : 11.   [6] Isa. 9 : 17.   [7] Jer. 11 : 16.   [9] Josh. 8 : 8.
[8] יָרָה, יָרֵא, יָדָה; *cf.* also the pausal form יְרֵשָׁה (Deut. 33 : 23).

Remark 3.—The verb הָלַךְ *walk* forms its Ḳăl Imperf., Imv. and Inf. Const. and its Hif. Perf. and Imperf. on the analogy of the Pē Wâw verb.

Remark 4.—The verb לָקַח *take* follows the analogy of this class of verbs in its Imperative and Inf. Const. Ḳăl where ל is dropped. In Ḳăl Imperf. it assimilates ל as some Pē Wâw verbs treat וֹ and as נ is regularly treated in Pē Nûn verbs.

3. The first radical (וֹ), when medial, remains; but

a. It appears as a consonant only when it would be doubled, as in the Nĭf'ăl Imperf., Imv. and Inf. Const. (§ 44. 5 *c*).

b. It unites with the preformative vowel ă, and forms וֹ (ă+w= ô), in the Nĭf'ăl Perfect and Participle, and throughout the Hĭf'îl (§ 44. 3. *a*).

c. It unites with the preformative vowel ŭ, and forms וֹ throughout the Hŏf'ăl (§ 44. 3. *e*).

Note.—The form יוּכַל (from יָכֹל *be able*) is regarded by some as a regular Hŏf'ăl Imperf.; by others, as a Ḳăl Passive Imperf.

4. In a few verbs ו"פ, the י (=וֹ) is assimilated, just as נ of verbs פ"נ (§ 78.) was assimilated.

81. *Verbs Pē Yôd* (פ"י)

[For full inflection, see Paradigm I, p. 202.]

TABULAR VIEW

	Ḳăl.	Nĭf'ăl.	Hĭf'îl.	Hŏf'ăl.
Perf.	יָטַל		הֵיטִיל	
Impf.	יִיטַל	No	יֵיטִיל	No
Imv.	——	forms	הֵיטֵל	forms
Inf. abs.	יָטוֹל	occur.	הֵיטֵל	occur.
Inf. const.	יְטַל		הֵיטִיל	
Part.	יֹטֵל		מֵיטִיל	

1. ¹תִּינְקוּ (34:18); יִיטְבוּ ;וַיִּיקַץ for (9:24); יִיטַב (12:13).

2. (4:7); תֵּיטִיב ;²הֵיטַבְתָּ (21:7); הֵינִיקָה (12:16); הֵיטִיב
הֵיטֵב (32:10); וְאֵיטִיבָה ;⁴הֵטִיבִי (32:13); אֵיטִיב ;³תֵּינִק
⁷מֵינֶקֶת ;⁶מֵיטִיב ;⁵לְהֵיטִיב (32:13).

Verbs whose first radical was originally י exhibit the following peculiarities:

1. In the Ķăl Imperfect the radical י unites with the vowel of the
preformative (ĭ) and gives î (§ **30. 2. a**).　No forms of an Imperative
occur.

2. In the Hîf'îl the radical י unites with the vowel of the preformative (ă) and gives ê (§ **30. 4. b**).

Note.—No Nĭf'ăl or Hŏf'ăl forms occur.

82.　*Verbs* ל"י *or* ל"ו, *called* ל"ה

[For full inflection, see Paradigm K, p. 204]

TABULAR VIEW

	Ķăl.	Nĭf'ăl.	Pĭ'ēl.	Pŭ'ăl.	Hîf'îl.	Hĭθpă'ēl.
Perf.	קָטָה	נִקְטָה	קִטָּה	קֻטָּה	הִקְטָה	הִתְקַטָּה
Impf.	יִקְטֶה	יִקָּטֶה	יְקַטֶּה	יְקֻטֶּה	יַקְטֶה	יִתְקַטֶּה
Imv.	קְטֵה	הִקָּטֵה	קַטֵּה	——	הַקְטֵה	הִתְקַטֵּה
Inf. abs.	קָטֹה	{ נִקְטֹה / הִקָּטֹה }	קַטֵּה	——	הַקְטֵה	——
Inf. const.	קְטוֹת	הִקָּטוֹת	קַטּוֹת	קֻטּוֹת	הַקְטוֹת	הִתְקַטּוֹת
Part. act.	קֹטֶה		מְקַטֶּה		מַקְטֶה	מִתְקַטֶּה
Part. pass.	קָטוּי	נִקְטֶה		מְקֻטֶּה		

⁹הָגְלָה ;⁸נִבְנָה (18:33); כָּלָה (2:6); הֻשְׁקָה (2:10); הָיָה

---

¹ Isa. 66 : 11.　　² Jer. 1 : 12.　　³ Ex. 2 : 7.　　⁴ Isa. 23 : 16.
⁵ Jer. 4 : 22.　　⁶ 1 Sam. 16 : 17.　　⁷ Ex. 2 : 7.　　⁸ 1 Kgs. 6 : 7.
⁹ Esth. 2 : 6.

b. יְהְיֶה (1:29); יַעֲלֶה (2:6); אֲכַלֶּה (24:45); אֶבְנֶה (30:3); יַכֶּה.¹

c. עָשָׂה (1:11); רָעֶה (4:2); מְכַלֶּה²; מַכֶּה³; מִשְׁתָּאֵה (24:21).

Remark.—עֹשֶׂה⁴; רֹעֶה (4:2); בֹּנֶה.⁵

d. הִכָּה⁹; בָּכֹה⁶; הָיֹה (18:18); נִגְלֹה⁷; קֹוֹה⁸; הַרְבֵּה (15:1);

e. הַחֲיוֹת (6:19); הַבָּנוֹת¹⁰; רְאוֹת (2:19); עֲשׂוֹת (2:3); הִתְחַלּוֹת¹¹

f. הֵרָאֵה¹⁶; הַכֵּה¹⁵; כַלֵּה¹⁴; הַחֲיֵה¹³; עֲנֵה¹²; עֲשֵׂה (6:14).

Verbs whose third radical is ן are very few, the ן in nearly every case having passed over into י. Verbs whose third radical is י present the following peculiarities:

1. When the third radical (י) would be final, it appears nowhere except in the Ḳăl passive Participle. Its place is generally supplied by the vowel-letter ה, and hence these verbs are commonly termed ל"ה. The following treatments of final י__ occur:

a. It is wholly rejected, and â, rounded from ă (§ 36. 2), appears as the vowel of the second radical in all *Perfects*.

b. It unites with the stem-vowel, and ê, contracted from ăy (§ 36. 6), appears as the vowel of the second radical in all *Imperfects*.

c. It unites with the stem-vowel, and ê, contracted from ăy (§ 36. 6), appears as the vowel of the second radical in all *Participles*, except the Ḳăl passive.

Remark.—In the construct form of the participle י__ contracts with the preceding vowel (ă), yielding the form ê (ה__).

d. It is lacking, and ô (rounded from â) and ē, the usual vowels, appear as the stem-vowels of the Infs. absolute (the latter (ē) in Hïf. Hŏf., and sometimes in Pĭ'ēl and Nĭf.).

e. It is lacking, and ô (either rounded from â, or contracted from ă and w) with the ending ת, appears as the ending of all Infs. Const.

---

¹ Ex. 21 : 20.   ² Job 9 : 22.   ³ Ex. 2 : 11.   ⁴ Mal. 2 : 17.
⁵ Ps. 147 : 2.   ⁶ 1 Sam. 1 : 10.   ⁷ 1 Sam. 2 : 27.   ⁸ Ps. 40 : 2.
⁹ Deut. 13 : 16.   ¹⁰ Hag. 1 : 2.   ¹¹ 2 Sam. 13 : 2.   ¹² Mic. 6 : 3.
¹³ Josh. 9 : 20.   ¹⁴ Ps. 59 : 14.   ¹⁵ Ezek. 6 : 11.   ¹⁶ 1 Kgs. 18 : 1.

f. It unites with the preceding vowel, and ê (written הֶ֫‍‍ָ‍‍),
arising from the contraction of יֶ‍‍ָ‍‍, appears in all Imvs. (2 masc. sg.).

2. יִרְדּוּ (1:26) *for* יִרְדּיוּ; יִכְלוּ (2:1); יִקּוּ (1:9); הָיוּ (1:14);
תִּבְעָיוּן⁴; יִבְכָּיוּן³; יֶאֱתָיוּן²; חָסָיוּ¹; פְּרוּ (1:22); (1:22); רְבוּ
יְרַבִּין⁶; יִכְסָיֽמוּ⁵.

3. *a.* הֵרָאֵית¹⁰; נִדְמֵית⁷; נִהְיֵיתָ⁸; חָלִיתָ⁹; צִוִּיתָה (45:19);

  b. הֻכִּיתָ¹¹; קָנִיתִי (4:1); עָשִׂיתָ (3:14); וֶהְיִיתֶם (3:5);
    כִּסִּיתִי¹⁵; הֶעֱלִיתָ¹⁴ *and* הֶעֱלִית¹³; הִשְׁתַּחֲוֵית¹²; *but cf.*
    and כִּסִּיתִי¹⁶; צִוִּיתִי¹⁷ *and* צִוִּיתָ (3:17).

  c. תְּהֶיֽין¹⁹; תֶּעֱשֶׂ֫ינָה¹⁸; וַתַּשְׁקֶ֫ין (19:33); תֶּעֱשֶׂ֫ינָה (41:36);
    בְּכֶ֫ינָה²⁰.

4. הָיְתָה (1:2); עָשְׂתָה (27:17); רָאֲתָה (38:14); נִרְאֲתָה (9:14);
   הִפְנְתָה²¹; כִּלְתָה²²; הִשְׁקְתָה (24:46).

2. *Before vowel-additions*, the radical י is usually lacking, together
with its preceding vowel; it appears, however, in pausal and emphatic forms.

3. *Before consonant-additions*, the radical י unites with the preceding stem-vowel, always ă, forming the diphthongal *ay*, which
appears as

  a. ê (יֵ‍‍ָ‍‍) in the Perfects of the passive stems (rarely it is יֶ‍‍ָ‍‍);

  b. î (יִ‍‍ָ‍‍), thinned from ê, generally in the Perfects of active
stems, though Pi'ēl and Hif'il stems very frequently have יֶ‍‍ָ‍‍;

  c. ê (יֶ‍‍ָ‍‍), contracted from *ay*, in Imperfects and Imperatives.

4. The Perfect 3 sg. fem. of all stems lacks the third radical (י)
and takes the old feminine ending ‍ָ‍‍ת, to which ‍ָ‍‍ה is added.

Note.—This ‍ָ‍‍ה is probably the usual feminine ending, added
after the analogy of other verbs.

¹ Deut. 32 : 37.	² Isa. 41 : 5.	³ Isa. 33 : 7.	⁴ Isa. 21 : 12.
⁵ Ex. 15 : 5.	⁶ Deut. 8 : 13.	⁷ Ezek. 32 : 2.	⁸ Deut. 27 : 9.
⁹ Isa. 14 : 10.	¹⁰ Ex. 26 : 30.	¹¹ Ex. 17 : 5.	¹² Deut. 4 : 19.
¹³ Ex. 32 : 7.	¹⁴ Ex. 33 : 1.	¹⁵ Ezek. 31 : 15.	¹⁶ Ps. 32 : 5.
¹⁷ Deut. 3 : 21.	¹⁸ Deut. 1 : 44.	¹⁹ Lev. 4 : 2.	²⁰ 2 Sam. 1 : 24.
²¹ Jer. 49 : 24.	²² Hos. 11 : 6.		

5. a. ;הַרְבֵּה for הַרְבֵּ ³הֶרֶב for הַרְבְּ; צַו² for צַוֵּה; גַּל¹ for גְּלֵה;
　　 ⁴הֶרֶף for הַרְפֵּ; הַרְפֵּה for הַעֵל⁵ for הַעֲלֵה.

b. (1) ⁷וַיִּשֶׁב; ⁶וַיִּפְתְּ.

(2) וַיֵּשְׁתְּ (9:21); וַיֵּבְךְּ (27:38); וָאֵשְׁתְּ (24:46).

(3) וַיִּבֶן (2:22); יָרֵב (1:22); וַיִּקֶר⁹;וַיִּפֶן⁸; וַיִּקֶן (33:19).

(4) וַתִּפֶן¹⁰;וַנִּפֶן¹¹; וַתֵּרֶא (3:6); וַתֵּרֶב (43:34).

(5) וַיֵּשַׁע (4:4); וַתֵּהַר (4:1); וַיִּחַר (4:5); וַיַּעַשׂ (1:7);
　　 תַּעַשׂ (22:12).

(6) תֵּגַל¹²;וַיִּרָא (12:7); וָאֵרָא¹³.

(7) וַיִּתְגַּל; וָאֶאֱצוֹ¹⁵;וָאָמָן¹⁴; וַיִּצֶו (2:16); וַיֵּכַל (2:2); (9:21).

(8) וַיִּפֶן¹⁶; יָפְתְּ (9:27); וַיִּשֶׁק (29:10).

5. Forms lacking any representation of the third radical are found
as follows:

　a. Without הָ in the Pī̆'ēl, Hĭf'ĭl and Hĭθpă'ēl Imperatives;
in Hĭf'ĭl forms, a helping -ֶ or -ֵ is often inserted.

　b. Without הָ in the Imperfect when used as a Jussive, or
with Wāw Conversive (§§ **69. 70.**).　In the absence of the הָ,
　　 (1) the verbal form may stand without change; or
　　 (2) it may have the vowel of the preformative modified; or
　　 (3) it may receive the helping-vowel -ֶ; or
　　 (4) it may receive the helping-vowel -ֵ, and also have the
　　　　 vowel of the preformative modified;
　　 (5) in laryngeal forms -ַ is employed as the helping-vowel;
　　 (6) in the Nĭf'ăl there is no further change;
　　 (7) in the Pī̆'ēl and Hĭθpă'ēl there is naturally the absence
　　　　 of the characteristic Dăğēš-fŏrtē;
　　 (8) in the Hĭf'ĭl the helping vowel -ֶ is frequently employed,
　　　　 in which case the -ַ of the preformative is deflected to
　　　　 ĕ (§ **36. 4.**)

---

¹ Ps. 119 : 18.　　² Deut. 3 : 28.　　³ Judg. 20 : 38.　　⁴ Deut. 9 : 14.
⁵ Ex. 8 : 1.　　⁶ Job 31 : 27.　　⁷ Num. 21 : 1.　　⁸ Ex. 2 : 12.
⁹ Ruth 2 : 3.　　¹⁰ 1 Kgs. 10 : 13.　　¹¹ Deut. 2 : 1.　　¹² Isa. 47 : 3.
¹³ Ex. 6 : 3.　　¹⁴ Jon. 2 : 1.　　¹⁵ Deut. 3 : 18.　　¹⁶ Judg. 15 : 4.

83. Verbs Lắmĕđ 'Ắlĕf (ל"א)

[For full inflection, see Paradigm N. p. 210.]

TABULAR VIEW

	Kăl.	Nĭfʻăl.	Pĭʻēl.	Hĭfʻil.	Hĭθpăʻēl.
Perf.	קָטָא	נִקְטָא	קִטֵּא	הִקְטִיא	הִתְקַטֵּא
Impf.	יִקְטָא	יִקָּטֵא	יְקַטֵּא	יַקְטִיא	יִתְקַטֵּא
Imv.	קְטָא	הִקָּטֵא	קַטֵּא	הַקְטֵא	הִתְקַטֵּא
Inf. abs.	קָטוֹא	נִקְטֹא	קַטֵּא	הַקְטֵא	——
Inf. const.	קְטֹא	הִקָּטֵא	קַטֵּא	הַקְטִיא	הִתְקַטֵּא
Part. act.	קֹטֵא		מְקַטֵּא	מַקְטִיא	מִתְקַטֵּא
Part. pass.	קָטוּא	נִקְטָא			

1. בָּרָא (1:1) for בָּרָא; ¹נִקְרָא; קְרָא² for קְרָא; מָצָא (2:20); תַּדְשֵׁא (1:11).

2. a. ³יִקְרָאֵנִי; וַיִּבְאֶה (2:22); ⁴יִמְלְאוּ (25:24); מִלְאוּ (1:28);

   b. ⁷לְהַבְרִיאֲכֶם; ⁶וַיּוֹצִיאֲךָ; יִשָּׁאֵךְ⁵; יִמְצָאֲךָ; נְשָׂאֲךָ⁴;

3. a. ⁸מְצָאתֶם; מָצָאנוּ (26:32); בְּרָאתִי (6:7); קָרָאתָ (17:19);

   b. ¹²שָׂנֵאת; יְרֵאתֶם¹¹; יָרֵאתִי¹⁰; מָלֵאתִי⁹; מָלֵאת (31:31); נַחְבֵּאתָ¹⁷; ¹⁶בֵּרֵאתָ; הֶחֱטֵאת¹⁴; טָמֵאת¹⁵; נִקְרֵאתִי¹³;

   c. ¹⁸תִּקְרֶאנָה (2 f. pl.); תִּקְרֶאנָה (3 f. pl.)¹⁹; ²⁰קָרָאן; ²¹תְּמַלֶּאנָה.

Remark 1.—צֵאת (24:11) for צֵאת; שֵׂאת (36:7) or שֵׂאת (4:7) for שֵׂאת.

---

¹ Deut. 28 : 10.   ² Isa. 58 : 12.   ³ Ps. 89 : 27.   ⁴ Deut. 1 : 31.
⁵ 1 Kgs. 18 · 12.   ⁶ Deut. 4 : 37.   ⁷ 1 Sam. 2 : 29.   ⁸ Judg. 14 : 12.
⁹ Job 36 : 17.   ¹⁰ Jer. 6 : 11.   ¹¹ Deut. 5 : 5.   ¹² Ps. 5 : 6.
¹³ Esth. 4 : 11.   ¹⁴ Ex. 29 : 36.   ¹⁵ Ezek. 5 : 11.   ¹⁶ Josh. 17 : 15.
¹⁷ 1 Sam. 19 : 2.   ¹⁸ Ruth 1 : 20, 21.   ¹⁹ Ruth 4 : 17.   ²⁰ Ruth 1 : 20.
²¹ Ex. 2 : 16.

Remark 2.—תִּשֶּׁנָה.[4]; צָמֵתִי.[3]; נַחְבֵּתֶם.[2]; בָּאנוּ for בָּנוּ[1]

Remark 3.—דִּכְאָת[8]; צָמֵאת for צָמֵת[7]; נָשׁוּי[6]; נִטְמִינוּ[5]; מָלֵאת.[9]

Verbs whose third radical is א exhibit the following peculiarities:

1. *Final* א always quiesces (§ 43. 1); this does not affect any preceding vowel except ă, which, in an open syllable, then becomes â, as in the Ḳăl Perf., Imperf. and Imv.; throughout the Pŭ'ăl and Hŏf'ăl forms, and in the Nĭf'ăl Perfect.

Note.—The Ḳăl Imperf. and Imv. have ă for their stem-vowel, after the analogy of verbs לֹ laryngeal (§ 76.).

2. *Medial* א *is treated as a consonant* (larynge),

    a. Before all vowel-additions.

    b. Before the Šᵉwâ which precedes the suffixes כֶן‎, כֶם‎, ךָ‎.

3. *Medial* א *quiesces* (*i. e.*, loses its consonantal character) before all consonant-additions, the preceding vowel becoming

    a. ָ, rounded from ă, in the Ḳăl Perfect (active).

    b. ֵ, lowered from ĭ, in the Ḳăl Perfect (stative), and in the remaining Perfects.

Note.—This use of ē in the Perfects parallels the usage in לֹ"ה verbs (§ 82.).

    c. ֶ (ĕ), after the analogy of the לֹ"ה verb, in the Imperfects and Imperatives.

Remark 1.—In addition to instances indicated under 3 (above), א shows a tendency to become silent in many isolated cases.

Remark 2.—א, losing its consonantal character, is frequently dropped.

Remark 3.—There are numerous examples of verbs לֹ"א with the inflection of verbs לֹ"ה (§ 82.), there being an evident confusion, in many cases, of the one class with the other.

---

[1] 1 Sam. 25 : 8.   [2] Josh. 2 : 16.   [3] Judg. 4 : 19.   [4] Ruth 1 : 14.
[5] Job 18 : 3.   [6] Ps. 32 : 1.   [7] Ruth 2 : 9.   [8] Ps. 89 : 11.
[9] Jer. 29 : 10.

XII. Bi-literal Verbs

84. Classes of Bi-literal Verbs

1. קַלּוּ (8:8); יִשְׁכּוּ (8:1); יֵרַע (21:12); וַיֶּחֱל (29:20); חַי (3:22).

2. יָשׁוּף (3:15); יָמוּת (38:11); שָׁב (18:33); תָּשׁוּב (3:19); וַיָּקָם (4:8).

The Semitic vocabulary in general and the Hebrew in particular are predominantly *tri-literal; i. e.,* words are, for the most part, made upon the basis of three radical consonants. Hebrew grammars have long taught that all Hebrew words might be explained upon the tri-literal basis; and many still so teach. But it now appears to be true that originally, not only in the Semitic languages as a whole, but also in Hebrew, there were two kinds of words, those organized as *tri-literals,* and those organized as *bi-literals.* But the tendency of the language was toward tri-literality. The bi-literals gradually yielded to this influence and sought in various ways to achieve tri-literality, or its equivalent, for themselves. Some carry the marks of their bi-literal origin more plainly visible than do others. It is probable indeed that all of the Weak Verbs were originally of the bi-literal order; but for the sake of convenience they have been treated here as tri-literals. But there are two classes of verbs which from every point of view are best treated frankly as bi-literals. These are:

1. The ʿĂyĭn-doubled (ע״ע) verb, the main characteristic of which is the doubling of the second radical.

Note.—An accurate name for this class awaits discovery. ʿĂyĭn must here be understood as designating the second radical, rather than the middle radical, since these roots have only two consonants.

2. The Middle-Vowel verbs, commonly called ʿĂyĭn Wåw (ע״ו) and ʿĂyĭn Yôd (ע״י).

Note.—The name "Middle-Vowel verb" is chosen here rather for convenience than for accuracy.

130

85. The 'Ăyin-Doubled Verb

[For full inflection, see Paradigm L, p. 206.]

TABULAR VIEW

	Ḳal.	Nif'al.	Hif'il.
Perf.	קַט קָטַט	נָקַט נָקַט	הֵקַט הֵקַט
Impf.	יָקֹט יִקֹּט	יִקַּט	יָקֵט
Imv.	קֹט	הִקַּט	הָקֵט
Inf. abs.	קָטוֹט	הִקֵּט הִקֵּט	הָקֵט
Inf. const.	קֹט	הִקֵּט	הָקֵט
Part. act.	קֹטֵט		מֵקֵט
Part. pass.	קָטוּט	נָקַט	
Hŏf'ăl: Pf. הוּקַט;	Impf. יוּקַט;		Part. מוּקָט

1. *a.* הַסֵּבִּי[2]; הֶחֱלָה[1]; נָסַבּוּ (19:4); רַבָּה (18:20); יָשֹׁכּוּ (8:1);
נָסַב[5]; יִּסֹּב[4]; מְסַבַּת[3];

b. יִקַּד (24:26). יִמָּלוּ[9]; יִתֹּם (47:15); אָכַּת[8]; יִסֹּב[7]; יִדֹּם[6];

Remark.—יֵכַּת[14]; תַּמֵּר[13]; יַכַּתּוּ[12]; יֻתַּם[11]; יִסַּב[10];

2. *a.* נָדְדָה[16]; צַלְלוּ[15]; גַּלְלוּ (29:3); חָנַן (33:5); בָּלַל (11:9);

b. שָׁדוּד[21]; שָׁדוֹד[20]; סוֹבֵב[19]; חָצֵץ[18]; זוֹלֵל[17];

c. יְלַבֵּב[27]; הַשְׁמֵם[26]; לַחֲמָם[25]; לִסְבֹּב[24]; לִשְׁדוֹד[23]; לִשְׁלֹל[22];

1 Judg. 20 : 40.   2 Cant. 6 : 5.   3 Ex. 28 : 11.   4 1 Kgs. 7 : 15.
5 Num. 34 : 4.   6 Ps. 30 : 13.   7 1 Sam. 5 : 8.   8 Deut. 9 : 21.
9 Job 24 : 24.   10 Ex. 13 : 18.   11 2 Kgs. 22 : 4.   12 Deut. 1 : 44.
13 Ex. 23 : 21.   14 Isa. 24 : 12.   15 Ex. 15 : 10.   16 Isa. 10 : 31.
17 Deut. 21 : 20.   18 Prov. 30 : 27.   19 2 Kgs. 6 : 15.   20 Mic. 2 : 4.
21 Judg. 5 : 27.   22 Isa. 10 : 6.   23 Jer. 47 : 4.   24 Num. 21 : 4.
25 Isa. 47 : 14.   26 Mic. 6 : 13.   27 Job 11 : 12.

One group of bi-literal verbs sought to approximate tri-literality by strengthening the consonantal element of the root. As a rule, the second radical was therefore doubled whenever possible. The vowel used before this doubled consonant was the same as that found as characteristic stem-vowel in the corresponding forms of the tri-literal strong verb.

1. *a.* The second radical is regularly doubled, except when final, throughout the Ķăl, Nïf'ăl, Hïf'îl and Hŏf'ăl stems.

b. Some verbs double the first instead of the second radical in the Ķăl Imperf. This is the regular form in Aramaic for these verbs; this form of the Imperf. therefore is commonly called the Aramaic Imperf.

Remark.—Such forms occur sporadically in the Hïf'îl and Hŏf'ăl.

2. Certain forms of the Ķăl, Nïf'ăl, Hïf'îl and Hŏf'ăl become fully tri-literal by writing the second radical twice and vocalizing as in the tri-literal strong verb. These are:

a. The Ķăl Perfect of verbs denoting action or movement in all the forms of the 3d pers.

b. The Ķăl Participles and Infin. Absol. The naturally long vowels of these forms made any other method of strengthening them impossible.

c. A few sporadic forms.

3. *a.* ;[6]הֲסִבּוֹת ;[5]הֲשִׁמּוֹת ;[4]נְקַלּוֹתִי ;[3]סַכּוֹת ;[2]סַבּוֹתָ ;[1]גַּלּוֹתִי

b. תְּסֻבֶּינָה[7] (37:7); (41:54)‏ וַתְּחִלֶּינָה ;תִּצֶּלֶינָה

c. .[הַקְטוֹתֶם ;נְקַטוֹתֶם] ;[9]מוּסַבּוֹת ;[8]וְסַבּוֹתֶם

4. *a.* ;[13]תְּסֻבֶּינָה (37:7); יְסֻבֵּנִי[10] ;בְּחָקוֹ[11] ;תֻּמִּי[12]
   רַבְּכֶם.[14]

b. .[18](רָנִּי but) רָנִּי[17] ;רֹנּוּ[16] ;וַיִּמַּד[15]

c. .אֲהַל[19]; יִסַּבּוּ[20]

---

[1] Josh. 5 : 9.	[2] 1 Sam. 22 : 22.	[3] Ex. 40 : 3.	[4] 2 Sam. 6 : 22.
[5] Job 16 : 7.	[6] 1 Kgs. 18 : 37.	[7] 1 Sam. 3 : 11.	[8] Josh. 6 : 3.
[9] Ezek. 41 : 24.	[10] Ps. 49 : 6.	[11] Prov. 8 : 27.	[12] Jer. 27 : 8.
[13] Ps. 139 : 13.	[14] Deut. 7 : 7.	[15] Ruth 3 : 15.	[16] Jer. 31 : 7.
[17] Isa. 54 : 1.	[18] Isa. 12 : 6.	[19] Ezek. 1 : 9.	[20] Ezek. 22 : 26.

d. הֶחֵל (6:1); ‹מֵחַל; ‹מֵסֵב; ‹הָסֵבִּי; ‹הַשִּׁמּוֹת⁴;
⁶וַתָּחֶל (9:20) וַיָּחֶל; ‹תִּצֶּלֶינָה; (41:54) תְּחֶלֶינָה.

3. When terminations beginning with a consonant are attached to forms containing a doubled second radical, a *separating vowel* is inserted to make it possible to retain the doubling of the radical.

    a. The forms in the perfect take ô as the separating vowel.

    b. The Imperfect takes *ê* (יָ_) before the termination נָה.

    c. The separating vowels regularly carry the tone except before the heavy terminations תֶּם_ and תֶּן_.

    Note.—The origin of these separating vowels is not clear, but the probability is that they arose after the analogy of the ל״ה verb forms.

4. The following variations from the form of the *stem-vowel* as it appears in corresponding forms of the tri-literal strong verb are found:

    a. The original ŭ regularly appears in the Ķăl Imperf., Inf., and Imperative, whenever the tone leaves the root-syllable by reason of the addition of affixes or suffixes.

    b. The original ŭ is deflected to ŏ in the Ķăl Imperf. when the tone recedes to the preformative upon the addition of Wâw-conversive; and frequently also in cases covered by 4 *a.*

    c. In the Nïf'ăl Imperf. and Imv., where ē appears in the strong verb, the original ă is retained unchanged.

    d. In the Hïf'îl stem throughout, the attenuated ĭ is not lengthened to î as in the strong verb, but

        (1) is lowered to ē when it has the tone;

        (2) is retained as ĭ when it loses the tone by reason of the addition of affixes or suffixes, and

        (3) is deflected to ĕ when the tone recedes on account of wâw-conversive.

    Note.—A naturally long vowel before a doubled consonant is contrary to usage in Hebrew, being rarely, if ever, found.

---

¹ Jer. 25 : 29.　　² Jer. 21 : 4.　　³ Cant. 6 : 5.　　⁴ Job 16 : 7.
⁵ 1 Sam. 3 : 11.　　⁶ Judg. 13 : 25.

5. *a.* יָסֹב[1], *but* תְּסֻבֶּינָה (37:7); נָסַב[2], *but* נְשַׁדֵּנוּ[3]; נָסֵב[4],
　　.הָחֵל[7]; הָסֵב[6]; וַיְסֻבֵּנִי[5], *but*

b. הַמֵּם[8]; יִסֹב[9]; יֻדַּם[10]; הֻבַּז תֻּבַּז[11]; תָּבוֹק תִּבּוֹק[11].

c. הָחֵל (6:1); מֵחַל[12]; הֲקַלֹּתַנִי[13]; הֲשִׁמֹּתָ[14]; וַהֲשִׁכֹּתִי[15].

Remark.—אֵקַל (16:5); יֵחַם[16]; יֵחַת[17].

d. הוּחַל (4:26); יוּשַׁד[18]; מוּסַבּוֹת[19].

5. Certain variations occur in the *vowel of the preformative syllable*
from the vowel forms in the corresponding places in the strong verb.
These are:

　　a. In the regular Ḳăl Imperf., the Nĭf'ăl Perf. and Part., and the
Hĭf'ĭl Imperf. and Imv., the original ă of the preformative syllable is
rounded to å when pretonic, but is reduced to Šᵉwâ when the tone
moves farther away.

　　b. In the Nĭf'ăl Imperf., Imv., and Infins. and in the so-called
Aramaic Imperf. of the Ḳăl, the ă of the preformative is attenuated to
ĭ in the unaccented sharpened syllable and remains without further
change.

　　c. In the Hĭf'ĭl Perf. and Part., the original ă of the preformative is attenuated to ĭ and then lowered to ē when pretonic; but when
the tone moves away original ă is reduced to compound Šᵉwâ (–͞).

　　Remark.—The *intransitive* Ḳăl Imperf. with ă as stem-vowel also
has ē in the preformative syllable, but probably here it arises from
an original ĭ.

　　d. The preformative ŭ of the Hŏf. stem regularly lengthens to
û. This is probably due to the influence of the Middle-Vowel verb
(§ 86.).

　　Remark.—Frequently forms appear with ŭ unchanged and the
first radical doubled; *e. g.*, הֻמְכוּ[20].

---

[1] 1 Kgs. 7 : 15.	[2] Num. 34 : 4.	[3] Mic. 2 : 4.	[4] 2 Chr. 14 : 6.
[5] Ezek. 47 : 2.	[6] 2 Sam. 5 : 23.	[7] Deut. 2 : 24.	[8] Ps. 68 : 3.
[9] 1 Sam. 5 : 8.	[10] Ps. 30 : 13.	[11] Isa. 24 : 3.	[12] Jer. 25 : 29.
[13] 2 Sam. 19 : 44.	[14] Job 16 : 7.	[15] Num. 17 : 20.	[16] Deut. 19 : 6.
[17] Isa. 7 : 8.	[18] Hos. 10 : 14.	[19] Ezek. 41 : 24.	[20] Job 24 : 24.

6. *a.* מְחֹקֵק (49:10); יְמֹלֵל¹; וְדֹמַמְתִּי²; יִתְרֹצְצוּ (25:22);
פּוֹרַרְתָּ³; יִרֹצְצוּ⁴

b. הִתְרֹעֲעָה⁷; הִתְפּוֹרְרָה⁷; מְחֹלָל⁶; עוֹלָל⁵

c. מְכַרְכֵּר¹²; עַרְעֵר¹¹; תְּצַפְצֵף¹⁰; גִּלְגַּלְתִּי⁹; קַלְקַל⁸
הִתְמַהְמָהְנוּ (43:10).

d. רְכְבָּה¹⁶; יִתְפַּלֵּל (20:7); יְקַלֵּל¹⁵; הַלְלוּ¹⁴; הִלֵּל¹³;
יְקַלֵּל¹⁷

7. See forms cited under 3 *a, b, c,* 4 *a, d,* 5 *a, c.*

8. אֲמֹשְׁךָ (27:21), *for* בְּחָקוֹ¹⁹, *for* בְּחֻקּוֹ; לָבֹר¹⁸, *for* לָבוּר
יָרֹץ, *for* יָרוּץ²², *for* יָרֹן; יִשֹׁד²¹, *for* יָשֹׁד; יָרֹן²⁰, *for* יֵרוֹן; אֲמֹשְׁךָ.

6. The *Intensive Stems* assume special forms in these verbs.　These are:

　a. The *Pôlēl* stem, as active intensive, with its reflexive *Hiθpôlēl.*

　b. The *Pôlăl* stem, as passive of the Pôlēl, with its reflexive Hiθpôlăl.

　c. The *Pĭlpēl* stem appears as an active intensive in a few verbs.

　Note.—These stems serve both for this verb and for the Middle-Vowel verb (§ 86.).　In the Pôlēl and Pôlăl forms, the double writing of the 2d radical gives the desired tri-literality; and to express the intensive idea, the vowel of the penult is lengthened (and rounded) in place of another doubling of the 2d radical.　In the Pĭlpēl, the entire bi-literal root is doubled.

　d. A few verbs write the 2d radical twice and make intensive stems from this lengthened root exactly as in the tri-literal verb proper. These are forms that developed late.

　7. The *tone* generally stays upon the stem-syllable.　As a rule, it

---

¹ Ps. 90 : 6.　　² Ps. 131 : 2.　　³ Judg. 10 : 8.　　⁴ Ps. 74 : 13.
⁵ Lam. 1 : 12.　　⁶ Isa. 53 : 5.　　⁷ Isa. 24 : 19.　　⁸ Eccl. 10 : 10.
⁹ Jer. 51 : 25.　　¹⁰ Isa. 29 : 4.　　¹¹ Jer. 51 : 58.　　¹² 2 Sam. 6 : 14.
¹³ Ps. 10 : 3.　　¹⁴ Ps. 104 : 35.　　¹⁵ Lev. 20 : 9.　　¹⁶ Isa. 1 : 6.
¹⁷ Isa. 65 : 20.　　¹⁸ Eccl. 9 : 1.　　¹⁹ Prov. 8 : 29.　　²⁰ Prov. 29 : 6.
²¹ Ps. 91 : 6.　　²² Isa. 42 : 4.

leaves that syllable only when the separating vowels are used or when pronominal suffixes are added.

8. The forms of this verb sometimes exchange with similar forms of the Middle-Vowel verb (§ 86.).

86. *The Middle-Vowel Verb*

[For full inflection, see Paradigm M, p. 208.]

TABULAR VIEW

	Kăl. Middle *û.*	Middle *î.*	Nif'äl.	Hif'il.	Hôf'äl.
Perf.	{ קָל / קֵל }	קַל	נָקוֹל	הֵקִיל	הוּקַל
Impf.	יָקוּל	יָקִיל	יִקּוֹל	יָקִיל	יוּקַל
Imv.	קוּל	קִיל	הִקּוֹל	הָקֵל	
Inf. abs.	קוֹל	קָל	{ הִקּוֹל / נָקוֹל }	הָקֵל	
Inf. const.	קוּל	קִיל	הִקּוֹל	הָקִיל	הוּקַל
Part. act.	קָל	{ קָל / קֵל }		מֵקִיל	
Part. pass.	קוּל	{ קִיל / קוּל }	נָקוֹל		מוּקַל

---

1. *a.* שָׁב (18:33); ¹קַמְתָּ; ²שַׁבְתִּי; ³סָרוּ; ⁴סָרָה; ⁵רָמָה; ⁶דָּשׁ ⁷שָׁבָה.

Remark.—מֵת (42:38); אוֹר (44:3); ⁸בּוּשׁ; ⁹טוֹב; מֵתוּ (7:22).

b. יִמּוֹל (17:12); הֵמוֹל (17:10); נָכוֹן (41:32); נָבוֹן (41:33);

¹²נְפוּגֹתִי; ¹¹נְסוּגֹתִי; ¹⁰נְקֹטֹתֶם (10:18); נָפֹצוּ.

---

[1] 2 Sam. 12:21.   [2] Zech. 1:16.   [3] Mal. 2:8.   [4] Deut. 9:12.
[5] 1 Sam. 2:1.   [6] Ruth 1:15.   [7] 1 Chr. 21:20.   [8] Jer. 48:39.
[9] Deut. 5:30.   [10] Ezek. 20:43.   [11] Isa. 50:5.   [12] Ps. 38:9.

c. נָאוֹת (34:15); ³יֵאָתוּ; ¹יֵבוֹשׁ; ²יְאֹר; יָבוֹא (32:9).

d. הֵבִיא (4:4); הֵשִׁיב (14:16); הָאִיר (1:17); אָקִים (17:21);
הֲקִמֹתִי; ⁴לְהָקִים (9:9); מֵקִים (9:9); יָשִׁיב (50:15);
תָּשֵׁב (50:15); הָשֵׁב (38:8); הָקֵם (44:8); הֲשִׁיבֹנוּ
⁷וַהֲקִמֹת; ⁶וַיָּקֶם; ⁵תְּשֻׁבֶנָה; יָבֵא (4:3); (24:8);
⁸וַהֲרֵמֹתָ; הֵבֵאתָ (20:9); וְהֵבֵאתִי (27:12).

e. שׁוּב (31:3); קוּם (13:17); תָּשׁוּב (3:19); יָמוּת (38:11);
¹⁰שֻׁבְנָה; ⁹קֻמְנָה; נָמוּת (42:2); סוּרוּ (19:2);

Remark.—וַיָּרֶץ (18:2); ¹⁴תָּקָץ; ¹³תָּנֹד; ¹²יֵשֵׁב; ¹¹יִירְם (4:8); וַיָּקֶם
¹⁵וַתֵּשֻׁבֶנָה; וַיָּנֶם (39:12); וַיָּגָר (20:1); וַיֵּשֶׁב (26:18);

f. לָלִין (24:23); ¹⁶יָדִין (49:16); אָשִׁית (3:15); יָשִׂים (30:42);
¹⁸בִּין; ¹⁷בִּינָה; ¹⁶יָבִין;

Remark.—וַיָּשֶׁת (30:40); וַיָּשֶׂם (2:8); ²¹יִשֵׂם; ²⁰יָגֵל; ¹⁹יָבֶן;
²²וַיָּבֶן

g. ²⁸לָאט; ²⁷זָב; ²⁶קָמָה; ²⁵קָמִים; ²⁴קָאם; ²³שָׁב;

The Middle-Vowel verb is a bi-literal verb which seeks to approximate tri-literality, mainly by emphasizing the characteristic stem-vowel. Hence

1. Wherever the stem-vowel is characteristic of the form, it becomes naturally long, if the consonantal environment permits.

　a. The ă of the Ḳăl Perf. becomes â, except before terminations beginning with a consonant.

　Remark.—Stative verbs have ē or ō in the Ḳăl Perf.

¹ Isa. 29 : 22.　　²² Sam. 2 : 32.　　³ 2 Kgs. 12 : 9.　　⁴ Num. 7 : 1.
⁵ Job 20 : 10.　　⁶ Judg. 2 : 16.　　⁷ Ex. 26 : 30.　　⁸ Num. 31 : 28.
⁹ Isa. 32 : 9.　　¹⁰ Ruth 1 : 8.　　¹¹ Num. 24 : 7.　　¹² Judg. 7 : 3.
¹⁰ Jer. 16 : 5.　　¹⁴ Prov. 3 : 11.　　¹⁵ 1 Sam. 7 : 14.　　¹⁶ Ps. 19 : 13.
¹⁷ Ps. 5 : 2.　　¹⁸ Prov. 23 : 1.　　¹⁹ Jer. 9 : 11.　　²⁰ Ps 13 : 6.
²¹ 1 Sam. 22 : 15.　　²² 1 Sam. 3 : 8.　　²³ Jer. 30 : 18.　　²⁴ Jer. 49 : 9.
²⁵ Mic. 7 : 6.　　²⁶ 2 Sam. 18 : 31.　　²⁷ Hos. 10 : 14.　　²⁸ Judg. 4 : 21.

b. The original ă of all Nĭf'ăl forms is lengthened to â and rounded to ô.

Note.—This ô gives way to û in some forms of the Perf., for the sake of euphony.

c. The same change to ô takes place in certain verbs having ă as the original stem-vowel of the Ķăl Imperf.

d. The original ă of the Hĭf'ĭl attenuates to ĭ, which lengthens to î in all forms except the Inf. Abs., the Imv. 2d sing. masc., the Jussive form of the Imperf., the Imperf. with Wâw-conversive, sometimes in the Imperf. before the ending נָ‍, and in some exceptional forms.

Note.—The î in Hĭf'ĭl of the tri-literal strong verb is probably due to the influence of this î in the Middle-Vowel verb.

e. An original ŭ is lengthened to û in the Ķăl Imperf. and Infin. Const., and in the Imv. except in the 2d fem. pl., where ŭ is lowered to ō before the affix נָ‍.

Remark.—In the Jussive form of the Ķăl Imperf., ŭ is merely lowered to ō; and in the form with Wâw-conversive, ŭ is deflected to ŏ, except where it carries the tone and becomes ō.

f. An original ĭ lengthens to î in the Ķăl Imperf., Imv. and Infin. Const. of the Middle î verb.

Remark.—In the Jussive this ĭ becomes ē; and with wâw-conversive ĭ is deflected to ĕ.

g. The Ķăl Active Part. takes â (sometimes with א as vowel-letter), the vowel so characteristic of the penult of this Part. in the tri-literal verb, though in its rounded form ô; here it remains as â. The Ķăl Infin. Absol. rounds its â into ô, as in the characteristic syllable of the corresponding tri-literal form.

2. *a.* הֲקִימֹת (6:18); ²הֲרִמֹתִי (14:22); ¹יְהֲקִיצֹתִי; הֲשִׁיבֹנוּ

(44:8); ²נְסוּגֹתִי; ³נְפוּגֹתִי; ⁴נְבֹנֹתִי

b. ⁷תְּמוּטֶינָה; ⁶תְּמוּטֶינָה; ⁵תְּעוּפֶינָה; ⁷תְּשֹׁבֶינָה; ⁵תְּמוּתֶנָה

¹⁰תְּבִיאֶינָה; ⁹תְּהִימֶנָה

---

¹ Ps. 139 : 18.   ² Isa. 50 : 5.   ³ Ps. 38 : 9.   ⁴ Isa. 10 : 13.
⁵ Isa. 54 : 10.   ⁶ Isa. 60 : 8.   ⁷ Ezek. 16 : 55.   ⁸ Ex. 13 : 19.
⁹ Lev. 7 : 30.   ¹⁰ Mic. 2 : 12.

2. Forms which lengthen the stem-vowel, as indicated above, take certain *separating vowels* before terminations beginning with a consonant. These make it possible to retain the lengthened stem-vowel and, in addition, give a longer form.

a. In the Nif'al and Hif'il Perfects the separating vowel is ô (וֹ).

b. In the Ḳal Imperf. and rarely in the Hif'il Imperf. the separating vowel ê (י‍ֶ) is used.

c. These separating vowels regularly carry the tone, except before the heavy terminations תֶּם__ and תֶּן__.

Note.—Just as in the ע"ע verb, the separating vowels are perhaps due to the analogy of the ל"ה verb.

3. *a.* יָמוּת (38:11); יְשׁוּפְךָ (3:15); נָמוּת (42:2); יְשׁוּבוּ (8:3); הָאִיר (1:17); הָשֵׁב (50:15); אָקִים (17:21); יָשִׁיב ⁴; נָפֻצוּ (10:18); יְנָסֹגוּ ;תְּשֻׁבֶנָה ;נְסוּגֹתִי ⁴ (50:15); נְפוּגֹתִי ;וַיָּקָם (4:8); נָבוֹן (41:33); נְבוֹנִים ⁵.

b. נָמוֹל (17:26); יִמּוֹל (17:12); הִמּוֹל (17:10); הִכּוֹן ;יִמָּלֵא; תְּלוֹנוּ ⁷ (34:24).

c. הֵבִיא (4:4); הָשֵׁיב (14:16); מֵקִים (9:9); הָקִים ⁸; הֵנִיף ;הֲקִמֹתִי (6:18); הֲרִמֹתִי (14:22); הֲבִיאוּךָ ¹⁰; הֲסִירָה ¹¹.

d. See examples cited under 1 *c* above.

3. The vowel of the preformative syllable, when the latter is open, necessarily undergoes change:

a. The original ă rounds to å when pretonic, and is reduced to Šᵉwâ when ante-pretonic, in the Ḳal Imperf., Nif'al Perf. and Part., Hif'il Imperf., Imv., and Infinitives.

b. The original ă attenuates to ĭ in the Nif'al Imperf., Imv., and Infinitives, and remains without further change in the sharpened syllable, just as in the tri-literal strong verb in the corresponding forms.

¹ Isa. 42 : 17.   ² Job 20 : 10.   ³ Isa. 50 : 5.   ⁴ Ps. 38 : 9.
⁵ Deut. 1 : 13.   ⁶ Ezek. 38 : 7.   ⁷ Ex. 16 : 7.   ⁸ Josh. 4 : 9.
⁹ Lev. 14 : 12.   ¹⁰ Ezek. 27 : 26.   ¹¹ 2 Chr. 15 : 16.

c. The original ă of the Hĭf'îl Perf. and Part. is attenuated to ĭ and lowered to ē when pretonic, but is reduced to Šᵉwâ when ante-pretonic.

d. In the preformative of the Ḳăl Imperf., with ă as stem-vowel (1 *c* above) of some *intransitive* verbs original ĭ undergoes the same changes as the attenuated ĭ of the preformative of the Hĭf'îl Perfect.

4. הוּשַׁב ;הֻכַן[1] ;הֻקַם[2] ;יוּמַת[3] ;יוּרַם[4]; הַמּוּשַׁב (42:28);
מוּסָר[5]; וַיּוּשַׁב[6]; (43:12).

5. *a.* יְעוֹפֵף (1:20); כוֹנֵן[7]; כּוֹנַנְתָּ[8]; יְכֹנֵן[9]; אֶתְבּוֹנָן[10]

b. כּוֹנְנוּ[11]; חוֹלָלְתָּ[12]; יִתְבֹּשָׁשׁוּ (2:24); יִתְכּוֹנָן[13]

c. יְכַלְכֵּל (47:12); וְכִלְכַּלְתִּי (45:11); כַּלְכֵּל[14]; כָּלְכְּלוּ[15];
תִּתְחַלְחַל[16]; מְטַלְטֶלְךָ[17]

d. קָיָם[18]; קָיְמוּ[19]; אֲקַיְּמָה[20]; קַיְּמֵנִי[21]; לְקַיֵּם[22]

4. The Hŏf'ăl stem, having its characteristic vowel in the pre-formative syllable, naturally strengthens that vowel rather than the stem-vowel. Consequently ŭ is lengthened to û (וּ), which is of course without further change. The inflection is otherwise as in the strong verb.

5. The Middle-Vowel verb, having no middle radical to double, forms its intensive stems in a different way.

a. The intensive actives, corresponding to the Pĭ'ēl and Hĭθpă'ēl of tri-literal verbs, are known as the *Pôlēl* and *Hĭθpôlēl*.

b. The corresponding intensive passive is known as the *Pôlăl*.

Note.—For an explanation of the origin of these forms, see § 85.

c. Some Middle-Vowel verbs make an intensive stem by simply doubling the bi-literal root as a whole and vocalizing the resulting form like a regular tri-literal Pĭ'ēl, etc. These forms are known as the *Pĭlpēl, Pĭlpăl,* and *Hĭθpălpēl.*

---

[1] Isa. 30 : 33.	[2] Ex. 40 : 17.	[3] Num. 15 : 35.	[4] Lev. 4 : 10.
[5] Ex. 10 : 8.	[6] Isa. 17 : 1.	[7] Ps. 9 : 8.	[8] Ps. 99 : 4.
[9] Isa. 62 : 7.	[10] Job 23 : 15.	[11] Ps. 67 : 23.	[12] Job 15 : 7.
[13] Prov. 24 : 3.	[14] Jer. 20 : 9.	[15] 1 Kgs. 20 : 27.	[16] Esth. 4 : 4.
[17] Isa. 22 : 17.	[18] Esth. 9 : 31.	[19] Esth. 9 : 27.	[20] Ps. 119 : 106.
[21] Ps. 119 : 28.	[22] Ruth 4 : 7.		

d. Pĭ'*ēl* forms of Middle-Vowel verbs are found only in the later literature. These were probably made after the analogy of genuine Middle-Wăw verbs, such as צָוָה, עָוַל, עָוַת, etc.

6. יִמְלֹוּ (10:18); נָפֹצוּ (7:22); מֵתוּ (7:9); בָּאוּ (8:3); יָשֻׁבוּ
   תְּשׁוּבֶינָה (14:22); הֲרִמֹתִי (6:18); הֲקִמֹתִי (34:24); [1]
   נָקֹטֹתֶם[3]; תָּעוּפֶינָה[2];

7. יָדִין (24:23); לָלִין (3:15); אָשִׁית (30:42); יָשִׂים (49:16);
   בִּינָה[4]; בִּין[5]; גִּילוּ[6]

Remark.—דִּיגוּ[7]; בִּינוֹתִי[8]; רִיבוֹת[9].

8. בֵּן[10] (from בּוּן; as if from בֵּן); נָמֵר[11] (for נָמוֹר, from מוּר;
   as if from רָמַם); (רָם from) יֵרֹומוּ[12] (from מְרֹר); as if from
   (from סוּג).

6. The tendency of the Middle-Vowel verb being to stress the stem-vowel, the tone naturally stays upon this strengthened vowel wherever possible. It loses the tone only when (*a*) the endings תֶּם and תֶּן are added, which carry the tone; or (*b*) the separating vowels ô or ê are used, which always carry the tone themselves except before תֶּם and תֶּן; or (*c*) in forms with Wăw-conversive, etc., in which the stem-vowel was never strengthened.

7. Middle-î verbs differ from Middle-û only in the Ḳăl Imperf., Imv. and Inf. Const., and sometimes in the Ḳăl Passive Part., in all of which î appears instead of û.

Remark.—A few Middle-î verbs seem to show a characteristic form of the Ḳăl Perf. with î instead of â. But these forms are perhaps better considered as *Hĭf'ĭls* with the preformative dropped.

8. Since the Middle-Vowel verb and the so-called 'Ăyĭn-doubled verb are fundamentally the same, it is natural that the two should often interchange forms. As a matter of fact, the same root some-

---

[1] Ezek. 16 : 55.   [2] Isa. 60 : 8.   [3] Ezek. 20 : 43.   [4] Ps. 5 : 2.
[5] Prov. 23 : 1.   [6] Ps. 2 : 11.   [7] Jer. 16 : 16.   [8] Dan. 9 : 2.
[9] Job 33 : 13.   [10] Zech. 4 : 10.   [11] Jer. 48 : 11.   [12] Ezek. 10 : 15, 17.
[13] Mic. 2 : 6.

times develops two sets of forms, one with strengthening of consonants, the other with strengthening of vowels, *e. g.*, בַּזַז and בָּזַ֑; צוּר and צָרַר, etc. More often, only sporadic forms of a second development appear.

87. *A Comparative View of the Verb Forms*

1. THE ḴĂL PERFECT AND IMPERFECT

	Perfect.	Impf. with ō.	Impf. with ă.	Impf. with ē.
	[kăṭăl]	[yăḵṭŭl]	[yăḵṭăl]	[yăḵṭĭl]
Active	קָטַל	יִקְטֹל	יִקְטַל	(יִקְטֵל)
Stative	{ קָטֵל / קָטֹל }			
פ׳ laryng.	עָטַל	[1] וַיֵּעָטֵל	[4] יֵעָטֵל	——
ע׳ laryng.	קָאַל	[2] יִקְאַל	יִקְאַל	——
ל׳ laryng.	קָטַח	——	יִקְטַח	——
פ״ן	נָטַל	יִטֹּל	יִטַּל	[5] יִטֵּל
פ״א	אָטַל	——	יֹאטַל	יֹאטֵל
פ״ו	יָטַל	——	יִיטַל	יִיטֵל
פ״י	יָטַל	——	יִיטַל	——
ע״ע	{ קָטַט / קַט }	{ יָקֹט / יִקֹּט }	יֵקַט	——
ל״א	קָטָא	——	יִקְטָא	——
ל״ה	קָטָה	——	יִקְטֶה	——
ע״ו	קָל (â)	{ יָקוּל / [3] יָקֹל }	(6) יָקֹל	——
ע״י	קָל (â)	——	——	יָקִיל

---

[1] Or יַעֲטֹל; also יֶעֱטַל.   [2] Only in verbs פ״ן and ע׳ laryng.

[3] Jussive and with Wâw-convers. in pause.

[4] Also יֶעֱטַל.   [5] Only in יִתֵּן.

2. THE PĬ'ĒL AND PŬ'ĂL PERFECTS AND IMPERFECTS

	Pĭ'ēl Perfect.	Pŭ'ăl Perfect.	Pĭ'ēl Impf.	Pŭ'ăl Impf.
	[kăttăl])	[kŭttăl]	[yᵉkăttăl]	[yᵉkŭttăl]
Strong	קַטֵּל ,¹יְקַטֵּל	קֻטַּל	יְקַטֵּל	יְקֻטַּל
פ' laryng.	עִטֵּל	עֻטַּל	יְעַטֵּל	יְעֻטַּל
ע' laryng.	קֵחַל, ¹קִחֵל ,קֵחַל	קֹחַל	⁷יְקָאֵל	⁹יְקֹאַל
ל' laryng.	²קִטַּח	קֻטַּח	⁸יְקַטַּח	יְקֻטַּח
פ"ן	נִטֵּל	נֻטַּל	יְנַטֵּל	יְנֻטַּל
פ"ו	יִטֵּל ,יִטֵּל	יֻטַּל	יִיטֵּל	יִיֻטַּל
ל"א	קִטֵּא	קֻטָּא	יְקַטֵּא	יְקֻטָּא
ל"ה	קִטָּה	קֻטָּה	יְקַטֶּה	יְקֻטֶּה
ע"ע	קִטֵּט	קֻטַּט	יְקַטֵּט	יְקֻטַּט
ע"ע	³קוֹטֵט	קוֹטַט	יְקוֹטֵט	יְקוֹטַט
ע"ע	⁴קְטַקְט	—	יְקַטְקֵט	—
ע"ו	⁵קַיֵּל	—	יְקַיֵּל	—
ע"ו	⁶קוֹלֵל	קוֹלַל	יְקוֹלֵל	יְקוֹלַל
ע"ו	⁴קַלְקֵל		יְקַלְקֵל	

3. THE HĬF'ÎL AND HŎF'ĂL PERFECTS AND IMPERFECTS

	Hĭf'il Perf.	Hŏf'ăl Perf.	Hĭf'il Impf.	Hŏf'ăl Impf.
	[hăktăl]	[hŭktăl]	[yăktăl]	[yŭktăl]
Strong	הִקְטִיל	¹¹(הָ')הָקְטַל	יַקְטִיל	יֻקְטַל
פ' laryng.	¹⁰הֶעֱטִיל	¹²הָעֳטַל	¹³יַעֲטִיל	יָעֳטַל
ע' laryng.	הִקְאִיל	הָקְאַל	יַקְאִיל	יָקְאַל
ל' laryng.	הִקְטִיחַ	הָקְטַח	יַקְטִיחַ	יָקְטַח

---

¹ Forms with *a* under the second radical are quite frequent.
² In pause קָמָח.   ³ Pô'ēl.   ⁴ Pilpēl.   ⁵ Rare.
⁶ Pôlēl.   ⁷ Also יְקָחַל.   ⁸ In pause יִקְמָח.   ⁹ Also יִקְחַל.
¹⁰ Also הֶעֱמִיל.   ¹¹ There are a few forms like הָקְטַל.
¹² Also הָעֳמַל.   ¹³ Also יַעֲמִיל.

	Hifʻil Perf.	Hŏfʻăl Perf.	Hifʻil Imperf.	Hŏfʻăl Imperf.
	[hăḳṭăl]	[hŭḳṭăl]	[yăḳṭăl]	[yŭḳṭăl]
פ״ן	הִטִּיל	הֻטַּל	יַטִּיל	יֻטַּל
פ״ו	הוֹטִיל	הוּטַל	יוֹטִיל	יוּטַל
פ״י	הֵיטִיל	—	יֵיטִיל	—
ל״א	הִקְטִיא	הֻקְטָא	יַקְטִיא	יֻקְטָא
ל״ה	הִקְטָה	הֻקְטָה	יַקְטֶה	יֻקְטֶה
ע״ע	הֵקֵט	הוּקַט	יָקֵט	יוּקַט
ע״ו	הֵקִיל	הוּקַל	יָקִיל	יוּקַל

4. THE NĬFʻĂL AND HĬθPĂʻĔL PERFECTS AND IMPERFECTS

	Nifʻăl Perf.	Nifʻăl Impf.	Hĭθpă. Perf.	Hĭθpă. Impf.
	[năḳṭăl]	[yĭḳḳăṭăl]	[hĭθḳăṭṭăl]	[yĭθḳăṭṭăl]
Strong	נִקְטַל	יִקָּטֵל[1]	הִתְקַטֵּל	יִתְקַטֵּל
פ׳ laryng.	נֶעֱטַל[2]	יֵעָטֵל	הִתְעַטֵּל	יִתְעַטֵּל
ע׳ laryng.	נִקְאַל	יִקָּאֵל	הִתְקָאֵל[3]	יִתְקָאֵל[4]
ל׳ laryng.	נִקְטַח	יִקָּטַח	הִתְקַטַּח	יִתְקַטַּח
פ״ן	נִטַּל	יִנָּטֵל	הִתְנַטֵּל	יִתְנַטֵּל
פ״ו	נוֹטַל	יִוָּטֵל	הִתְיַטֵּל	יִתְיַטֵּל
ל״א	נִקְטָא	יִקָּטֵא	הִתְקַטֵּא	יִתְקַטֵּא
ל״ה	נִקְטָה	יִקָּטֶה	הִתְקַטָּה	יִתְקַטֶּה
ע״ע	נָקַט	יִקַּט	הִתְקַטֵּט	יִתְקַטֵּט
ע״ע			הִתְקוֹטֵט	יִתְקוֹטֵט
ע״ו	נָקוֹל	יִקּוֹל	הִתְקוֹלֵל	יִתְקוֹלֵל
ע״ו			הִתְקַלְקֵל	יִתְקַלְקֵל

---

[1] Rarely יָקֵּטֵל.   [2] Also נֶעֲטַל.   [3] Also הִתְקָחֵל.   [4] Also יִתְקַחֵל.

5. THE VARIOUS INFINITIVES CONSTRUCT

	Ḳäl.	Nif'äl.	Pī'ēl.	Hif'il.	Hŏf'äl.
	[ḳᵉṭŭl]	[hĭḳḳäṭăl]	[ḳäṭṭăl]	[hăḳṭăl]	[hŭḳṭăl]
Strong	קְטֹל ¹	הִקָּטֵל	קַטֵּל	הַקְטִיל	הָקְטַל
פ' laryng.	עֲטֹל	הֵעָטֵל	עַטֵּל	הַעֲטִיל	הָעֳטַל
ע' laryng.	קָאֹל	הִקָּאֵל	{ קָאֵל / קַהֵל }	הַקְאִיל	הָקְאַל
ל' laryng.	קְטֹחַ	הִקָּטֵחַ	קַטֵּחַ	הַקְטִיחַ	הָקְטַח
פ"ן	{ נְטֹל / טֶלֶת }	הִנָּטֵל	נַטֵּל	הַטִּיל	—
פ"ו	{ יְטֹל / טֶלֶת }	הִוָּטֵל	יַטֵּל	הוֹטִיל	הוּטַל
פ"י	יְטֹל	—	—	הֵיטִיל	—
ל"א	קְטֹא	הִקָּטֵא	קַטֵּא	הַקְטִיא	הָקְטֵא
ל"ה	קְטוֹת	הִקָּטוֹת	קַטּוֹת	הַקְטוֹת	הָקְטוֹת
ע"ע	קֹט	הִקֵּט	קוֹטֵט	הָקֵט	—
ע"ו	קוּל	הִקּוֹל	קוֹלֵל	הָקִיל	—
ע"י	קִיל	—	—	—	—

¹ Rarely קְטַל.

XIII. Nouns

88. The Inflection of Nouns

1. אֹמֶר *Saying,* from אמר; דָּבָר *Word,* from דבר; מָוֶת *Death,*
   from מות.

2. אֹתֹת—אוֹת (1:24); חַיָּה (1:1); יָמִים—יָם (1:22); רֵאשִׁית (1:1);
   (1:14); עֵינַיִם (3:6).

3. פְּנֵי—פָּנִים (1:2); רְקִיעַ—רָקִיעַ (1:14); דְּגַת—דָּגָה (1:26); פָּנִים (1:2);
   מַלְכִּי־צֶדֶק (14:18); חַיְתוֹ־אֶרֶץ (1:24).

4. אִישָׁהּ—אִישׁ (3:16); עֵינֵיכֶם—עַיִן (3:5); יָדוֹ־יָד (3:22);
   אַרְצָה (20:1); צָפֹנָה (13:14).

The inflection of nouns includes,

1. The formation of the noun-stems from the root, or from other
nouns;

2. The addition of affixes for gender and number;

3. The changes of stem and termination in the formation of the
construct state;

4. The addition of pronominal suffixes and affixes.

89. Nouns with One, Originally Short, Formative Vowel

1. *a.* קֶטֶל [for ḳăṭl]; אֶרֶץ *Earth;* עֶרֶב *Evening;* אֶבֶן *Stone;*
   שֶׁרֶץ *Swarm.*

b. קֵטֶל [for ḳĭṭl]; עֵשֶׂב *Herb;* סֵפֶר *Book;* עֵזֶר *Help;* עֵדֶן *Eden.*

c. קֹטֶל [for ḳŭṭl]; בֹּקֶר *Morning;* חֹשֶׁךְ *Darkness;* אֹמֶר
   Saying.

2. *a.* זֶרַע *Seed;* נֶצַח *Perpetuity;* אֹרַח *Path;* נַעַר *Youth;* תַּחַת
   Under.

b. אַף (=אַנְף) (cf. אַנְפִּי=אַפִּי) *Nose;* עֵז (=עֶנְז) *Goat.*

c. פְּרִי *Fruit;* תֹּהוּ *Desolation;* בֹּהוּ *Waste;* בֶּכֶה *Weeping.*

146

3. דְּבַשׁ *Honey;* מְעַט *A little;* בְּאֹשׁ *Stench;* בְּאֵר *Well.*

4. *a.* מַלְכָּה *Queen;* נַעֲרָה *Maiden;* שְׁלָוָה *Rest.*

　b. סִתְרָה *Covert;* שִׂמְחָה *Gladness;* אִמְרָה *Saying;* מִנְחָה *Gift.*

　c. אָכְלָה *Food;* חָכְמָה *Wisdom.*

1. These nouns, called *Seğolates*, had, originally, one short vowel (ă, ĭ or ŭ), which, generally, stood with the first radical. A helping-vowel was then inserted under the second radical, and the formative vowel was then changed: ă to ĕ; ĭ to ē; ŭ to ō.

2. When the root contains one or more weak radicals, certain changes occur:

　a. In 'ע or 'ל laryngeal stems, ă is the helping-vowel, instead of ĕ; and, in 'ע laryngeal *a*-class stems, the original formative *a* stands unchanged.[1]

　b. In ע"ן stems, נ is assimilated, represented in the following consonant by Dâğeš-fŏrtē, and then rejected from this consonant whenever it is not followed by a vowel.

　c. In ל"ה stems occur formations ending in ִי, ְו and הָ.

Note.—For so-called ע"ע, ע"ו and ע"י Seğolates, see §§ 100. and 109.

3. In a small number of nouns, the formative vowel stands under the second radical, instead of under the first; in these, ă suffers no change; but ĭ and ŭ, under the tone, become ē and ō; no helping-vowel is needed.

4. Many feminine nouns are formed from Seğolate stems; the feminine ending being added to the primary form (קְטַל, קְטֶל, קְטֹל); but an original ŭ is generally deflected to ŏ.

Note 1.—The Ḳăl Infinitive Const. (ḳŭṭŭl = ḳᵉṭŭl and ḳŭṭl) is with some suffixes treated like a Seğolate noun; while the Inf. Const. of verbs פ"ן and פ"ו (מְלַת = שְׁלַת) is a Seğolate formation.

---

[1] *Cf.*, however, לֶחֶם *bread,* רֶחֶם *womb.*

Note 2.—Seǧolates in the plural form look like two-vowel nouns. Whether this is a survival of an original two-vowel form in these nouns or is a later development of a one-vowel form by analogy is not clear.

90. Nouns with Two, Originally Short, Formative Vowels

1. *a.* [קְטָל for kặtặl]; אָדָם *Man;* חָכָם *Wise;* דָּבָר *Word;* יָשָׁר *Upright;* בָּשָׂר *Flesh;* גָּמָל *Camel;* דָּגָן *Corn;* חָמָס *Violence.*

　　שָׂדֶה (=sằdằy) *Field;* יָפֶה *Beautiful;* הָרָה *Pregnant.*

b. [קְטֵל for kặtĭl]; זָקֵן *Old man;* כָּבֵד *Heavy;* אָמֵן *Truly;* עָקֵב *Heel;* עָיֵף *Weary;* דָּשֵׁן *Fat;* חָסֵר *Deficient.*

c. [קְטֹל for kặtŭl]; עָגֹל *Round;* עָמֹק *Deep;* נָקֹד *Spotted;* עָרֹם *Naked;* קָטֹן (cf. קְטַנִּים) *Small;* אָדֹם *Red.*

d. [קְטָל for kĭtặl]; לֵבָב *Heart;* צֵלָע *Rib;* חֵמָר *Bitumen.*

2. [קְטָלָה]; צְדָקָה *Righteousness;* אֲדָמָה *Ground;* עֲגָלָה *Chariot;* אֲחֻזָּה [קְטֻלָּה]; *Possession;* בְּהֵמָה [קְטֵלָה]; *Cattle.*

A second class includes nouns which are formed by the employment of two, originally short, vowels, ă—ă, ă—ĭ, ă—ŭ, ĭ—ă. These nouns are, for the most part, adjectives or participles:

1. *a.* Original ă—ă, in strong stems, are rounded to å—å; in ל״ה stems, the second ă is deflected, after the loss of ן or י, to ě; in a few cases of ל״ה stems, the final הָ is lacking.

b. Original ă—ĭ, in strong stems, are changed to å—ē.

c. Original ă—ŭ are changed to å—ō; the latter (ō), however, goes back to ŭ before additions for gender and number, a Dåǧēš-fŏrtē being inserted in the final consonant.

d. Original ĭ—ă are changed to ē—å.

2. The feminines of these stems are made by the addition of הָ; this addition requiring a change of tone, the vowel of the first radical is reduced to Šᵉwâ.

91. Nouns with One Short and One Long Formative Vowel

1. *a.* [קָטוֹל = קָטָל for ḳăṭâl]; גָּדוֹל *Great;* קָדוֹשׁ *Holy;* כָּבוֹד
   Honor; שָׁלוֹם *Peace;* אָדוֹן *Lord;* טָהוֹר *Pure;* מָתוֹק
   Sweet.

b. [קָטִיל for ḳăṭîl]; אָסִיר *Captive;* יָמִין *Right hand;* נָשִׂיא
   Prince; מָשִׁיחַ *Anointed;* נָבִיא *Prophet;* פָּקִיד *Overseer;*
   צָעִיר *Little.*

c. [קָטוּל for ḳăṭûl]; אָרוּר *Cursed,* and all Ḳăl pass. parts.;
   עָצוּם *Strong;* עָרוּם *Cunning;* שָׁבוּעַ *Week;* עָבוּר *Grain;*
   שָׁכוּל *Bereaved.*

d. [קָטוֹל or קָטָל for ḳiṭâl]; כָּתָב *Writing;* קְרָב *War;* עֲבָד
   Work; אֱלֹהַּ *God;* אֱנוֹשׁ *Man;* חֲמוֹר *Ass;* חֲלוֹם *Dream;*
   יְאֹר *River.*

e. [קָטִיל for ḳiṭîl or ḳuṭîl]; בְּדִיל *Tin;* כְּסִיל *Fool;* נְצִיב
   Column; פְּסִיל *Idol;* חֲזִיר *Swine.*

f. [קָטוּל for ḳiṭûl or ḳuṭûl]; גְּבוּל *Limit;* לְבוּשׁ *Dress;* גְּמוּל
   Benefit; עֱזוּז *Strength;* כְּרוּב *Cherub;* רְכוּשׁ *Property.*

2. גְּדוֹלָה *Great* (f.); נְבִיאָה *Prophetess;* אֲרוּרָה *Cursed* (f.);
   בְּתוּלָה *Virgin;* חֲגוֹרָה *Girdle;* נְחִילָה *Flute;* אֱמוּנָה *Truth.*

A third class includes nouns which are formed by the employment of an originally short vowel in the penult, and an originally long vowel in the ultima. These nouns are, for the most part, abstract substantives, neuter adjectives, or passive participles:

1. *a.* Original ă—â become å—ô, the first vowel being rounded to å, the second to ô; this formation is to be distinguished from that with ō, described in § 90. Here belongs the Ḳăl Infinitive absolute.

b. Original ă—î become å—î; here belong many nouns with a *passive,* and a few with an active signification.

c. Original ă—û become å—û; here belong all Ḳăl passive participles.

d. Original ĭ—â become ᵉ—â or ᵉ—ô, the first vowel being reduced, the second (â) being sometimes retained, but more frequently rounded to ô.

e. Original ĭ—î or ŭ—î become ᵉ—î, the first vowel being reduced.

f. Original ĭ—û or ŭ—û become ᵉ—û, the first vowel being reduced.

2. The feminines of these stems are generally made by the addition of הָ‍ָ, the vowel of the first radical becoming Šᵉwâ.

92. *Nouns with One Long and One Short Formative Vowel*

1. [קוֹטָל *for* ḳâṭăl]; עוֹלָם *Eternity;* אוֹצָר *Treasury;* עֹשֶׂה (*for* 'ôsăy) *Making;* רֹמֶשֶׂת (*for* רוֹמֶשֶׂת) *Creeping.*

2. [קוֹטֵל *for* ḳâṭĭl]; אוֹיֵב *Enemy;* חוֹבֵל *Pilot;* כֹּהֵן *Priest;* יֹצֵא *Going forth;* רֹמֵשׂ *Creeping;* הֹלֵךְ *Walking,* etc.

3. [קוֹטָל *for* ḳûṭăl]; עוּגָב *Flute, organ;* שׁוּעָל *Fox.*

Remark.—[קִיטוֹל *for* ḳîṭâl]; קִיטוֹר *Smoke;* שִׁיחוֹר *Nile;* קִימוֹשׁ *Nettle.*

A fourth class includes nouns with a naturally long vowel in the penultima, and an originally short vowel in the ultima.

1. Original â—ă become ô—å; here belong, besides some substantives, all לה″ Ḳăl active participles, and also the Ḳăl act. part. fem. (in ת‍ָ‍ or ת‍ָ‍) of strong forms. The vowels do not change before *af*-fixes of gender and number.

2. Original â—ĭ become ô—ē; here belong a few substantives, and all strong Ḳăl participles; also those feminines of the form קְטֵלָה.

3. Original û—ă become û—å.

Remark.—There are a few nouns with an originally long vowel in both penult and ultima; the former, however, is probably long in compensation for an omitted Dåğěš-fŏrtē (§ **30.** 2. *c*).

93. Nouns with the Second Radical Reduplicated

1. [קְטָל for ḳặṭṭặl]; אַיָּל Hart; שַׁבָּת Sabbath; סַבָּל Burden;
יַבֶּשֶׁת ,יַבָּשָׁה Dry land; חַטָּאָה Sin; אַדֶּרֶת Magnificence.

Remark.—גַּנָּב Thief; טַבָּח Cook; חָרָשׁ Artificer; קַנָּא Jealous.

2. [קְטָל for ḳặṭṭîl]; מַקֵּל Shoot, rod; קַדֵּשׁ To consecrate.

3. [קְטָל for ḳiṭṭîl]; אִלֵּם Dumb; עִוֵּר Blind; חֵרֵשׁ Deaf; עִקֵּשׁ
Perverse; פִּקֵּחַ Clear-sighted; חִבֵּל Mast; אִוֶּלֶת Folly;
עִוֶּרֶת Blindness.

4. a. [קְטָל = ḳặṭṭâl]; see examples under 1. R. above.

   b. [קְטָל = ḳiṭṭâl from ḳặṭṭâl]; אִכָּר Husbandman; 1. R. above.

   c. [קְטוֹל = ḳiṭṭôl]; גִּבּוֹר Hero; שִׁכּוֹר Drunkard; צִפּוֹר Sparrow.

5. [קַטִּיל]; אַדִּיר Great; אַמִּיץ Strong; צַדִּיק Righteous; אָסִיר
Fettered.

6. [קַטּוּל]; עַמּוּד Pillar; שַׁכּוּל Childless; חַנּוּן Merciful.

7. [קַטּוּל]; לִמּוּד Learner; נִחֻמִים Consolation.

Remark.—שִׁקּוּץ Abomination; גִּלּוּל Idol; צִיּוּן Pillar; פִּגּוּל
Unclean Thing.

A fifth class includes nouns whose second radical is reduplicated. This doubling intensifies the root-idea, giving it greater force or greater firmness:

1. Formations like ḳặṭṭâl are frequent, but with no special significance.

Remark.—It is a question whether nouns of this form indicative of occupation have ặ or â (see 4. a below); the corresponding Arabic have â, yet some of these have ặ in the Construct state.

2. Formations like ḳặṭṭēl are rare, except as Piʿēl Infinitives Construct.

3. Formations like ḳ ĭ ṭ ṭ ē l are, mostly, adjectives designating deformities and faults, physical or moral.

4. *a.* Formations like ḳ ă ṭ ṭ â l are, properly, nouns indicative of occupation; but see 1. R. above.

b. The form ḳ ĭ ṭ ṭ â l is the same as ḳ ă ṭ ṭ â l with the penultimate ă attenuated to ĭ.

c. The form ḳ ĭ ṭ ṭ ô l is the same as ḳ ĭ ṭ ṭ â l with â rounded to ô.

5. Formations like ḳ ă ṭ ṭ î l are adjectives expressing a personal quality.

6. Formations like ḳ ă ṭ ṭ û l are descriptive epithets of persons or things.

7. Formations like ḳ ĭ ṭ ṭ û l are, for the most part, abstracts, and are often used in the plural.

Remark.—This is a favorite formation for terms designating or characterizing idolatrous objects and ideas.

94. Nouns with the Third Radical Reduplicated

1. שַׁאֲנָן *Tranquil;* רַעֲנָן *Green;* נָאוֶה (=נָאֲוִי) *Comely;* אֻמְלַל *Faint;* שִׁפְרוּר *Splendor;* חֲכְלִיל *Dark;* נַהֲלֹל *Pasture;* נַאֲפוּפִים *Adulteries.*

2. פְּתַלְתֹּל *Full of twists;* הֲפַכְפַּךְ *Full of turns;* אֲדַמְדָּם *Reddish;* שְׁחַרְחֹר *Blackish;* אֲסַפְסוּף *Rabble;* עֲקַלְקַל *Crooked.*

A sixth class, closely related to the fifth class, includes:

1. Noun-formations with the third radical reduplicated, the signification being, in general, the same as when the second radical is doubled.

2. A few words in which the second and third radicals are reduplicated, the signification being that of intensity, or repetition; in the case of adjectives of color, there is a diminutive force.

95. Nouns with א and י Prefixed

1. אֶצְבַּע *Finger;* אֶגְרוֹף *Fist;* אֵיתָן *Lasting;* אַכְזָר *Violent.*

2. יִצְהָר *Oil;* יַלְקוּט *Pouch; cf.* the proper names יִצְחָק, יִפְתָּח.

A seventh class includes nouns formed by prefixing א, or י:

1. A few nouns are formed by means of a prosthetic א; this א is merely euphonic and has no significance.

2. Nouns with a prefixed י occur rarely as appellatives; but frequently as proper names, where however they are really verbal forms.

96.   Nouns with מ Prefixed

1. מַאֲכֶלֶת Kingdom; מַמְלָכָה Food; מַאֲכָל [וּמַקְטָל for מַקְטָל]; Knife; מַרְאֶה Exit; (מֹוצָא=) מוֹצָא Gift; (מִנְתָּן=) מַתָּן Appearance. (מַרְאִי=)

2. מִדְבָּר [וּמַקְטָל for מַקְטָל]; Dwelling-place; מִשְׁכָּן Desert; מִקְנֶה Judgment; מִלְחָמָה War; מִשְׁמֶרֶת Watch; מִשְׁפָּט Property. (מִקְנִי=)

3. מַזְלֵג [וּמַקְטָל for מַקְטָל]; Stall; מַרְבֵּק Key; מַפְתֵּחַ Flesh-hook; (מוֹקֵשׁ=) מוֹקֵשׁ Smiting; מַגֵּפָה Plough; מַרְחֵשָׁה Snare.

4. מִזְבֵּחַ [וּמַקְטָל for מַקְטָל]; Altar.

5. מַאֲכֹלֶת [וּמַקְטָל for מַקְטָל]; Fuel.

6. מַלְקוֹחַ [וּמַקְטֹל ,מַקְזוֹל for מַקְטָל]; Want; מַחְסוֹר Booty; מִכְשׁוֹל Song; מִזְמוֹר Stumbling-block.

7. מַמְטִיר [וּמַקְטִיל ,מַקְטִיל]; Dividing; מַבְדִּיל Raining.

8. מַאֲבוּס [וּמַקְטוֹל]; Garment; מַלְבּוּשׁ Bolt; מַנְעוּל Granary.

An eighth class includes nouns formed by prefixing מ, the same element which is used in the formation of participles. So far as concerns the vowels employed the following combinations may be noted:

1. ă—å, the latter of which is rounded from ă. Feminines in ◌ָה and ◌ֶת occur. In פ"ן stems, ן is assimilated; in פ"ו stems, aw

becomes ô; in לְ"הַ forms, the second ă becomes ê (probably a contraction of ăy).

2. ĭ—â, the former of which is attenuated, the latter rounded from an original ă; the usual vowel changes take place in weak stems.

3. ă—ē, the latter of which is lowered from ĭ; the usual vowel changes take place in weak stems.

4. ĭ—ē, the ĭ of which is the attenuation of ă (cf. 3.).

5. ă—ō, the ō of which is lowered from an original ŭ.

6. ă—ô, ĭ—ô, of which ô is rounded from â, while ĭ is attenuated from ă.

7. ă—î, used only in the formation of Hîf'îl participles (m.).

8. ă—û, not used to any great extent.

For מ-formations from bi-literal roots, see § 100.

97. *The Signification of Nouns with* מ *Prefixed*

1. מַשְׁחִית *Destroyer;* מַשְׂכִּיל *A didactic poem* (= *instructor*); מַעֲרִיץ *He who inspires terror;* מַפָּל *What falls off, chaff;* מִכְסֶה *Covering.*

2. מִצְעָר *Food;* מַאֲכָל *Food;* מַלְקוֹחַ *Booty;* מַתָּן *Gift;* מִזְמוֹר *Psalm;* *That which is small;* מֶרְחָק *That which is remote.*

3. מַאֲכֶלֶת *Knife;* מַפְתֵּחַ *Key;* מַלְמֵד *Goad.*

4. מִשְׁכָּן *Dwelling-place;* מִדְבָּר *Desert;* מִזְבֵּחַ *Altar.*

5. מַגֵּפָה *Smiting;* מַדְוֶה *Sickness;* מֵישָׁר *Straightness;* מִלְחָמָה *War.*

The letter מ is from מִי (*who*) or מָה (*what*), and is used in the formation of nouns:

1. To denote the *subject* of an action; cf. its use denoting agency in Pĭ'ēl, Hîf'îl and Hĭθpă'ēl participles.

2. To denote the *object* of an action, or the *subject* of a quality; cf. its use in Pŭ'ăl and Hŏf'ăl participles.

3. The *instrument* by which an action is performed.

4. The *place* (or *time*) in which an action is performed.

5. The *action* or *quality* which is contained in the root.

98. Nouns Formed by Prefixing ת

1. תּוֹכַחַת Reproof [for תַּקְטָל וְתַקְטָל]; תַּחְמָס (?); תּוֹשָׁב Tenant; תֵּימָן South; תּוֹדָה Thanks; תּוֹרָה Law.

2. תִּקְוָה Hope [for תַּקְטָל וְתַקְטָל]; תִּדְהָר Elm; תִּפְאָרָה Glory.

3. תַּרְדֵּמָה Deep sleep [for תַּקְטָל וְתַקְטָל]; תַּשְׁבֵּץ Checkered cloth.

4. תַּכְלִית Completeness; תַּכְרִיךְ Cloak; תַּלְמִיד Disciple [וְתַקְטִיל].

5. תַּלְאָבָה Drought; תַּחֲלָאִים Diseases; תַּנְחוּם Consolation [וְתַקְטוּל]; תַּעֲצֻמוֹת Might.

Remark.—תִּפְאֶרֶת Glory; תְּשׁוּעָה Deliverance; תַּרְדֵּמָה Deep sleep.

A ninth class of nouns includes those with the prefix ת. This prefix is the same as that used in the Impf. 3 fem. It is used in a neuter sense, and is employed in the formation of abstract nouns, but rarely of concrete nouns. The cases cited above exhibit the various forms assumed by nouns of this class, as well as the vowel changes which take place in formations from weak stems.

Remark.—Nouns with ת prefixed have also, in the majority of instances, the feminine ending ָה.

99. Nouns Formed by means of Affixes

1. כַּרְמֶל Garden; בַּרְזֶל Iron; גְּבִעַל Cup of a flower; קַרְסֹל Ankle; חַרְטֹם (?) Sacred scribe.

2. *a.* אַחֲרוֹן Last; רִאשׁוֹן First; אֶבְיוֹן Poor; עֶלְיוֹן Most high.

   b. אַבְדָּן Destruction; קָרְבָּן Offering; שֻׁלְחָן Table; קִנְיָן Gain.

c. פִּתְרוֹן *Interpretation;* כִּשְׁרוֹן *Success;* עִוָּרוֹן *Blindness;*
גָּאוֹן בִּטָּחוֹן *Confidence;* זִכָּרוֹן *Memorial;* עִצָּבוֹן *Pain;* גָּאוֹן
Majesty.

A tenth class of nouns includes those with affixes, ל, מ and נ:

1. Nouns formed by the addition of ל and מ are few, and have no special significance; they should perhaps be regarded as quadri-literals and may reflect some foreign influence.

2. Nouns formed by the addition of נ are numerous, including

   a. Adjectives formed either from a noun-stem or from a root.

   b. Abstract substantives ending in ân.

   c. Abstract substantives ending in ôn, rounded from ân.

100. *Nouns from Bi-Literal Roots*

1. *a.* רַב *Great;* רַךְ *Tender;* דַּל *Weak;* מַר *Bitter;* תָּם *Complete;*
כַּלָּה *Bride;* מַצָּה *Unleavened bread;* כַּפַּיִם *Hands.*

אֵם *Mother;* תֵּל *Mound;* לֵב *Heart;* שֵׁן *Tooth;* צֵל *Shadow;*
מִדָּה *Measurement;* מִלָּה *Word;* בִּצָּה *Swamp;* בִּזָּה *Spoil;*
אִמּוֹ *His mother.*

תֹּם *Completeness;* כֹּל *All;* חֹק *Statute;* דֹּב *Bear;* רֹב *Mul-*
titude; תֻּמָּה *Integrity;* חֻקָּה *Statute;* כֻּלָּם *All of them.*

   b. קָם ;רָם ;בָּן; Ḳăl act. ptcp. of ע״וּ and ע״י verbs.

מֹץ *Chaff;* תּוֹר *Turn;* שׁוֹר *Ox;* שׁוֹק *Leg.*

גֵּר *Stranger;* נֵר *Lamp;* מֵת *Dead;* רֵעַ *Noise.*

רוּם ;קוּם ;גוּר ;מוּת; Inf. Const. of ע״וּ verbs.

בִּינָה *Understanding;* דִּין *Judgment;* רִיב *Strife;* גִּיל, גִּילָה
Joy; מִין *Sort;* קִינָה *Dirge.*

2. גַּלְגַּל *Wheel;* חַתְחַת *Frightful;* כַּדְכֹּד *Ruby;* קָדְקֹד *Crown*
of head; גֻּלְגֹּלֶת *Skull;* בַּקְבּוּק *Flask;* קַלְקַל *Worthless;*
תַּעְתֻּעִים *Scorn.*

3. *a.* מָסָךְ *Cover;* מֵסַב *Circle;* מֵרַע *Evil;* מֵצַר *Distress;* מְשַׂמָּה
Desolation; מָגֵן *Shield;* מְגִלָּה *Roll;* מִגְנָה *Covering;*
מְזִמָּה *Purpose;* מְסִלָּה *Highway;* מְחִתָּה *Terror;* מֵסַב
Divan; מְשֻׂכָּה *Covering;* מְשׂוּכָה *Hedge.*

b. מָאוֹר *Luminary;* מָרוֹם *Height;* מָקוֹם *Place;* מָגוֹר *Terror;*
מְנוֹרָה *Lamp-* stand; מָנוֹחַ *Rest;* מָנוֹס *Flight;* מָבוֹא *Entrance;*
מְגוֹרָה *Terror;* מְחוֹלָה *Dancing;* מָצוּק *Pillar;*
מְרוּצָה *Running;* מְשׁוּבָה *Apostasy;* מְנוּחָה *Rest;*
מְבוּכָה *Weeping;* מֵקִים *Raising;* מְרִיבָה *Strife;* מְדִינָה
Province.

c. מוּסָר *Removed;* מוּסָךְ *Coverer (?);* מוּסָב *Surrounding (?).*

d. מְתֹם *Soundness;* מֹרֶךְ *Weakness.*

4. *a.* תְּפִלָּה *Praise;* תְּחִלָּה *Beginning;* תְּחִנָּה *Favor;* תְּהִלָּה
Prayer.

b. תְּבוּנָה *Understanding;* תְּרוּמָה *Offering;* תְּמוּנָה *Likeness;*
תְּבוּסָה *Ruin;* תְּמוּרָה *Exchange;* תְּמוּתָה *Death;*
תְּבוּאָה *Product.*

5. הָאִיר *To shine;* הֲנָפָה *Waving;* הֲנָחָה *Rest;* הֲפוּגָה *Cessation;* הָקֵם *To raise;* הָסֵב *To cause to turn.*

6. נָכוֹן, נְכוֹנָה *Established;* נְשַׁמָּה *Desolated.*

7. יְקוּם *Being;* יָרִיב *Adversary.*

8. סֻלָּם *Ladder;* אוּלָם *Porch;* עֵירֹם *Naked;* עָרֹם *Naked.*

9. תֶּמֶס *Melting;* תֹּפֶת *Contempt.*

Under this head are treated those nouns which are formed upon
the foundation of two radicals and have not progressed to complete
tri-literality by actually writing one of those radicals twice and vocalizing the resultant form as a tri-literal noun, *e. g.* מִכְלוֹל. There
is a relatively wide range of forms in bi-literal nouns.

1. Monosyllabic nouns of various forms:

a. Those with one of the original short-vowels as the primary form. The vowels ĭ and ŭ, and occasionally ă, change under the tone to ē, ō and å respectively. When affixes are added, the second radical takes Dåğēš-fŏrtē and the stem-vowel remains short. These all come from so-called ע״ע roots.

b. Those with an unchangeable vowel, which of course is unaffected by the addition of affixes; but â regularly is rounded to ô, except in the Ḳăl act. ptcp. These all come from Middle-Vowel roots.

2. Nouns made by reduplication of the bi-literal stem.

3. Nouns with the prefix מ. These assume several forms:

a. Those which in the primary form have the prefix mă with a short stem-vowel. These (1) regularly change both vowels, măḳăl becoming måḳål; măḳĭl becoming måḳēl; and măḳŭl becoming måḳōl; (2) when affixes are added, the second radical of the stem receives Dåğēš-fŏrtē, the original stem-vowel remains unchanged, and the ă of the preformative syl. is reduced to Šᵉwâ (—); (3) those having ă as the original stem-vowel generally retain it without change, but the preformative syllable has ē, probably from an original ĭ. This formation occurs only in the so-called ע״ע roots.

b. Those which in the primary form have the prefix mă and a naturally long stem-vowel. The preformative ă becomes å in the absolute singular form, but is reduced to Šᵉwâ whenever affixes are added. This formation is characteristic of Middle-Vowel roots.

(1) The stem-vowel may be either ô (וֹ), û (וּ), or î (י_).

(2) With the stem-vowel î (י_), the preformative vowel becomes ē, either by assimilation to the stem-vowel, or after the analogy of the Hĭf'îl perfect. This is the form of the Hĭf'îl ptcp. of ע״ו and י״ע verbs.

c. Those having the prefix mû, with the stem-vowel ă, which is rounded to å. This is the form of the Hŏf'ăl participle of bi-literal verbs.

d. A few exceptional forms.

4. Nouns with the prefix ת. These nearly all have the feminine ending and fall into two classes:

a. Those having ĭ as stem-vowel followed by Dåğēš-fŏrtē in the second radical of the stem. The preformative vowel is reduced to Š•wâ upon the addition of the feminine affix.

b. Those having û as stem-vowel, without a following Dåğēš-fŏrtē, but with the same reduction of the preformative ă to Š•wâ upon the addition of the feminine affix.

5. Nouns with the prefix הּ. These are few, aside from the Infinitives of the Hĭf'îl, Hŏf'ăl and Nĭf'ăl of bi-literal verbs and are practically all verbal nouns.

6. Nouns with the prefix nă. These are practically confined to the Nĭf'ăl participle and Infin. of bi-literal verbs, in which the ă of the prefix regularly is rounded to å before the tone and is reduced to Š•wâ when not pretonic.

7. A few nouns are made with the prefix y (יִ).

8. A few bi-literal nouns with affixes occur, viz. (a) the affix ăm; (b) the affix ŭm. There is room for doubt as to the origin of these nouns.

9. A few isolated formations appear.

101. Nouns Having Four or Five Radicals

1. עַקְרָב Scorpion; גִּזְבָּר Treasurer; חֶרְמֵשׁ Sickle; חֲנָמָל Frost; חַלָּמִישׁ Flint; פִּלֶגֶשׁ Concubine; עֲטַלֵּף Bat.

2. אַרְגָּמָן Purple; שַׁעַטְנֵז A kind of cloth; אֲחַשְׁתְּרָן Mule.

1. Nouns with four radicals are comparatively few; they have no special classification or signification.

2. Nouns with five or more radicals are still fewer, and, for the most part, of foreign origin.

102. Compound Nouns

1. מְאוּמָה Anything; בְּלִיַּעַל Worthlessness; אֶתְמוֹל Formerly.

2. מַלְכִּי־צֶדֶק King of righteousness; יִשְׁמָעֵאל God hears.

1. Compound words, as common nouns, are few and doubtful.
2. Compound words, as proper names, are very numerous.

103. Nouns Formed from Other Nouns

1. שֹׁעֵר *Porter* (cf. שַׁעַר *Gate*); כֹּרֵם *Vine-dresser* (cf. כֶּרֶם *Vine-yard*).

2. מַעְיָן *Place of the fountain* (cf. עַיִן *Fountain*); מַרְגְּלוֹת *Place of feet* (cf. רֶגֶל *Foot*).

3. אַחֲרוֹן *Last* (cf. אַחַר *After*); עִוָּרוֹן *Blindness* (cf. עִוֵּר *Blind*). לִוְיָתָן *Coiled, serpent* (cf. לִוְיָה *Wreath*); נְחֻשְׁתָּן *Brazen* (cf. נְחֹשֶׁת *Bronze*).

4. *a.* שְׁלִישִׁי *Third* (cf. שָׁלֹשׁ); חֲמִישִׁי *Fifth;* etc.

   b. עִבְרִי *Moabite;* אֲרַמִּי *Aramæan;* גֵּרְשֻׁנִּי *Gershonite;* מוֹאָבִי *Hebrew.*

   צְפוֹנִי *Northerner;* נָכְרִי *Foreigner;* פְּרָזִי *Villager.*

5. רֵאשִׁית *Beginning;* מַלְכוּת *Kingdom;* אַלְמָנוּת *Widowhood.*

Nouns formed from other nouns, and not directly from the root, are termed denominatives. The most common formations are:

1. Nouns with the form of the Ḳăl active participle, indicating *agency.*

2. Nouns with the prefix מ, indicating the *place* where a thing is found.

3. Adjectives and nouns formed by the affix וֹן or וָן (seldom וּן).

4. Adjectives formed by the affix יִ; these are,

   a. Ordinals formed from cardinals;

   b. Gentilics and patronymics; and a few others.

5. Nouns formed by the affixes יִת and וּת, designating abstract ideas.

104. The Formation of Noun-Stems

From §§ 88–103. it has been seen that noun-stems are formed,

1. *Directly from the root:*

   a. By means of *vowels* given to the root; as in the case of

      (1) nouns with one, originally short, vowel (§§ 89, 100.);

(2) nouns with one originally long vowel (§ **100.**);

(3) nouns with two (originally) short vowels (§ **90.**);

(4) nouns with one (originally) short and one long vowel (§ **91.**);

(5) nouns with one long and one (originally) short vowel (§ **92.**);

b. By a reduplication of one or more of the consonants of the root; as in the case of

(1) nouns with the second radical doubled (§ **93.**);

(2) nouns with the third, or the second and third radicals doubled (§ **94.**);

(3) nouns with the entire root doubled (§ **100.**);

c. By prefixing vowels and consonants to the root; as in the case of

(1) nouns with א, ה or י prefixed (§§ **95, 100.**);

(2) nouns with מ prefixed (§§ **96, 97, 100.**);

(3) nouns with ת prefixed (§§ **98, 100.**);

d. By affixing vowels and consonants to the root; as in the case of

(1) nouns with ל, מ or נ affixed, with a vowel (§§ **99, 100.**);

(2) nouns with four or five radicals (§ **101.**);

(3) nouns compounded of two distinct words (§ **102.**).

2. *From other nouns* (and called denominatives), by the various means indicated above (§ **103.**).

105. The Formation of Cases

1. מְתוּ in מְתוּשָׁאֵל (4:18); שְׁמוּ in שְׁמוּאֵל[1]; פְּנוּ in פְּנוּאֵל (32:32).

Remark.— מֵעֵינוּ; בְּנוּ צִפֹּר[3]; בְּנוֹ בְעֹר[2]; חַיְתוֹ־אֶרֶץ (1:24); מֵימ[4].

2. *a.* הָאֹהֱלָה; יָמָּה (13:14); אַרְצָה הַנֶּגֶב (20:1); צָפֹנָה (13:14); (18:6).

b. שְׁלִישׁוֹ־ם (31:2) *for* šilšâm; חִנָּ־ם (29:15); יוֹמָ־ם[5];

---

[1] 1 Sam. 1:20　　　[2] Num. 24:3, 15.　　　[3] Num. 23:18.　　　[4] Ps. 114:8.
[5] Ex. 13:21.

Very slight evidence of case-endings is found in Hebrew:

1. The only possible case of a nominative ending is the û in the first part of a few proper names; as in the examples cited above, מְתוּ = *man of;* שְׁמוּ = *name of;* פְּנוּ = *face of.* This is open to serious doubt since the words to which û is attached do not function as nominatives in these cases.

> **Remark.**—An old ending וֹ = ô, appears in a few forms, but its origin and significance are unknown.

2. The *accusative* had the ending *a* and appears only

   a. In the so-called Hē *directive* (הָ‍ַ), which

      (1) is used to denote *direction* or *motion;* but

      (2) is often used in a weaker sense to designate the place *where,* and

      (3) in many cases seems to be entirely without force.

   b. In the syllables âm and ôm (the latter by the rounding of â), which are found in certain adverbs.

3. No *genitive* ending appears in our texts.

106. *Affixes for Gender and Number*

1. אוֹר (1:3); רָקִיעַ (1:6); בֹּקֶר (1:5); יוֹם (1:5); טוֹב (1:4); (1:6).

2. *a.* אִמְרָתִי (4:23); אִשְׁתּוֹ (2:24); מִנְחָתוֹ (4:5).

   דְּנַת (31:39); גְּנַבְתִּי (1:24); חַיָּתוֹ (1:25); (חַיָּה) חַיַּת (דָּגָה) (1:26); (נְשָׁמָה) נִשְׁמַת (2:7).

   b. רֶמֶשׂ (1:2); מְרַחֶפֶת (1:26); דְּמוּת (1:1); רֵאשִׁית (1:21).

   דַּעַת (4:2); לֶדֶת (1:16); מֶמְשֶׁלֶת (3:24); מִתְהַפֶּכֶת (2:9); קְהָת (4:11).

   c. אֲדָמָה (2:5); חַיָּה (1:24); בְּהֵמָה (1:24); יַבָּשָׁה (1:9); אִשָּׁה (3:4).

3. אֹתֹת (1:14); חֲגֹרֹת (3:7); תּוֹלְדוֹת (2:4).

4. *a.* אֱלֹהִים (1:1); יָמִים (1:22); יָמִים (1:14); מוֹעֲדִים (1:14); שָׁנִים (1:14).

b. פְּנֵי (1:2); יֹדְעֵי (3:5); נְשֵׁי (4:23); בְּנֵי (6:4); אַנְשֵׁי (6:4).

5. שְׁנַיִם, whence שְׁנֵי (1:16); עֵינַיִם (3:6), but עֵינֵי (3:7).

The Hebrew has two genders,—masculine and feminine; and three numbers,—singular, dual and plural.

1. The *masculine singular* has no particular indication.

2. The sign of the *feminine singular* is תְ_. This feminine sign has a threefold treatment:

　　a. It is retained, with such change of its vowel as may be necessary, whenever the noun of which it is a part is in close connection with what follows; as when it (the feminine-sign, תְ) stands

　　　　(1) before a pronominal suffix (§ 108);

　　　　(2) at the end of a noun in the Construct state (§ 107.).

　　b. It appears as תָ_ (with laryngeals תַ_), in the formation and inflection of many nouns, participles and infinitives.

　　c. תָ gives way to ה, which then ceases to be pronounced, but is retained orthographically as a mere symbol of final â rounded from ă. *This form is the more usual indication of the feminine gender.*

3. The *feminine plural* is indicated by the ending וֹת (ôθ for âθ), which is unchangeable.

4. The *masculine plural* is indicated by the endings,

　　a. יִם_ (îm) in the Absolute state (§ 107.).

　　b. ֵי_ (ê) in the Construct state (§ 107.).

Note.—Many masculine nouns have plurals in ôθ, and many feminine nouns have plurals in îm.

5. The *dual,* used chiefly of objects which go in pairs, is indicated by the endings,

　　a. יִם_ (ăyĭm) in the Absolute state.

　　b. ֵי_ (ê) in the Construct state.

107. The Absolute and Construct States

1. אֱלֹהִים (1:1); הַשָּׁמַיִם (1:1); הָאָרֶץ (1:1); הָאוֹר (1:3); רָקִיעַ (1:6).

2. פְּנֵי תְהוֹם (1:2) *faces-of abyss;* רוּחַ אֱלֹהִים (1:2) (the) *spirit-of God;* בִּרְקִיעַ הַשָּׁמַיִם (1:14) *in-(the)-expanse-of the heavens.*

Of two nouns closely related, the second, in Latin or Greek, is in the genitive, *e. g.*, *dominus dominorum*. The same relation is indicated in Hebrew by pronouncing the second noun in close connection with the first. The effort thus to unite the two words in pronunciation as one phrase results invariably in a shortening of the *first* word, because the tone hastens on to the second, but involves also a retention of some old endings which hold their place in the phrase.

1. A noun which is not thus dependent upon a following substantive or pronoun is said to be in the *Absolute state*.

2. A noun which *is* thus dependent on a following substantive or pronoun is said to be in the *Construct* state.

Note.—It is the *first* of two nouns, therefore, and not the *second*, which suffers change.

3. רֹעֶה (4:2), *cf.* רֹעֵה; מִקְוֶה (1:10), *cf.* מִקְוֵה; עָלֶה (3:7), *cf.* עָלֵה; חַי (42:15), *cf.* חֵי; גַּיְא[1] *cf.* גֵּיא.[2]

4. דָּגָה (1:25) *instead of* חַיָּה; דְּגַת (1:26) *instead of* חַיַּת.

5. חַיְתוֹ (1:24); גְּנַבְתִּי (31:39); בְּנוֹ;[3] מַעְיָנוֹ;[4] בְּנִי (49:11); עֹזְבִי;[5] שֹׁכְנִי.[6]

6. פְּנֵי (1:2), *cf.* פָּנִים; יְמֵי (3:17), *cf.* יָמִים; דְּמֵי (4:11), *cf.* דָּמִים; עֵינֵי (3:7), *cf.* עֵינַיִם; שְׁנֵי (1:16), *cf.* שְׁנַיִם; דָּמִים.

Remark.—*Abs.*, פְּרִי (1:11), *Const.*, פְּרִי (1:29); *Abs.*, צָבָא,[7] *Const.*, צְבָא;[8] *Abs.*, יָרֵא (32:12), *Const.*, יְרֵא (22:12); *Abs.*, מֶלֶךְ (14:17), *Const.*, מֶלֶךְ (14:1); *Abs.*, סֵפֶר,[9] *Const.*, סֵפֶר (5:1); *Abs.*, נַעַר (37:2), *Const.*, נַעַר.[10]

So far as concerns *endings* or *affixes*, the Construct state differs from the Absolute in the following particulars:

3. Final הֶ‏ (*i. e.*, ê = ay) gives place to הֵ‏ (*i. e.*, ê = ay).

Note.—Compare with this the fact that in ל״ה verbs, the Imperfect ends in הֶ‏ (ê), but the Imperative in הֵ‏ (ê).

---

[1] Josh. 15 : 8.　[2] Num. 21 : 20.　[3] Num. 23 : 18.　[4] Ps. 114 : 8.
[5] Deut. 33 : 16.　[6] Zech. 11 : 17.　[7] Num. 1 : 3.　[8] Deut. 4 : 19.
[9] 2 Kgs. 5 : 5.　[10] 1 Sam. 2 : 13.

4. The original form of the feminine affix ‏תְ‎, preserved by its close connection with what follows, appears instead of the later ‏הָ‎.

5. The endings ô (‏וֹ‎) and î (‏י‎) appear occasionally in Construct forms, serving as connecting vowels binding the Construct to its genitive.

6. The affix ‏יַ‎ (= ay) appears instead of the ordinary plural and dual endings ‏יִם‎ and ‏יִם‎.

Remark 1.—The feminine plural affix ôθ is the same in Absolute and Construct.

Remark 2.—Final vowels, other than those just mentioned, as well as final å when followed by ‏א‎, and Seğolates in the singular (strong and laryngeal) do not suffer change in the Construct state.

Remark 3.—The Construct form may best be explained by understanding that it is really a constituent element of a phrase which tends somewhat toward becoming a compound word. The Construct itself, therefore has no primary tone, the tone having passed on to the next word.

108. The Pronominal Suffixes
[See Paradigms **A**. and **C**.]
TABULAR VIEW

	Masc. sg.	Masc. plur.	Fem. sg.	Fem. plur.
Absolute	סוּס	סוּסִים	סוּסָה	סוּסוֹת
Construct	סוּס	סוּסֵי	סוּסַת	סוּסוֹת
Sing. 1 c.	סוּסִי	סוּסַי	סוּסָתִי	סוּסוֹתַי
2 m.	סוּסְךָ	סוּסֶיךָ	סוּסָתְךָ	סוּסוֹתֶיךָ
2 f.	סוּסֵךְ	סוּסַיִךְ	סוּסָתֵךְ	סוּסוֹתַיִךְ
3 m.	סוּסוֹ	סוּסָיו	סוּסָתוֹ	סוּסוֹתָיו
3 f.	סוּסָהּ	סוּסֶיהָ	סוּסָתָהּ	סוּסוֹתֶיהָ
Plur. 1 c.	סוּסֵנוּ	סוּסֵינוּ	סוּסָתֵנוּ	סוּסוֹתֵינוּ
2 m.	סוּסְכֶם	סוּסֵיכֶם	סוּסַתְכֶם	סוּסוֹתֵיכֶם
2 f.	סוּסְכֶן	סוּסֵיכֶן	סוּסַתְכֶן	סוּסוֹתֵיכֶן
3 m.	סוּסָם	סוּסֵיהֶם	סוּסָתָם	סוּסוֹתֵיהֶם
3 f.	סוּסָן	סוּסֵיהֶן	סוּסָתָן	סוּסוֹתֵיהֶן

1. *a.* צאנו; יָדְ־הוּ (3:22) *for* יָדוֹ; לְמִינֵ־הוּ (1:11) *for* לְמִינוֹ (4:4).

זַרְעָה; אִישָׁ־הָ (3:6) *for* אִישָׁהּ; לְמִינֵ־הָ (1:24) *for* לְמִינָהּ (3:15).

⁶לָבֵ־ן; ⁵קוֹלְ־ן; ⁴יוֹמָ־ם; ³דַּרְכָּ־ם; ²אַרְצָ־ם; ¹קוֹלָ־ם;
אֲכָלְכֶם (3:5); זַרְעֵךְ (3:15); גְּחֹנְךְ (3:14); קֹלֶךְ (3:10).

b. צַלְמֵ־נוּ; אִישֵׁ־ךְ (3:16); הֵרֹנֵ־ךְ (3:16); שָׁדֵ־הוּ (23:9); (1:26).

פִּיהֻ (4:11); אָחִיו (4:8); אָחִיךָ (4:9); אָבִיו (2:24).

2. חַבֵּרְתִי הַבְּרָה *but* (4:23); אִמְרָתִי (4:23); אָמְרָה *but* (4:23); תְּשׁוּקָתוֹ (4:7).

The relation existing between a noun and its pronominal suffix is really the Construct relation. The form of the noun, however, is not always identical with that of the Construct, but varies with the position of the tone. In this section only the *endings* of the noun, as affected by the suffix, are treated.

1. Masculine nouns in the singular take,

     a. A connecting vowel ă

         (1) in the form of å, before הוּ, הָ, ם and ן, the suffixes of the 3d person;

         (2) in the form of ־ַ, before ךָ, כֶם, כֶן.

     b. A connecting vowel ĭ

         (1) in the form of ē before הוּ (in ל״ה stems and a few poetical forms), נוּ, ךָ.

         (2) in the form of î before all suffixes in the words אָב *father,* אָח *brother,* פֶּה *mouth.*

Remark 1.—Certain changes take place, viz., ־ֵהוּ to ו, ־ֶהָ to הָ, the final vowel of the latter form having been dropped.

Remark 2.—Before ךָ, כֶם, כֶן ă is deflected to ĕ in pause.

---

¹ Num 14:1.   ² Deut. 4:38.   ³ 1 Kgs. 2:4.   ⁴ Jer. 15:9.
⁵ Ruth 1:9.   ⁶ Ex. 35:26.

2. Feminine nouns in the singular preserve before suffixes the earlier form of the feminine affix, which is תְ_; but the _ when standing in an open syllable is rounded.

Note.—The feminine affix is followed by the same connecting vowels as those which occur with masculine nouns (see above, 1. *a*, *b*).

3. *a.* עֲצָמִי (2:23); [1]דְּרָכַי; [2]דְּרָכֶיךָ; [3]פָּנֶיךָ; [4]כְּנָפֶיךָ.

   b. [5]לְמִינֵהֶם (4:4); חֶלְבְּהֶן (3:5); עֵינֵיכֶם (2:25); שְׁנֵיהֶם (1:21).

   c. [6]פָּנֶיהָ (4:6); פָּנֶיךָ (3:19); אַפֵּיךָ (3:14); חַיַּיִךְ.

   d. [8]כְּנָפָיו (4:5); פָּנָיו; [7]דְּרָכָיו (2:7); אַפָּיו.

4. [10]בְּנוֹתַי; [9]אֹתִי; אֹתִי (6:9); דֹּרֹתָיו (2:21); צַלְעֹתָיו.
   בְּנֹתֶיךָ (19:12); [11]בְּנֹתֶיךָ (34:9); בְּנוֹתֵינוּ (31:26).

Remark.—[12]אֲבוֹתָם and [13]אֲבוֹתֵיהֶם; *cf.* also שְׁמוֹתָם (25:16);
דֹּרוֹתָם[14]; אֹתָם (17:7).

3. The masculine plural has before all suffixes the ending ay, which, in the Construct, appears in the form of ê. But certain modifications in the form of this ending take place, due to the character of the following consonants:

   a. The form ay (ַי) appears unchanged
      (1) in the 1 c. sg. ַי, the י of the suffix having been absorbed by the final י of the ending.
      (2) in the 2 f. sg. יִךְ, ךְ being joined by the helping-vowel _.
   b. The form ay (ַי) is contracted to ê (ֵי) before all plural suffixes.
   c. The form ay (ַי) is contracted to ֵי (ê) before ךָ and הָ.
   d. The original form ay (ַי) loses י and rounds ă to â before (הֶן changed according to § 44. 4. *c.* to) ן, the י being generally retained orthographically.

---

[1] Isa. 58 : 2.   [2] Jer. 2 : 33.   [3] 1 Sam. 25 : 35.   [4] Jer. 2 : 34.
[5] With ָ written defectively, instead of יָ.   [6] 1 Sam. 1 : 18.
[7] Deut. 10 : 12.   [8] Deut. 32 : 11.   [9] Ex. 7 : 3.   [10] Ps. 74 : 9.
[11] Ezek. 16 : 20.   [12] Ex. 4 : 5.   [13] 1 Chron. 4 : 38.   [14] Ps. 74 : 4.

4. The feminine plural with suffixes has (1) **ת**ֹ, the usual affix of the fem. plur., (2) the masculine plural ending **ַי**, which is modified in the manner just described (see above, 3. *a–d*); and then (3) the same suffixes as were used with the masc. plur.

Remark.—Very frequently the suffix is attached directly to **ת**ֹ; this is done probably in order to obtain a shorter form.

109. *Stem-Changes in the Inflection of Nouns*

1. ;לִבְבוֹת[5] *but* שְׁלֵמָה[2]; מָאוֹר[3] *but* מְאֹרֹת[4]; לֵבָב *but* שָׁלֵם[1]
כְּנָפַיִם[10] *but* גְּדוֹלָה[7] *and* גְּדוֹלִים[8]; כָּנָף[9] *but* גָּדוֹל[6]
שְׁכָרָה[16] *but* שָׂכָר[15]; בְּשָׂרִי[14]; בָּשָׂר[13] *but* גָּחוֹן[11] גְּחֹנְךָ[12]; בָּשָׂר
חֲצֵרֶיהָ[22] *but* חָצֵר[21]; זְקֵנָיו[20]; זָקֵן[19] *but* דְּבָרַי[18]; דָּבָר[17]

2. חֲצֵרוֹת[25] *but* חָצֵר[21]; דִּבְרֵי[23]; זָקֵן[19] *but* דָּבָר[17]
לֵבָב[4] *but* זָקֵן[19]; זִקְנֵיכֶם[27]; דִּבְרֵיהֶם[26]; דָּבָר[17] *but*
לִבְבֵיהֶן[28]

3. זָהָב[34] *but* זָקֵן[32]; זָקֵן[31] *but* דְּבַר[30]; דָּבָר[29] *but* זָהָב[33]
דָּם[40] *but* דָּם[39]; יָד[38]; יָד[37] *but* רְקִיעַ[36]; רְקִיעַ[35]
לֵבָב[44] *but* לְבַבְכֶם[42]; בְּשַׂר[43] *but* בְּשַׂרְכֶם[41]

Remark 1.—לְבָבְכֶם[42] *and* בְּשַׂרְךָ[46] *but* בְּשַׂרְכֶם[44] *and* לִבְּךָ[45].

Remark 2.—(2) בְּרָכֹות[47], (1) בָּרֵךְ[47] *from* (12:2) בְּרָכָה; (3) בִּרְכַת (28:4), (49:25).

Remark 3.—כֹּהֵן[48] *but* כֹּהֲנִים[49]; מָצָא[50] *but* מְצָאִי[51]; שֹׁפֵט[52] *but*
שֹׁפְטִים[53].

[1] Gen. 15 : 16.	[2] Deut. 25 : 15.	[3] Gen. 1 : 16.	[4] Deut. 28 : 28.
[5] 1 Chron. 28 : 9.	[6] Gen. 1 : 16.	[7] Gen. 15 : 12.	[8] Gen. 1 : 21.
[9] Ex. 25 : 20.	[10] Gen. 1 : 16.	[11] Lev. 11 : 42.	[12] Gen. 3 : 14.
[13] Gen. 2 : 21.	[14] Gen. 2 : 23.	[15] Num. 18 : 31.	[16] Jon. 1 : 3.
[17] Gen 18 : 14.	[18] Gen. 24 : 33.	[19] Gen. 19 : 4.	[20] Isa. 24 : 23.
[21] 1 Kgs. 7 : 8.	[22] Josh. 21 : 12.	[23] Gen. 24 : 30.	[24] Gen. 50 : 7.
[25] 2 Kgs. 21 : 5.	[26] Gen. 24 : 52.	[27] Deut. 29 : 9.	[28] Nah. 2 : 8.
[29] Gen. 18 : 4.	[30] Gen. 20 : 18.	[31] Gen. 19 : 4.	[32] Gen. 24 : 2.
[33] Gen. 2 : 11.	[34] Gen. 2 : 12.	[35] Gen. 1 : 6.	[36] Gen. 1 : 20.
[37] Gen. 38 : 28.	[38] Gen. 41 : 35.	[39] Gen. 37 : 22.	[40] Gen. 9 : 6.
[41] Deut. 28 : 28.	[42] Deut. 10 : 16.	[43] Gen. 2 : 21.	[44] Gen. 17 : 13.
[45] Gen. 20 : 6.	[46] Gen. 40 : 19.	[47] Ps. 21 : 7.	[48] Gen. 14 : 18.
[49] Gen. 47 : 22.	[50] Ps. 119 : 162.	[51] Gen. 4 : 14.	[52] Gen. 18 : 25.
[53] Deut. 16 : 18.			

The noun-stem, if it contains two changeable vowels (§ 7. 4), is subject to change,

(1) when terminations of gender and number are added;

(2) when the noun stands in the Construct relation with a following word;

(3) when pronominal suffixes are added.

The changes which take place are due to the shifting of the tone:

1. With affixes for gender and number (*Absolute*), viz., הָ֫, וֹת, םִי֫, םִי֫, and with the light (§ 51. 1. *a*) suffixes, *the tone is shifted one place;* in which case,

a. An original ă or ĭ, which had become å or ē[1] before the tone is reduced to Šᵉwâ;

b. An ultimate tone-*long* å or ē is retained, since it stands now directly before the *tone*.

2. With affixes for gender and number in the *Construct*, viz., י֫֫, וֹת (also the sing. fem. ה֫֫), and with the grave suffixes when attached to plural nouns, *the tone is shifted two places;* in which case,

a. The penultimate vowel being now in a closed unaccented syllable remains short, but ă is often attenuated to ĭ;

b. The ultimate vowel reduces to Šᵉwâ.

3. In the case of the Construct singular of masculine nouns and with the grave suffixes (כֶם, כֶן) when attached to singular nouns, *the tone is shifted one place;* in which case,

a. The penultimate vowel is reduced to Šᵉwâ.

b. An ultimate tone-long (originally short) å or ē gives way to ă.

Remark 1.—While an original ă is rounded to å before הָ֫, it remains short before כֶם֫.

Remark 2.—The principles here given apply also to the formation and inflection of feminine nouns.

Remark 3.—Ḳăl active participles and nouns of like formation (§ 92.), in whose inflection the final vowel becomes Šᵉwâ before all affixes (except ךָ, כֶם, כֶן), furnish an important exception to the principle stated in 1. *b* above. The difference in treatment is due to the fact that the participial forms have an unchangeable vowel in the penult.

---

[1] The vowel *o*, except in *u*-class Seğolates, is generally unchangeable.

4. *a.* סֵ֫פֶר [1] *abs.;* סֵ֫פֶר (14:1) *Const.;* מֶ֫לֶךְ (14:17) *abs.;* מֶ֫לֶךְ
    נַ֫עַר [2] (5:1);

b. סִפְרִי [4]; מַלְכִּי [3]; זַרְעֲךָ (3:15); צַלְמוֹ (1:27); צַלְמֵ֫נוּ (1:26);
    יַקְבְךָ [6]; אָכְלְךָ [5];

c. מְלָכִים (14:9); מַלְכוֹת; יְלָדִים (33:1); בִּקְרִים [8];

d. מַלְכֶ֫יהָ [9]; עֲצָמַי (2:23); יְלָדַי (30:26); נְדָרֶ֫יךָ [10]; קָדָשֶׁ֫יךָ [11];

e. מַלְכֵי [14]; קָדָשַׁי [13]; נִדְרֵיכֶם [12]; קָדָשֵׁיכֶם [14];

f. צָהֳרַ֫יִם [17]; מָתְנַ֫יִם [16]; קַרְנַ֫יִם [15] *but* קְרָנַ֫יִם (43:16).

5. *a.* מוֹת, מָ֫וֶת [19] (25:11), תּוֹךְ, תָּ֫וֶךְ [18] (1:2), תּוֹכָה (41:48); מוֹתָיו [20]; בַּ֫יִת (17:12), בֵּית (12:15), בֵּיתִי
    מוֹתִי (27:2); בֵּיתוֹ (15:2), (12:17).

b. אִמּוֹ (3:20), אֵם (21:34); רַבִּים (6:5), רַבָּה (24:25), רַב
    חֻקִּים [22], (47:22) חֻקָּם (47:22), חֹק; אֻמָּתָם [21], (2:24),
    חֻקָּה [23].

6. שָׂדֶה [25] (2:5) *but* שָׂדֶה (14:7), שָׂדוֹת [24], שָׂדֵי; פָּנֶה (*not in use*), פָּנִים (9:23), (32:31), פָּנֵ֫ימוֹ [26] (6:13), *but* פְּנֵי (1:2); פְּנֵיהֶם.

4. *Seğolate-stems* (§ 89.) deserve particular attention:

a. The form assumed in the absolute, viz., קֶ֫טֶל *from* קַטְל,
קֵ֫טֶל *from* קִטְל, קֹ֫טֶל *from* קֻטְל, remains unchanged in the Construct singular of words with strong consonants or laryngeals.

b. In the singular before *all* suffixes the noun takes the primary form (§ 89.); ă is sometimes attenuated and ŭ regularly becomes ŏ.

c. Before the plural affixes (absolute) a pretonic å appears, and the primary vowel becomes Šᵉwâ.

---

1 2 Kgs. 5 : 5.   2 1 Sam. 2 : 13.   3 2 Sam. 19 : 44.   4 Ex. 32 : 33.
5 Lev. 25 : 37.   6 Deut. 15 : 14.   7 Cant. 6 : 8.   8 Ps. 73 : 14.
9 Isa. 7 : 16.   10 Deut. 12 : 17.   11 Deut. 12 : 26.   12 Deut. 12 : 6.
13 Lev. 22 : 15.   14 Ezek. 20 : 40.   15 Dan. 8 : 6.   16 Hab. 3 : 4.
17 Deut. 33 : 11.   18 Judg. 16 : 29.   19 Josh. 2 : 13.   20 Isa. 53 : 9.
21 Jer. 16 : 3.   22 Deut. 4 : 5.   23 Ex. 13 : 10.   24 Neh. 12 : 29.
25 Ruth 1 : 2.

d. In the plural before light suffixes the pretonic å is retained.

e. In the plural Const. and before grave suffixes the å disappears, and the primary vowel is retained, though sometimes in attenuated or deflected form.

f. In the dual the form is generally that which is found in the plural (see *c*), sometimes that used in the sing. before suffixes (see *b*).

5. *a.* Nouns from bi-literal roots (§ 100.) of the Middle-Vowel class have monosyllabic forms with ô, ê and î everywhere except in some absol. sing. forms in which ן and י appear as middle consonants. *Cf.* a similar development of diphthongs to consonants in English *bower* from older *būr; dowel* from older *dowl; fire,* often pronounced *fiyur,* from older *fyr.*

b. ʿĂyin Doubled (ע״ע) Seğolate-stems, before affixes of gender and number, and before suffixes, take Dåğēš-fŏrtē in the second radical, the preceding vowel remaining short.

6. Låmĕd Hē (ל״ה) nouns ending in ה_ lack this before affixes and suffixes beginning with a vowel; the tone-long å of the first radical,

a. Is retained when it would be pretonic, but

b. Yields to Šᵉwâ in the Construct (sing. or plur.), and when it would be ante-pretonic.

110. *Classification of Noun-Stems*

1. אֶרֶץ‎, סֵפֶר‎, בְּקֶר‎, נַעַר‎, אֵם‎, מָוֶת‎, פְּרִי‎, תֹּהוּ‎.

2. דָּבָר‎, אָדָם‎, בָּשָׂר‎, זָקֵן‎, כָּבֵד‎, לֵבָב‎, שָׂדֶה‎, עָרֹם‎.

3. עוֹלָם‎, אוֹיֵב‎, עָשָׂה‎, שַׁבָּת‎, אִלֵּם‎, מִשְׁפָּט‎, עַקְרָב‎.

4. גָּדוֹל‎, אָסִיר‎, נָבִיא‎, אָרוּר‎, מָאוֹר‎, מֵקִים‎.

5. כְּתָב‎, חֲמוֹר‎, גִּבּוֹר‎, עַמּוּד‎, סוּס‎, שׁוֹר‎, דִּין‎, רָם‎.

For purposes of inflection, nouns may conveniently be divided into five classes:

1. The *first* class includes the so-called Seğolates, nouns which originally had one changeable vowel (§ 89.);

2. The *second* class includes nouns which have two changeable

vowels; here belong stems which had originally the vowels ă—ă, ă—ĭ, ă—ŭ, ĭ—ă, etc. (§ 90.).

3. The *third* class includes nouns which have an unchangeable vowel, whether by nature or position, in the penult, and a changeable vowel in the ultima (§ 92.).

4. The *fourth* class includes nouns which have a changeable vowel in the penult, and an unchangeable vowel in the ultima (§ 91.).

5. The *fifth* class may, for convenience, include all nouns of whatever origin, the vowel, or vowels, of which are unchangeable.

111. Nouns of the First Class
1. STRONG AND LARYNGEAL STEMS.—TABULAR VIEW

	mălk (*king*)	sĭfr (*book*)	kŭdš (*holiness*)
Sg. abs.	מֶלֶךְ	סֵפֶר	קֹדֶשׁ
const.	מֶלֶךְ	סֵפֶר	קֹדֶשׁ
1. suf.	מַלְכִּי	סִפְרִי	קָדְשִׁי
gr. suf.	מַלְכְּכֶם	סִפְרְכֶם	קָדְשְׁכֶם
Pl. abs.	מְלָכִים	סְפָרִים	קָדָשִׁים
const.	מַלְכֵי	סִפְרֵי	קָדְשֵׁי
1. suf.	מְלָכַי	סְפָרַי	קָדָשַׁי
gr. suf.	מַלְכֵיכֶם	סִפְרֵיכֶם	קָדְשֵׁיכֶם
	(*feet*)	(*two-fold*)	(*loins*)
Du. abs.	רַגְלַיִם	כִּפְלַיִם	מָתְנַיִם
const.	רַגְלֵי		מָתְנֵי

	nă'r (*a youth*)	nĭṣḥ (*perpetuity*)	pŭ'l (*work*)
Sg. abs.	נַעַר	נֵצַח	פֹּעַל
const.	נַעַר	נֵצַח	פֹּעַל
1. suf.	נַעֲרִי	נִצְחִי	פָּעֳלִי
gr. suf.	נַעַרְכֶם	נִצְחֲכֶם	פָּעָלְכֶם

	nă'r (a youth)	niṣḥ (perpetuity)	pŭ'l (work)
Pl. abs.	נְעָרִים	נְצָחִים	פְּעָלִים
const.	נַעֲרֵי	נִצְחֵי	פְּעָלֵי
1. suf.	נְעָרַי	נִצְחַי	פְּעָלַי
gr. suf.	נַעֲרֵיכֶם	נִצְחֵיכֶם	פְּעָלֵיכֶם
	(sandals)		(noon)
Du. abs.	נַעֲלַיִם		צָהֳרַיִם
const.	נַעֲלֵי		

REMARKS

[For general remarks concerning the inflection of Seḡolates see § 109.]

1. Instead of the original pure vowel ־ֵ, there appears everywhere in *u*-class stems the deflected vowel ־ָ (ŏ), the latter always representing the former in closed, as distinguished from sharpened, syllables.

2. Instead of simple S̆ᵉwâ as a reduction of the original ŭ in the pl. abs. and the pl. with light suffixes, a compound S̆ᵉwâ (־ֳ) is generally found.

3. In the laryngeal stems, ־ֲ and ־ֳ before ־ָ become ־ַ and ־ָ (ŏ).

NOTES[1]

1. In reference to the *a*-class stems, it may be noted that,

a. In pause the ă generally becomes â (וְרָע),[2] though sometimes ĕ remains (קֶדֶם)[3];

b. In such forms as דְּשֶׁא (1:11), פֶּרֶא (16:12), the א is to be treated as a full consonant.

c. In many forms, the original ă, before suffixes and before the dual ending, is attenuated to ĭ (וִבְחִי).[4]

d. In a few *a*-class stems, especially 'פ laryngeal, before suffixes, ĕ (־ֶ) stands under the first radical instead of the primary ă (נֶגְדּוֹ).[5]

---

[1] Under "Notes" there are given the more important variations from the paradigm-forms.

[2] Gen. 1:29.　　　[3] Gen. 2:8.　　　[4] Ex. 23:18.　　　[5] Gen. 2:20.

e. In a few plurals, like תִּשְׁעִים, שִׁבְעִים, pretonic ◌ָ does not appear.

f. There are a few forms, especially ל׳ laryngeal, which make a Construct like קְטַע instead of קֶטַע (*cf.* זֶרַע).[1]

2. In reference to *i*-class stems it may be noted that,

a. In a few cases, ◌ֶ (ĕ) stands under the first radical instead of the original ◌ַ (עֶגְלֵי,[2] עֶזְרִי).[3]

3. In reference to *u*-class stems it may be noted that,

a. The ō is sometimes retained before suffixes (תְּאָרוֹ).[4]

b. The writing ◌ֹ (ŏ) is sometimes found as a substitute for ◌ֻ (ŏ) (קֳדָשִׁים).[5]

4. Seğolates with the vowel under the second radical,

a. In some cases have the usual inflection (שִׁכְבָה *from* שֶׁכֶב).[6]

b. In others treat this vowel as unchangeable (זְאֵבִי).[7]

c. In still others preserve it by an artificial doubling of the final consonant before affixes (מְעַטִּים).[8]

2. ע״ע AND ל״ה, ע״י, ע״ו STEMS.—TABULAR VIEW

Sg. abs.	מָוֶת	זַיִת	פְּרִי	יָם	אֵם	חֹק
const.	מוֹת	זֵית	פְּרִי	יָם ,יַם	אֵם	חָק־
1. suf.	מוֹתִי	זֵיתִי	פִּרְיִי	יָמִי	אִמִּי	חֻקִּי
gr. suf.	מוֹתְכֶם	זֵיתְכֶם	פֶּרְיְכֶם	יַמְּכֶם	אִמְּכֶם	חֻקְּכֶם
Pl. abs.	מוֹתִים	זֵיתִים	צְבָיִים	יַמִּים	אִמּוֹת	חֻקִּים
const.	מוֹתֵי	זֵיתֵי		יַמֵּי	אִמּוֹת	חֻקֵּי
1. suf.	מוֹתַי	זֵיתַי		יַמַּי	אִמּוֹתַי	חֻקַּי
gr. suf.	מוֹתֵיכֶם	זֵיתֵיכֶם		יַמֵּיכֶם	אִמּוֹתֵיכֶם	חֻקֵּיכֶם
Du. abs.	עֵינַיִם	לְחָיַיִם	כַּפַּיִם			שִׁנַּיִם
const.	עֵינֵי	לְחָיֵי	כַּפֵּי			שִׁנֵּי

[1] Num. 11:7. [2] Ex. 18:4. [3] 1 Kgs. 12:28. [4] Isa. 52:14.
[5] Ex. 30:36. [6] Gen. 19:33. [7] Zeph. 3:3. [8] Ps. 109:8.

REMARKS

1. The absolute forms of Middle-Vowel stems are perhaps developments from diphthongal forms which were the basis of both Absolute and Construct forms; $mau\theta$ or $maw\theta$, e. g., becoming $m\hat{o}\theta$ and $m\mathring{a}w\breve{e}\theta$; $bayt$ or $bai\theta$ becoming both $b\acute{a}yi\theta$ and $b\hat{e}\theta$; cf. the analogous case of the Middle-Vowel Pïʻēl forms.

2. In פְּרִי, the ־ְ is a reduction of the original ־ַ, while î = ĭy, the third radical with a helping vowel; the ĭ of פ in פִּרְיִי is an attenuation of the original ־ַ, while the ־ְ of פְּרִיכֶם is a deflection of ă.

3. In ע״ע stems, the original vowel, ă, ĭ, ŭ, is generally changed in the abs. sg.; but before affixes the second radical is doubled and the original vowel retained, though ŏ is rarely found for ŭ.

NOTES

1. In reference to Middle-Vowel stems, it may be noted that,

   a. Full tri-literal forms sometimes occur in the plural (חֲיָלִים),[1] and before suffixes and Hē directive (בֵּיתָה).[2]

   b. Stems ע״א, (e. g., צֹאן = צָאֹן[4], רֹאשׁ, רָאֹשׁ = רֹאשׁ[3]) are a-class Seǧolates, the ă, lengthened to â, becoming ô; these also will be included in the fifth class.

2. In reference to ל״ה stems, it may be noted that,

   a. Forms like פְּרִי become, in pause, פֶּרִי,[5] the ĕ being a deflection of the original ă.

   b. Inflected forms like אֲרָיוֹת[9], שְׁלָיִם[8], שַׁלְוֹת[7], שַׁלְוִי[6], תֵּחוּ[12], בָּכֹה[11], for צְבָיִם, occur; cf. also forms like צְבָאִים[10] for צְבָיִם, occur; cf. also forms like בָּכֹה[11], תֵּחוּ[12]; these are some of the irregular forms assumed by ל״ה stems.

3. In reference to ע״ע stems, it may be noted that,

   a. While הַר[13] stands even in Abs., יִם[14] stands even in Const.

   b. Forms like חַי have Const. like חֵי.[15]

   c. ־ַ is often attenuated to ־ִ (פֶּתַח[16] for פִּתַח).

---

[1] 1 Kgs. 15 : 20. [2] Ex. 28 : 26. [3] Gen. 3 : 15. [4] Gen. 4 : 2.
[5] Eccl. 2 : 5. [6] Ps. 30 : 7. [7] Jer. 22 : 21. [8] Num. 11 : 31.
[9] Judg. 14 : 5. [10] 1 Chron. 12 : 8 [11] Ezra 10 : 1. [12] Gen. 1 : 2.
[13] Jer. 50 : 6. [14] Gen. 14 : 3. [15] Gen. 42 : 15. [16] Ruth 2 : 14.

d. Many fully tri-literal forms are in use.

e. ע״ן forms like אַף (='ănp) are inflected like ע״ע forms (אַפִּין).[1]

112. Nouns of the Second Class
TABULAR VIEW

	dă-vǎr (word)	ḥă-χăm (wise)	ză-ḳīn (old)	ḥă-ṣīr (court)	să-dăy (field)	'ă-mŭḳ (deep)
Sg. abs.	דָּבָר	חָכָם	זָקֵן	חָצֵר	שָׂדֶה	עָמֹק
const.	דְּבַר	חֲכַם	זְקַן	חֲצַר	שְׂדֵה	עֲמֹק
1. suf.	דְּבָרִי	חֲכָמִי	זְקֵנִי	חֲצֵרִי	שָׂדִי	
gr. suf.	דְּבַרְכֶם	חֲכַמְכֶם	זְקַנְכֶם	חֲצַרְכֶם	שָׂדְכֶם	
Pl. abs.	דְּבָרִים	חֲכָמִים	זְקֵנִים	חֲצֵרִים	[שָׂדִים]	עֲמָקִים
const.	דִּבְרֵי	חַכְמֵי	זִקְנֵי	חַצְרֵי	שְׂדֵי	עִמְקֵי
1. suf.	דְּבָרַי	חֲכָמַי	זְקֵנַי	חֲצֵרַי	שָׂדַי	
gr. suf.	דִּבְרֵיכֶם	חַכְמֵיכֶם	זִקְנֵיכֶם	חַצְרֵיכֶם		

	(wings)	(loins)	(thighs)
Du. abs.	כְּנָפַיִם	חֲלָצַיִם	יְרֵכַיִם
const.	כַּנְפֵי		

REMARKS

1. This class includes all nouns with two, orig. short, vowels.

2. While the original penultimate ă, in Const. pl. and before grave suffixes, is generally attenuated to ĭ, it is retained unchanged under laryngeals.

3. In ḳă-ṭĭl forms, there appears in the Const. sg., ă instead of ĭ, because the latter cannot stand in a closed accented syllable;[2] in the sg. with grave suffixes, this ĭ is deflected to ĕ.

4. The הַ and הָ in the Abs. and Const. of ל״ה stems is for ăy; this ăy is entirely lacking before affixes of gender and number, and before suffixes.

---

[1] Gen. 2 : 7.

[2] This principle is known as Philippi's law, after the scholar who first formulated it.

5. Many words artificially double the last consonant before all affixes; the preceding vowel is then necessarily sharpened. Here may be included,

　　a. Adjectives in ō, אָדֹם, נָקֹד, עָגֹל, etc.

　　b. Nouns in ā, גָּמָל, the adjective form קָטָן, etc.

NOTES

1. The אַ_ of ל״א stems stands unchanged even in the Construct.

2. Some words of this class assume in the Construct state a Seğolate form, *e. g.*, כָּתֵף[1] from כָּתֵף, יֶרֶךְ[2] from יָרֵךְ; some of these words have also the regular form in the Const., *e. g.*, כָּבֵד, both כְּבַד[3] and כָּבֵד.[4]

3. In some verbal adjectives the ē, lowered from ĭ, is retained even in the Construct state, *e. g.*, יָשֵׁן[7], שָׂמֵחַ[6], חָפֵץ[5].

113. Nouns of the Third Class
TABULAR VIEW

	'ô-lăm (eternity)	mĭš-păṭ (judgment)	'ô-yĭv (enemy)	'îl-lĭm (blind)	ḥô-zăy (prophet)	'ô-făn (wheel)
Sg. abs.	עוֹלָם	מִשְׁפָּט	אֹיֵב	אִלֵּם	חֹזֶה	אוֹפָן
const.	עוֹלָם	מִשְׁפַּט	אֹיֵב		חֹזֵה	אוֹפַן
1. suf.	עוֹלָמִי	מִשְׁפָּטִי	אֹיְבִי		חֹזִי	אוֹפַנִּי
gr.suf.	עוֹלַמְכֶם	מִשְׁפַּטְכֶם	אֹיִבְכֶם		חֹזְכֶם	
Pl. abs.	עוֹלָמִים	מִשְׁפָּטִים	אֹיְבִים	אִלְּמִים	חֹזִים	אוֹפַנִּים
const.	עוֹלְמֵי	מִשְׁפְּטֵי	אֹיְבֵי		חֹזֵי	
1. suf.	עוֹלָמַי	מִשְׁפָּטַי	אֹיְבַי		חֹזַי	
gr.suf.	עוֹלְמֵיכֶם	מִשְׁפְּטֵיכֶם	אֹיְבֵיכֶם		חֹזֵיכֶם	

	(tongs)	(balances)
Du. abs.	מֶלְקָחַיִם	מַאֲזְנַיִם
const.		מַאֲזְנֵי

---

[1] Num. 34 : 11.　　[2] Gen. 24 : 9.　　[3] Ex. 4 : 10.　　[4] Isa. 1 : 4.
[5] Ps. 35 : 27.　　[6] Ps. 35 : 26.　　[7] Dan. 12 : 2.

REMARKS

1. This class includes nouns with an unchangeable vowel in the penult; this may be a naturally long vowel, or a short vowel in a closed syllable.

2. The following formations are included: קוֹטָל, קוֹטֵל, קוֹטָל, קְטָל, קְטֵל, קְטָל, קְטָל; many nouns with the third, or the second and third radicals reduplicated; some nouns with א, ה and י prefixed; תָּקְטָל, מַקְטֵל, מִקְטֵל, מִקְטָל, מַקְטֵל, מַקְטָל, תַּקְטֵל, תַּקְטָל; many nouns formed by affixes; some nouns with four radicals.

The existence of the form *ḳôṭăl* from *ḳâṭăl* is questioned by many scholars, who trace such words to a *ḳăuṭăl* form. But many proper names and the *ḳăl* active participle seem to make this form secure.

3. Original ă in the sg. Const., and in the sg. with grave suffixes remains unchanged; it is reduced in the pl. Const., and in the pl. with grave suffixes.

4. An original ĭ in the sg. before כֶן, כֶם, ךָ is usually unchanged, but sometimes is deflected to ĕ; *before all other suffixes and before affixes it is reduced.*

5. The Ḳăl act. participle of verbs ל"ה has the same ending (ה_ֶ), as was seen in certain nouns of the second class, like שָׂדֶה; but its first vowel is unchangeable.

6. Many nouns of this class treat the ultimate changeable vowel in the manner described in § 112. R. 5, *i. e.*, artificially double the following consonant, and sharpen the vowel:

a. אוֹפָן (§ 92.); שׁוֹשָׁן (§ 99.); מִשְׂגָּב (§ 96.); and others.

b. רַעֲנָן, שַׁאֲנָן (§ 94.); אֲדַמְדַּם (§ 94. 2); and others.

c. בַּרְזֶל, כַּרְמֶל (§ 99. 1. *a*); גַּלְגַּל (§ 100. 1); and others.

d. עַקְרָב, חַרְטֹם, קַרְדֹּם (§ 101. 1); and others.

114. Nouns of the Fourth and Fifth Classes
TABULAR VIEW

	gă-dôl (great)	pă-ḳiḍ (overseer)	'ă-nîy (poor)	sûs (horse)	tăl-miḍ (disciple)	kĭ-θâv (writing)
Sg. abs.	גָּדוֹל	פָּקִיד	עָנִי	סוּס	תַּלְמִיד	כְּתָב
const.	גְּדוֹל	פְּקִיד	עֲנִי	סוּס	תַּלְמִיד	כְּתָב
1. suf.		פְּקִידִי		סוּסִי	תַּלְמִידִי	כְּתָבִי
gr. suf.		פְּקִידְכֶם		סוּסְכֶם	תַּלְמִידְכֶם	כְּתָבְכֶם
Pl. abs.	גְּדוֹלִים	פְּקִידִים	עֲנִיִּים	סוּסִים	תַּלְמִידִים	כְּתָבִים
const.	גְּדוֹלֵי	פְּקִידֵי	עֲנִיֵּי	סוּסֵי	תַּלְמִידֵי	כְּתָבֵי
1. suf.		פְּקִידַי		סוּסַי	תַּלְמִידַי	כְּתָבַי
gr. suf.	פְּקִידֵיכֶם	עֲנִיֵּיכֶם		סוּסֵיכֶם	תַּלְמִידֵיכֶם	כְּתָבֵיכֶם

REMARKS ON NOUNS OF THE FOURTH CLASS

1. The fourth class includes nouns which have a changeable vowel in the penult and an unchangeable vowel in the ultima. Here belong many adjectives like קָטוֹל and קָטִיל (§ 91. 1. *a, b*); passive participles like קָטוּל (§ 91. 1. *c*); formations in which a —, originally in a closed syllable, has become — in an open syllable; and a few nouns ending in ôn with a pretonic — (99. 2. *c*).

2. In a few ל"ה stems with the form קָטִיל (§ 91. 1. *b*) the radical י, when final, in the absence of an affix, is absorbed in the formative vowel î; but when affixes of any kind are attached, it appears in the form of Dăḡĕš-fŏrtē; עֲנִיִּים.

REMARKS ON NOUNS OF THE FIFTH CLASS

1. This class includes those nouns which do not suffer change of any kind in inflection.

2. Here belong monosyllabic nouns like שׁוֹר, דִּין, סוּס, with an unchangeable vowel; participles like קָם and מֵת; formations like

קְטָל, קְטִיל, קְטוֹל (§ 91. *d–f*) which have an unchangeable vowel, with a Šᵉwâ reduced from an original ĭ or ŭ; formations
like מַקְטוֹל, מַקְטִיל, מַקְטוֹל (§ 96. 6–8); formations like
תַּקְטִיל, תַּקְטוֹל (§ 98. 4, 5); some formations with the affix
ôn (§ 99. 2); and a few denominatives (§ 103.).

115. *Feminine Nouns*

I. FEMININES OF THE FIRST CLASS

TABULAR VIEW

	măl-kăθ (queen)	ḥir-păθ (reproach)	ḥŭr-băθ (ruin)	ḥŭḳ-ḳăθ (statute)	gᵉvărt (mistress)
Sg. abs.	מַלְכָּה	חֶרְפָּה	חָרְבָּה	חֻקָּה	גְּבֶרֶת
const.	מַלְכַּת	חֶרְפַּת	חָרְבַּת	חֻקַּת	גְּבֶרֶת
1. suf.	מַלְכָּתִי	חֶרְפָּתִי	חָרְבָּתִי	חֻקָּתִי	גְּבִרְתִּי
gr. suf.	מַלְכַּתְכֶם	חֶרְפַּתְכֶם	חָרְבַּתְכֶם	חֻקַּתְכֶם	גְּבִרְתְּכֶם
Pl. abs.	מְלָכוֹת	חֲרָפוֹת	חֲרָבוֹת	חֻקּוֹת	[גְּבָרוֹת]
const.	מַלְכוֹת	חֲרָפוֹת	חֲרָבוֹת	חֻקּוֹת	
		(embroidery)			(cymbals)
Du. abs.		רִקְמָתַיִם			מְצִלְתַּיִם

REMARKS

1. The feminine ending is added to the ground form, ĕ and ŏ appearing in *i*-class and *u*-class stems in closed syllables; the older
form תְּ appears in the Const. and before suffixes.

2. The pretonic â is found in the feminine declension as well as in
the masculine.

3. Examples of weak feminine Segolates and monosyllabic nouns
with feminine ending are (1) נַעֲרָה, (2) טָהֳרָה, (3) עוֹלָה,
(4) צֵידָה, (5) בִּינָה, (6) סוּפָה, (7) אֱלִיָּה, (8) חַיָּה, (9) מִדָּה,

(10) זִמָּה, (11) חֻקָּה, of which those numbered 3–6, 8–11 suffer no change of stem, following the inflection of חֻקָּה given above.

4. Just as מֶלֶךְ is derived from מַלְךְ, so גְּבֶרֶת is derived from גְּבַר by the addition of ־ת, and the deflection of ă to ĕ. Before suffixes the original ־ֶ is attenuated to ĭ.

2. FEMININES OF THE SECOND CLASS

TABULAR VIEW

	șă-ḏă-ḳăθ (righteousness)	ză-'ă-ḳăθ (cry)	šă-năθ (year)	'ă-ṭă-răθ (crown)	gᵉzl-lăθ (violence)
Sg. abs.	צְדָקָה	זְעָקָה	שָׁנָה	עֲטָרָה	גְּזֵלָה
const.	צִדְקַת	זַעֲקַת	שְׁנַת	עֲטֶרֶת	גְּזֵלַת
1. suf.	צִדְקָתִי	זַעֲקָתִי	שְׁנָתִי	יְבָמָה (sister-in-law)	
gr. suf.	צִדְקַתְכֶם	זַעֲקַתְכֶם	שְׁנַתְכֶם		
Pl. abs.	צְדָקוֹת		שָׁנוֹת	עֲטָרוֹת	
const.	צִדְקוֹת		שְׁנוֹת	עֲטְרוֹת	
			(lips)		
Du. abs.			שְׂפָתַיִם		
const.			שִׂפְתֵי		

REMARKS

1. The same stem-changes take place before the ending ה־ as before the plural endings (§ 109.).

2. In the Const. sg. and pl., as well as before suffixes, the original ă of the first syl., while retained with laryngeals, is generally attenuated to ĭ.

3. The Šᵉwâ before the endings ת־ (Const. sg.) and וֹת (Const. pl.) is silent, except in laryngeal nouns where it serves as a helping-vowel.

4. Before the fem. ending the final ־ִי of ל"ה forms is lacking; in this case the ă of the first syl. is rounded or reduced according to the position of the accent.

5. Several nouns with the form קְטָלָה in the Abs. have קְטֶלֶת in the Const.; these in the singular as well as those which have the form קְטֶלֶת in the Abs., attenuate the original ă to ĭ before suffixes.

6. Nouns of the form קְטָלָה frequently retain the ־ in the Construct.

NOTES

1. Forms like ḳă-ṭĭl become ḳă-ṭăl when the fem. ending is added.

2. Forms like מֵתָה, זִבָה, גִּרָה, from bi-literal roots in which the stem-vowel is naturally long, retain it in the Const.

3. FEMININES OF THE THIRD AND FOURTH CLASSES

TABULAR VIEW

	yô-nĕḳt (sprout)	gŭl-gŭlt (skull)	ḳô-ṭĭ-lăθ (killing f.)	gᵉđô-lăθ (great f.)	tᵉhĭl-lăθ (praise)	mᵉnû-ḥăθ (rest)
Sg. abs.	יוֹנֶקֶת	גֻּלְגֹּלֶת	קוֹטְלָה	גְדֹלָה	תְּהִלָּה	מְנוּחָה
const.	יוֹנֶקֶת	גֻּלְגֹּלֶת	קוֹטֶלֶת	גְדֹלַת	תְּהִלַּת	מְנוּחַת
1. suf.	יוֹנַקְתִּי	גִּלְגָּלְתִּי	קוֹטַלְתִּי		תְּהִלָּתִי	מְנוּחָתִי
gr. suf.	יוֹנַקְתְּכֶם	גִּלְגָּלְתְּכֶם			תְּהִלַּתְכֶם	
Pl. abs.	[יוֹנְקוֹת]	גְּלְגָּלוֹת	קוֹטְלוֹת	גְדֹלוֹת	תְּהִלּוֹת	מְנוּחוֹת
const.	יוֹנְקוֹת	גְּלְגָּלוֹת		גְדֹלוֹת	תְּהִלּוֹת	

REMARKS

1. Feminines in תְ־ of the third class arise in the same manner as those described in § 115. 1. R. 4, the ground-form generally having ă in the ultima, though sometimes ŭ.

2. As before, the original ă (or ŏ deflected from ŭ) appears before suffixes.

3. The feminine participle most frequently assumes the form קֹטֶלֶת, though קֹטְלָה is common; the form יֹלֵדְתְּ (Gen. 16:11) is of interest.

4. Feminines of the fourth class present no points of difficulty.

116. Irregular Nouns

1. אָב *Father;* Const. אֲבִי; with suf., אָבִי (*my father*), אָבִיךָ,
אֲבוֹת ,plur. ;Const., אֲבִיכֶם ,אָבִיהָ ,אָבִיו or אָבִיהוּ.

2. אָח *Brother;* Const., אֲחִי; with suf., אָחִי (*my brother*), אָחִיךָ,
אֲחִיךָ ,אָחִי; plur., אַחִים; Const., אֲחֵי; with suf.,
אֲחֵיכֶם, etc.

3. אֶחָד אַחַד (for אֶחָד, with D. f. implied) *One;* Const., אַחַד (used
also before מִן); fem., אַחַת (= אַחְדַת), in pause, אֶחָת;
plur., אֲחָדִים *Some, the same.*

4. אָחוֹת *Sister;* Const., אֲחוֹת; with suf., אֲחוֹתִי; plur. with suf.,
אֲחֹיתָיו; also אַחְיוֹתֵיכֶם ,אַחְוֹתַי from אָחָה.

5. אִישׁ *Man;* plur., אֲנָשִׁים (three times אִישִׁים); Const., אַנְשֵׁי.

6. אָמָה *Maid-servant;* with suf., אֲמָתֶךָ; plur., אֲמָהוֹת; Const.,
אַמְהוֹת.

7. אִשָּׁה *Woman;* Const., אֵשֶׁת = 'ĭšt; with suf., אִשְׁתִּי ,אִשְׁתְּךָ;
plur., נָשִׁים; Const., נְשֵׁי; with suf., נָשָׁיו ,נְשֵׁיהֶם.

8. בַּיִת *House;* Const., בֵּית; plur., בָּתִּים; Const., בָּתֵּי; with suf.,
בָּתֵּיהֶם.

9. בֵּן *Son;* Const., בְּנִי ,בֶּן־,בִּן־ (Gen. 49:11), בְּנוֹ (Num. 23:18);
with suf., בְּנִי ,בִּנְךָ; plur., בָּנִים; Const., בְּנֵי; with suf.,
בָּנַי ,בָּנֶיךָ ,בְּנֵיהֶם.

10. בַּת (for בְּנַת, fem. of בֵּן) *Daughter;* with suf., בִּתִּי (= בְּנָתִי
=בְּנָתִי); plur., בָּנוֹת (*cf.* בָּנִים *sons*); Const., בְּנוֹת.

11. חָם *Father-in-law;* with suf., חָמִיךָ; חָמוֹת *Mother-in-law;*
cf. אָח ,אָחִיךָ ,אָחוֹת.

12. יוֹם *Day;* plur., יָמִים; Const., יְמֵי and יְמוֹת; dual, יוֹמַיִם.

13. כְּלִי *Vessel;* plur., כֵּלִים; Const., כְּלִי; with suf., כְּלִי ,כְּלֵיהֶם.

14. מַיִם (plur.) *Water;* Const., מֵי, מֵימֵי; with suf., מֵימָיו, מֵימֵיהֶם.

15. עִיר *City;* plur., עָרִים; Const., עָרֵי.

16. פֶּה *Mouth;* Const., פִּי (*cf.* אֲבִי, אֲחִי); with suf., פִּיךָ, פִּי; plur., פֵּיוֹת; פִּיכֶם, פִּיהָ, פִּיו or פִּיהוּ.

17. רֹאשׁ (רֵאשׁ=רֹאשׁ) (*for*) *Head;* plur., רָאשִׁים (*for* רְאָשִׁים); Const., רָאשֵׁי; with suf., רָאשֵׁנוּ.

18. שָׁמַיִם (plur.) *Heavens;* Const., שְׁמֵי.

117. Numerals

GENERAL VIEW

		With the Masculine.		With the Feminine.	
		Absolute.	*Construct.*	*Absolute.*	*Construct.*
1		אֶחָד	אַחַד	אַחַת	אַחַת
2		שְׁנַיִם	שְׁנֵי	שְׁתַּיִם	שְׁתֵּי
3		שְׁלֹשָׁה	שְׁלֹשֶׁת	שָׁלֹשׁ	שְׁלֹשׁ
4		אַרְבָּעָה	אַרְבַּעַת	אַרְבַּע	אַרְבַּע
5		חֲמִשָּׁה	חֲמֵשֶׁת	חָמֵשׁ	חֲמֵשׁ
6		שִׁשָּׁה	שֵׁשֶׁת	שֵׁשׁ	שֵׁשׁ
7		שִׁבְעָה	שִׁבְעַת	שֶׁבַע	שְׁבַע
8		שְׁמֹנָה	שְׁמֹנַת	שְׁמֹנֶה	
9		תִּשְׁעָה	תִּשְׁעַת	תֵּשַׁע	תְּשַׁע
10		עֲשָׂרָה	עֲשֶׂרֶת	עֶשֶׂר	עֶשֶׂר

	With the Masc.	With the Fem.
11	אַחַד עָשָׂר עַשְׁתֵּי עָשָׂר	אַחַת עֶשְׂרֵה עַשְׁתֵּי עֶשְׂרֵה

12	שְׁנֵים עָשָׂר שְׁנֵי עָשָׂר	שְׁתֵּים עֶשְׂרֵה שְׁתֵּי עֶשְׂרֵה
13	שְׁלֹשָׁה עָשָׂר	שְׁלֹשׁ עֶשְׂרֵה

100 מֵאָה *fem.*; *Const.*,   4,000 אַרְבַּעַת אֲלָפִים

מֵאַת ;*pl.*, מֵאוֹת

200 מָאתַיִם *dual (for*   10,000 { רְבָבָה, but in later books,

(מָאתַיִם)   רִבּוֹ, רִבּוֹא; *plural,*

(contracted רְבָאוֹת) רִבּוֹת}

300 שְׁלֹשׁ מֵאוֹת   20,000 רִבֹּתַיִם (*dual*) also שְׁתֵּי

400 אַרְבַּע מֵאוֹת   רִבּוֹת

1,000 אֶלֶף; *plural,* אֲלָפִים   30,000 שְׁלֹשׁ רִבּאוֹת

2,000 אַלְפַּיִם (*dual*)   40,000 אַרְבַּע רִבּאוֹת

3,000 שְׁלֹשֶׁת אֲלָפִים   60,000 שֵׁשׁ־רִבּאוֹת

REMARKS

1. The numeral אֶחָד *one* is an *adjective*, standing after and agreeing with its noun.

2. The numeral שְׁנַיִם (fem. שְׁתַּיִם, pronounced štă-yĭm) is a *noun*, used either in the appositional or Construct relation with the word which it enumerates, and agreeing with it.

3. The numerals from *three* to *ten* are abstract feminine substantives, used in appositional construction with the noun which they enumerate. The *feminine* form is used with masculine nouns; the masculine is a shorter form used with feminines.

4. The numerals from *eleven* to *nineteen* are formed by uniting עָשָׂר *ten* (or the feminine form עֶשְׂרֵה) with the units; here it may be noted:

a. In *eleven,* אַחַד and אַחַת have a form like that of the Construct.

b. עַשְׁתֵּי, in the second form of *eleven,* is to be connected with an Assyrian word *išten* (=one).

c. In *twelve*, שְׁנֵים is a contraction of שְׁנַיִם, and שְׁנֵי a shortened form of שְׁנַיִם, the contraction and shortening being due to the close connection of the words; these forms cannot be called Constructs.

d. The feminines from *thirteen* upward have a shortened, but not a real Construct, form.

5. The numerals *thirty* to *ninety* are formed by adding the masc. plur. ending ים_ to the units, but *twenty* (עֶשְׂרִים) is the plural of *ten* (עֶשֶׂר).

6. The units are added to the tens by means of וְ; in the earlier books preceding the tens, in later books following them.

7. The units take the noun in the plural; the tens, when before it, take the noun in the singular, when after it, in the plural.

8. The numerals *eleven* to *nineteen* take the noun in the plural, except in the case of a few very common nouns like *day*, *man*, etc.

9. The ordinal *first* is רִאשׁוֹן (cf. רֹאשׁ, *head*).

10. The ordinals from *two* to *ten* are formed from the corresponding cardinals by means of the termination י_, another י_ being inserted between the second and third consonants. Note that רְבִיעִי lacks the initial א.

11. Above *ten*, cardinals are used for ordinals.

12. The feminines of the ordinals are used to express fractional parts.

XIV. Separate Particles

118. Adverbs

1. a. אֵי *Where?*; אָן *There*; לֹא *Not*; שָׁם *There*; אַל *Not*.

   b. זֶה *Here*; הֵנָּה *Hither*; שָׁלֹשׁ *Thrice*; שֶׁבַע *Seven times*.

   c. מְאֹד *Very*; חוּץ *Abroad*; לְבַד *Alone*; מִבַּיִת *Within*.

   d. הַרְבֵּה *Much*; הֵיטֵב *Well*; הַשְׁכֵּם *Early*; מַהֵר *Speedily*.

   e. אָמֵן *Firmly*; טוֹב *Well*; רִאשׁוֹנָה *Formerly*; נִפְלָאוֹת *Wonderfully*.

   f. מִן with מַעֲלָה (=מִלְמַעְלָה) *Why?*; (מַה־יָּדוּעַ=) מַדּוּעַ and לְ) *Upward*; לָמָּה *Wherefore?*

2. a. הֵן *Here is*; הִנָּם, הִנְּכֶם, הִנֶּנּוּ, הִנְּךָ, הִנְנִי, etc.

   b. יֵשׁ *There is*; יֶשְׁכֶם, יֶשְׁנוֹ, יֶשְׁךָ.

   c. אַיִן *There is not*; אֵינְכֶם, אֵינֶנּוּ, אֵינְךָ, אֵינֶנִּי, etc.

   d. אַיֵּה *Where is?*; אַיִם, אַיּוֹ, אַיֵּכָה.

   e. עוֹד *Still is*; עוֹדָם, עוֹדֶנּוּ, עוֹדֶנָּה, עוֹדֵנוּ, עוֹדְךָ, עוֹדֶנִּי.

1. Adverbs, and words used adverbially, may be briefly classified as follows:

   a. Those which may be called primitive.

   b. Pronouns and numerals used in an adverbial sense.

   c. Nouns, either alone or with a preposition.

   d. Infinitives absolute, especially of Hif'il and Pi'ēl stems.

   e. Adjectives of all formations, especially in the feminine.

   f. Words formed by the composition of two or more distinct words.

2. Certain adverbial particles, involving a verbal idea and thus

often dispensing with the copula, take suffixes. The suffixes attached
are, in most cases, the verbal suffixes. The so-called Nûn Demonstrative (§ 71. 2. *c.* (3) and N. 1) is of frequent occurrence.

119. Prepositions

1. אַחַר *After;* בֵּין *Between;* בַּעַד *About;* זוּלָתִי *Besides;* יַעַן
On account of; מוּל *Over against;* נֶגֶד *Before;* עַד *During,
until;* עַל *Upon;* עִם *With;* תַּחַת *Under, in place of.*

2. מִתַּחַת *From under;* לְמִן *Since;* אֶל־בֵּין *Till between;* לִפְנֵי
Before; לְפִי *According to;* לְמַעַן *For the sake of;* בִּבְלִי *Without;* מִבְּלִי *For lack of, without;* בְּעוֹד *During;* כְּדִי *According to measure of.*

3. *a.* אַחַר *After,* more often אַחֲרֵי; with suf., אַחֲרִין ,אַחֲרֵי, etc.

   b. אֶל־ *Unto,* poet., אֱלֵי; with suf., אֵלַי ,אֵלֶיךָ ,אֲלֵיכֶם,
   אֲלֵיכֶן, etc.

   c. בֵּין *Between;* with sg. suf., בֵּינוֹ ,בֵּינְךָ ,בֵּינִי, (K⁼rî בֵּינָיו);
   with plur. suf., בֵּינוֹתָם ,בֵּינוֹתֵינוּ, also בֵּינֵיכֶם ,בֵּינֵינוּ.

   d. סָבִיב *Around;* with suf., סְבִיבָיו ,סְבִיבֶיךָ, also with fem.
   סְבִיבֹתָיו ,סְבִיבֹתַי ,סְבִיבֹתֵיהֶם, etc.

   e. עַד *Unto,* poet., עֲדֵי; with suf., עָדַי ,עָדֶיךָ ,עָדָיו.

   f. עַל *Upon,* poet., עֲלֵי; with suf., עָלַי ,עָלֶיךָ ,עָלָיו ,עָלֶיהָ,
   עֲלֵיהֶם ,עֲלֵיכֶם.

   g. תַּחַת *Under;* with suf., תַּחְתִּי ,תַּחְתָּיו ,תַּחְתֵּיהֶם ,תַּחְתָּם;
   cf. also the form with Nûn Demonstrative תַּחְתֶּנָּה.

1. Prepositions were originally, in most cases, nouns; they were
generally Constructs, governing the following noun as if it were a
genitive.

   Note.—Many words in common use as prepositions still retain
their original force as substantives.

2. Prepositional phrases, composed of two prepositions or of a preposition and a noun, or of a preposition and an adverb, occur frequently.

3. Many prepositions, especially those denoting space and time, are in reality plural nouns; some of them, when standing alone, have the form of the plural Construct, ending in ‎יִ‎; before pronominal suffixes, most of them assume this form.

Note.—For the inseparable prepositions, see §§ 47. 1–5; 51. 3–5.

120. Conjunctions

1. ‎וְ‎ And; ‎אוֹ‎ Or; ‎אַף‎ Also; ‎אִם‎ When, if, or.

2. ‎כִּי‎ That, because, for, when.

3. ‎אֲשֶׁר‎. Before that; ‎בְּטֶרֶם‎ That not, lest; ‎פֶּן‎ That not; ‎אַל‎ That not;

4. ‎עֵקֶב אֲשֶׁר, תַּחַת כִּי, תַּחַת אֲשֶׁר, עַל־כִּי, עַל־אֲשֶׁר, כַּאֲשֶׁר‎ In order that; ‎לְמַעַן אֲשֶׁר, עֵקֶב כִּי‎, Because, since; According as.

Conjunctions may be classified as to their origin as follows:

1. Certain words used *only* as conjunctions, the origin of which is, in most cases, doubtful.

2. Certain words which were originally pronouns.

3. Certain words which were originally substantives, or composed of a substantive and a preposition.

4. Prepositions which, by the addition of ‎אֲשֶׁר‎ or ‎כִּי‎, become themselves a part of a compound conjunction.

Note 1.—In general it may be said that any preposition may be followed by ‎אֲשֶׁר‎ or ‎כִּי‎, and be used as a conjunction.

Note 2.—In many cases the ‎אֲשֶׁר‎ or ‎כִּי‎ is omitted, and the preposition standing alone used as a conjunction.

121. Interjections

1. ‎אֲהָהּ, אָח‎ Ah! ‎הֶאָח‎ Ho! aha! ‎הַס‎ Hush! ‎אִי‎ Alas!

2. ‎אוֹי, הוֹי‎ Woe! ‎הֵן, הִנֵּה‎ Behold! ‎רְאֵה‎ Lo! ‎הָבָה‎ Come on! ‎נָא‎ Pray! ‎בִּי‎ I beseech! ‎חָלִילָה‎ Far be it! ‎לְכָה‎ Come on!

Interjections may be divided into two classes:

1. Those which were originally interjections, "natural sounds called forth by some impression or sensation."

2. Those which were originally substantives or verbal forms, which have become interjections by usage.

PARADIGMS

Paradigm A. The Personal

Nominative of the Pronoun or Separate Pronoun.	Genitive of the Pronoun, or *Suffix of the Noun* (*possessive Pron.*).	
	With Nouns Singular.	With Nouns Plur. and Dual.
Sing. 1. *com.* אָנֹכִי, in pause אֲנִי; אָנֹכִי, in pause אָנִי *I*.	ִי__ *my* (prop. Gen. *mei*).	ַי__ *my.*
2. { *m.* (אַתְּ) אַתָּה, in pause אָתָּה *thou.* *f.* אַתְּ (אַתִּי). }	ךָ ,ךְ ,ךָ__, in pause ךָ__ (ךָ__) ,ךְ__ ,ךָ. *thy* (*tui*).	ֶיךָ__ ,ַיִךְ__ *thy.*
3. { *m.* הוּא *he.* *f.* הִיא *she.* }	הוּ__ ,וֹ ;הוּ__ ,וֹ (ה)__ *his* (*ejus* and *suus*). הָ__ ,הָ ;הָ__ *her.*	ָיו__ ,ַו__ ,ֵיהוּ__ *his.* ֶיהָ__ *her.*
Plur. 1. *com.* (נַחְנוּ) אֲנַחְנוּ, (אָנוּ) *we.*	נוּ__ ;נוּ__ ;נוּ__ (נוּ__) *our.*	ֵינוּ__ *our.*
2. { *m.* אַתֶּם *f.* אַתֵּנָה ,אַתֵּן } *ye.*	כֶם; כֶם__ ;כֶם__ כֶן ;כֶן__ ;כֶן } *your.*	ֵיכֶם__ ֵיכֶן__ } *your.*
3. { *m.* הֵם ,הֵמָּה *f.* הֵן ,הֵנָּה } *they.*	מוֹ__ ;הֶם__ ;הֶם__ הֶן ,הֵן__ ,ָן__ } *their.*	ֵימוֹ__ ;ֵיהֶם__ ֵיהֶן__ } *their.*

Pronoun and Pronominal Suffixes

Accusative of the Pronoun, or *Suffix of the Verb*.

By itself.	With Nûn demonstrative.
נִי; נִֽי‑ֶ; נִֽי‑ֵ *me.*	נִֽי‑ֵֶ, נִֽי‑ֶ
ךָ; ךָֽ‑ֶ, in p. ךָֽ‑ֶ, ךָֽ‑ֶ ךָ; ךָֽ‑ֶ; ךָֽ‑ֵ, ךָֽ‑ֶ } *thee.*	(ךָֽ‑ֶ‑ֶ), ךָֽ‑ֶ not found.
הוּ‑ֵ (ה)‑ֶ, וֹ; הוּ‑ֵ, וֹ, הוּ *him.*	(נוּ)‑ֶ, נֽוּ‑ֶ, נְהוּ‑ֶ
הָ; הָ‑ֶ; הָֽ‑ֶ *her.*	נָּה‑ֶ
נוּ; נֽוּ‑ֶ; נֽוּ‑ֵ *us.*	נֽוּ‑ֶ(?)
כֶם; כֶם‑ֶ כֶן; כֶן‑ֵ } *you.*	These forms do not occur.
(הֵם)‑ֶ, ם; ם‑ֶ, ם‑ֵֶ; ם‑ֵ, ם‑ֵֶ; מוֹ‑ֶ, מוֹ‑ֵ. } *them.* (הֵן)‑ֶ, ן; ן‑ֵ‑ן‑ֶ; ן‑ֵ *them.*	

Ķăl.		Hiθpă'ēl.	Hŏf'ăl.	Hif'il.
Middle O.	Middle E.	*Intensive middle*	*e. Pass*	*Causative act*
קָטֹל	קָטֵל	הִתְקַטֵּל	הָקְטַל	הִקְטִיל
קָטְלָה	קָטְלָה	הִתְקַטְּלָה	הָקְטְלָה	הִקְטִילָה
קָטַלְתָּ	קָטַלְתָּ	הִתְקַטַּלְתָּ	הָקְטַלְתָּ	הִקְטַלְתָּ
קָטַלְתְּ	etc.	הִתְקַטַּלְתְּ	הָקְטַלְתְּ	הִקְטַלְתְּ
קָטַלְתִּי		הִתְקַטַּלְתִּי	הָקְטַלְתִּי	הִקְטַלְתִּי
קָטְלוּ		הִתְקַטְּלוּ	הָקְטְלוּ	הִקְטִילוּ
קְטַלְתֶּם		הִתְקַטַּלְתֶּם	הָקְטַלְתֶּם	הִקְטַלְתֶּם
קְטַלְתֶּן		הִתְקַטַּלְתֶּן	הָקְטַלְתֶּן	הִקְטַלְתֶּן
קָטַלְנוּ		הִתְקַטַּלְנוּ	הָקְטַלְנוּ	הִקְטַלְנוּ
יִקְטֹל etc.	יִקְטֵל	יִתְקַטֵּל	יָקְטַל	יַקְטִיל
	תִּקְטֵל	תִּתְקַטֵּל	תָּקְטַל	תַּקְטִיל
	תִּקְטֵל	תִּתְקַטֵּל	תָּקְטַל	תַּקְטִיל
	תִּקְטְלִי	תִּתְקַטְּלִי	תָּקְטְלִי	תַּקְטִילִי
	אֶקְטֵל	אֶתְקַטֵּל	אָקְטַל	אַקְטִיל
	יִקְטְלוּ	יִתְקַטְּלוּ	יָקְטְלוּ	יַקְטִילוּ
	תִּקְטֵלְנָה	תִּתְקַטֵּלְנָה	תָּקְטֵלְנָה	תַּקְטֵלְנָה
	תִּקְטְלוּ	תִּתְקַטְּלוּ	תָּקְטְלוּ	תַּקְטִילוּ
	תִּקְטֵלְנָה	תִּתְקַטֵּלְנָה	תָּקְטֵלְנָה	תַּקְטֵלְנָה
	נִקְטֵל	נִתְקַטֵּל	נָקְטַל	נַקְטִיל
	קְטֵל	הִתְקַטֵּל		הַקְטֵל
	קִטְלִי	הִתְקַטְּלִי	wanting	הַקְטִילִי
	קִטְלוּ	הִתְקַטְּלוּ		הַקְטִילוּ
	קְטֵלְנָה	הִתְקַטֵּלְנָה		הַקְטֵלְנָה
	קָטוֹל	(הִתְקַטֵּל)	הָקְטֵל	הַקְטֵל
	קְטֹל (קֶטֶל)	הִתְקַטֵּל		הַקְטִיל
	קֹטֵל	מִתְקַטֵּל	הָקְטָל מָקְטָל	מַקְטִיל

Paragraph 58

Strong Verb

Pŭʿal.	Piʿel.	Nifʿal.	Kal.		
קֻטַּל	קִטֵּל	נִקְטַל	קָטַל	Sg. 3 m.	
קֻטְּלָה	קִטְּלָה	נִקְטְלָה	קָטְלָה	3 f.	
קֻטַּלְתָּ	קִטַּלְתָּ	נִקְטַלְתָּ	קָטַלְתָּ	2 m.	Perfect.
קֻטַּלְתְּ	קִטַּלְתְּ	נִקְטַלְתְּ	קָטַלְתְּ	2 f.	
קֻטַּלְתִּי	קִטַּלְתִּי	נִקְטַלְתִּי	קָטַלְתִּי	1 c.	
קֻטְּלוּ	קִטְּלוּ	נִקְטְלוּ	קָטְלוּ	Pl. 3 c.	
קֻטַּלְתֶּם	קִטַּלְתֶּם	נִקְטַלְתֶּם	קְטַלְתֶּם	2 m.	
קֻטַּלְתֶּן	קִטַּלְתֶּן	נִקְטַלְתֶּן	קְטַלְתֶּן	2 f.	
קֻטַּלְנוּ	קִטַּלְנוּ	נִקְטַלְנוּ	קָטַלְנוּ	1 c.	
יְקֻטַּל	יְקַטֵּל	יִקָּטֵל	יִקְטֹל	Sg. 3 m.	
תְּקֻטַּל	תְּקַטֵּל	תִּקָּטֵל	תִּקְטֹל	3 f.	
תְּקֻטַּל	תְּקַטֵּל	תִּקָּטֵל	תִּקְטֹל	2 m.	
תְּקֻטְּלִי	תְּקַטְּלִי	תִּקָּטְלִי	תִּקְטְלִי	2 f.	
אֲקֻטַּל	אֲקַטֵּל	אֶקָּטֵל	אֶקְטֹל	1 c.	Imperfect.
יְקֻטְּלוּ	יְקַטְּלוּ	יִקָּטְלוּ	יִקְטְלוּ	Pl. 3 m.	
תְּקֻטַּלְנָה	תְּקַטֵּלְנָה	תִּקָּטַלְנָה	תִּקְטֹלְנָה	3 f.	
תְּקֻטְּלוּ	תְּקַטְּלוּ	תִּקָּטְלוּ	תִּקְטְלוּ	2 m.	
תְּקֻטַּלְנָה	תְּקַטֵּלְנָה	תִּקָּטַלְנָה	תִּקְטֹלְנָה	2 f.	
נְקֻטַּל	נְקַטֵּל	נִקָּטֵל	נִקְטֹל	1 c.	
	קַטֵּל	הִקָּטֵל	קְטֹל	Sg. 2 m.	
	קַטְּלִי	הִקָּטְלִי	קִטְלִי	2 f.	
wanting	קַטְּלוּ	הִקָּטְלוּ	קִטְלוּ	Pl. 2 m.	Imperative.
	קַטֵּלְנָה	הִקָּטַלְנָה	קְטֹלְנָה	2 f.	
קֻטַּל	קַטֵּל; קַטֹּל	הִקָּטֹל; נִקְטֹל	קָטוֹל	abs.	
	קַטֵּל	הִקָּטֵל	קְטֹל	Const.	Infin.
	מְקַטֵּל		קֹטֵל	act.	
מְקֻטָּל		נִקְטָל	קָטוּל	pass.	Part.

3 pl. f.	3 pl. m.	2 pl. m.	1 pl. c.	3 sg. f.
קָטְלָן	קְטָלָם		קְטָלָנוּ	קָטְלָה
	קְטַלְתֶּם	—	קְטַלְתָּנוּ	קְטָלַתָּה
	קְטַלְתֶּם	—	קְטַלְתָּנוּ	קְטָלָתָה
	קְטַלְתִּים		קְטַלְתִּינוּ	קְטַלְתִּיהָ
קְטַלְתִּין	קְטַלְתִּים	קְטַלְתִּיכֶם	—	קְטַלְתִּיהָ
קְטָלוּן	קְטָלוּם	—	קְטָלוּנוּ	קְטָלוּהָ
	קְטַלְתּוּם	—	קְטַלְתּוּנוּ	
	קְטָלְנוּם	קְטָלְנוּכֶם		קְטָלְנוּהָ
קְטֵלָן	קְטֵלָם	קְטֵלְכֶם	קְטֵלָנוּ	קְטֵלָה
	יִקְטְלֵם	יִקְטְלְכֶם	יִקְטְלֵנוּ	{ יִקְטְלָהּ / יִקְטְלָהּ
—	—	—	יִקְטְלֵנוּ	יִקְטְלֶנָּה
	יִקְטְלוּם	יִקְטְלוּכֶם	יִקְטְלוּנוּ	יִקְטְלוּהָ
	תִּקְטְלוּם		תִּקְטְלוּנוּ	תִּקְטְלוּהָ
—	קָטְלֵם	—	קָטְלֵנוּ	{ קָטְלָהּ / קָטְלָהּ
קָטְלָן	קָטְלָם	{ קָטְלְכֶם / קָטְלְכֶם	קָטְלָנוּ	קָטְלָהּ

with Suffixes

3 sg. m.	2 sg. f.	2 sg. m.	1 sg. c.	
קְטָלָהוּ קְטָלוֹ	קְטָלֵךְ	קְטָלְךָ	קְטָלַנִי	Kăl 3 m.
קְטָלַתְהוּ קְטָלַתּוּ	קְטָלַתֶךְ	קְטָלָתֶךָ	קְטָלַתְנִי	3 f.
קְטַלְתָּהוּ קְטַלְתּוֹ	—	—	קְטַלְתָּנִי	2 m.
קְטַלְתִּיהוּ	—	—	קְטַלְתִּינִי	2 f.
קְטַלְתִּיו קְטַלְתִּיהוּ	קְטַלְתִּיךְ	קְטַלְתִּיךָ	—	1 c.
קְטָלוּהוּ	קְטָלוּךְ	קְטָלוּךָ	קְטָלוּנִי	Pl. 3 c.
קְטַלְתּוּהוּ	—	—	קְטַלְתּוּנִי	2 m.
קְטַלְנוּהוּ	קְטַלְנוּךְ	קְטַלְנוּךָ	—	1 c.
קְטֵלוֹ	קְטֵלֵךְ	קְטֵלְךָ	קְטֵלַנִי	Sg. 3 m. Middle E
יִקְטְלֵהוּ	יִקְטְלֵךְ	יִקְטְלְךָ	יִקְטְלֵנִי	Sg. 3 m. With Nûn
יִקְטְלֶנּוּ	—	יִקְטְלֶךָּ	יִקְטְלֵנִי	Epenthet.
יִקְטְלוּהוּ	יִקְטְלוּךְ	יִקְטְלוּךָ	יִקְטְלוּנִי	Pl. 3 m.
תִּקְטְלוּהוּ	—	—	תִּקְטְלוּנִי	2 f.
קְטָלֵהוּ	—	—	קְטָלֵנִי	Sg. 2 m.
קְטָלוֹ	קְטָלֵךְ	קָטְלָךְ קָטְלֶךָ	קָטְלִי קְטָלֵנִי	Construct

Right margin labels: Perfect. · Perf. · Imperfect. · Impv. · Inf.

Höfʿäl.	Hifʿîl.	Nifʿäl.	Käl.		
הָעְטַל	הֶעְטִיל	נֶעְטַל	עָטַל	Sg. 3 m.	Perfect.
הָעְטְלָה	הֶעְטִילָה	נֶעְטְלָה	עָטְלָה	3 f.	
הָעְטַלְתָּ	הֶעְטַלְתָּ	נֶעְטַלְתָּ	עָטַלְתָּ	2 m.	
הָעְטַלְתְּ	הֶעְטַלְתְּ	נֶעְטַלְתְּ	עָטַלְתְּ	2 f.	
הָעְטַלְתִּי	הֶעְטַלְתִּי	נֶעְטַלְתִּי	עָטַלְתִּי	1 c.	
הָעְטְלוּ	הֶעְטִילוּ	נֶעְטְלוּ	עָטְלוּ	Pl. 3 c.	
הָעְטַלְתֶּם	הֶעְטַלְתֶּם	נֶעְטַלְתֶּם	עֲטַלְתֶּם	2 m.	
הָעְטַלְתֶּן	הֶעְטַלְתֶּן	נֶעְטַלְתֶּן	עֲטַלְתֶּן	2 f.	
הָעְטַלְנוּ	הֶעְטַלְנוּ	נֶעְטַלְנוּ	עָטַלְנוּ	1 c.	
יָעְטַל	יַעְטִיל	יֵעָטֵל	יַעְטֹל יֶעְטַל	Sg. 3 m.	Imperfect.
תָּעְטַל	תַּעְטִיל	תֵּעָטֵל	תַּעְטֹל תֶּעְטַל	3 f.	
תָּעְטַל	תַּעְטִיל	תֵּעָטֵל	תַּעְטֹל תֶּעְטַל	2 m.	
תָּעְטְלִי	תַּעְטִילִי	תֵּעָטְלִי	תַּעְטְלִי תֶּעְטְלִי	2 f.	
אָעְטַל	אַעְטִיל	אֵעָטֵל	אֶעְטֹל אֶעְטַל	1 c.	
יָעְטְלוּ	יַעְטִילוּ	יֵעָטְלוּ	יַעְטְלוּ יֶעְטְלוּ	Pl. 3 m.	
תָּעְטַלְנָה	תַּעְטֵלְנָה	תֵּעָטַלְנָה	תַּעְטֹלְנָה תֶּעְטַלְנָה	3 f.	
תָּעְטְלוּ	תַּעְטִילוּ	תֵּעָטְלוּ	תַּעְטְלוּ תֶּעְטְלוּ	2 m.	
תָּעְטַלְנָה	תַּעְטֵלְנָה	תֵּעָטַלְנָה	תַּעְטֹלְנָה תֶּעְטַלְנָה	2 f.	
נָעְטַל	נַעְטִיל	נֵעָטֵל	נַעְטֹל נֶעְטַל	1 c.	
	הַעְטֵל	הֵעָטֵל	עֲטֹל עַטֵל	Sg. 2 m.	Imperative.
	הַעְטִילִי	הֵעָטְלִי	עִטְלִי עַטְלִי	2 f.	
wanting	הַעְטִילוּ	הֵעָטְלוּ	עִטְלוּ עַטְלוּ	Pl. 2 m.	
	הַעְטֵלְנָה	הֵעָטַלְנָה	עֲטֹלְנָה עַטֵלְנָה	2 f.	
הָעְטֵל	הַעְטֵל	⌠נַעְטוֹל⌡ ⌊הֵעָטֵל⌋	עָטוֹל	abs.	Infin.
	הַעְטִיל	הֵעָטֵל	עֲטֹל	Const.	
	מַעְטִיל		עָטֵל	act.	Part.
מָעְטַל		נֶעְטַל	עָטוּל	pass.	

Hĭþpăʿēl.	Pŭʿăl.	Pĭʿēl.	Nifʿăl.	Ḳăl.		
הִתְקָאֵל	קֹאַל	קֵאַל,קֵאַל	נִקְאַל	קָאַל	Sg. 3 m.	
הִתְקָאֲלָה	קֹאֲלָה	קֵאֲלָה	נִקְאֲלָה	קָאֲלָה	3 f.	
הִתְקָאַלְתָּ	קֹאַלְתָּ	קֵאַלְתָּ	נִקְאַלְתָּ	קָאַלְתָּ	2 m.	
הִתְקָאַלְתְּ	קֹאַלְתְּ	קֵאַלְתְּ	נִקְאַלְתְּ	קָאַלְתְּ	2 f.	Perfect.
הִתְקָאַלְתִּי	קֹאַלְתִּי	קֵאַלְתִּי	נִקְאַלְתִּי	קָאַלְתִּי	1 c.	
הִתְקָאֲלוּ	קֹאֲלוּ	קֵאֲלוּ	נִקְאֲלוּ	קָאֲלוּ	Pl. 3 c.	
הִתְקָאַלְתֶּם	קֹאַלְתֶּם	קֵאַלְתֶּם	נִקְאַלְתֶּם	קָאַלְתֶּם	2 m.	
הִתְקָאַלְתֶּן	קֹאַלְתֶּן	קֵאַלְתֶּן	נִקְאַלְתֶּן	קָאַלְתֶּן	2 f.	
הִתְקָאַלְנוּ	קֹאַלְנוּ	קֵאַלְנוּ	נִקְאַלְנוּ	קָאַלְנוּ	1 c.	
יִתְקָאֵל	יְקֹאַל	יְקָאֵל	יִקָּאֵל	יִקְאַל	Sg. 3 m.	
תִּתְקָאֵל	תְּקֹאַל	תְּקָאֵל	תִּקָּאֵל	תִּקְאַל	3 f.	
תִּתְקָאֵל	תְּקֹאַל	תְּקָאֵל	תִּקָּאֵל	תִּקְאַל	2 m.	
תִּתְקָאֲלִי	תְּקֹאֲלִי	תְּקָאֲלִי	תִּקָּאֲלִי	תִּקְאֲלִי	2 f.	
אֶתְקָאֵל	אֲקֹאַל	אֲקָאֵל	אֶקָּאֵל	אֶקְאַל	1 c.	Imperfect.
יִתְקָאֲלוּ	יְקֹאֲלוּ	יְקָאֲלוּ	יִקָּאֲלוּ	יִקְאֲלוּ	Pl. 3 m.	
תִּתְקָאֵלְנָה	תְּקֹאַלְנָה	תְּקָאֵלְנָה	תִּקָּאֵלְנָה	תִּקְאַלְנָה	3 f.	
תִּתְקָאֲלוּ	תְּקֹאֲלוּ	תְּקָאֲלוּ	תִּקָּאֲלוּ	תִּקְאֲלוּ	2 m.	
תִּתְקָאֵלְנָה	תְּקֹאַלְנָה	תְּקָאֵלְנָה	תִּקָּאֵלְנָה	תִּקְאַלְנָה	2 f.	
נִתְקָאֵל	נְקֹאַל	נְקָאֵל	נִקָּאֵל	נִקְאַל	1 c.	
הִתְקָאֵל		קָאֵל	הִקָּאֵל	קְאַל	Sg. 2 m.	
הִתְקָאֲלִי	wanting	קָאֲלִי	הִקָּאֲלִי	קְאֲלִי	2 f.	Imperative.
הִתְקָאֲלוּ		קָאֲלוּ	הִקָּאֲלוּ	קְאֲלוּ	Pl. 2 m.	
הִתְקָאֵלְנָה		קָאֵלְנָה	הִקָּאֵלְנָה	קְאַלְנָה	2 f.	
——	——	קָאֵל	נִקְאוֹל	קָאוֹל	abs.	Infin.
הִתְקָאֵל	——	קָאֵל	הִקָּאֵל	קְאַל	Const.	
מִתְקָאֵל		מְקָאֵל		קָאֵל	act.	Part.
	מְקֹאַל		נִקְאַל	קָאוּל	pass.	

Hiθpă‘ēl.	Hif‘il.	Pĭ‘ēl.	Nif‘ăl.	Ḳăl.		
הִתְקַטַּח	הִקְטִיחַ	קִטַּח	נִקְטַח	קָטַח	*Sg.* 3 *m.*	
הִתְקַטְּחָה	הִקְטִיחָה	קִטְּחָה	נִקְטְחָה	קָטְחָה	3 *f.*	
הִתְקַטַּחְתָּ	הִקְטַחְתָּ	קִטַּחְתָּ	נִקְטַחְתָּ	קָטַחְתָּ	2 *m.*	
הִתְקַטַּחַתְּ	הִקְטַחַתְּ	קִטַּחַתְּ	נִקְטַחַתְּ	קָטַחַתְּ	2 *f.*	Perfect.
הִתְקַטַּחְתִּי	הִקְטַחְתִּי	קִטַּחְתִּי	נִקְטַחְתִּי	קָטַחְתִּי	1 *c.*	
הִתְקַטְּחוּ	הִקְטִיחוּ	קִטְּחוּ	נִקְטְחוּ	קָטְחוּ	*Pl.* 3 *c.*	
הִתְקַטַּחְתֶּם	הִקְטַחְתֶּם	קִטַּחְתֶּם	נִקְטַחְתֶּם	קְטַחְתֶּם	2 *m.*	
הִתְקַטַּחְתֶּן	הִקְטַחְתֶּן	קִטַּחְתֶּן	נִקְטַחְתֶּן	קְטַחְתֶּן	2 *f.*	
הִתְקַטַּחְנוּ	הִקְטַחְנוּ	קִטַּחְנוּ	נִקְטַחְנוּ	קָטַחְנוּ	1 *c.*	
יִתְקַטַּח	יַקְטִיחַ	יְקַטַּח	יִקָּטַח	יִקְטַח	*Sg.* 3 *m.*	
תִּתְקַטַּח	תַּקְטִיחַ	תְּקַטַּח	תִּקָּטַח	תִּקְטַח	3 *f.*	
תִּתְקַטַּח	תַּקְטִיחַ	תְּקַטַּח	תִּקָּטַח	תִּקְטַח	2 *m.*	
תִּתְקַטְּחִי	תַּקְטִיחִי	תְּקַטְּחִי	תִּקָּטְחִי	תִּקְטְחִי	2 *f.*	
אֶתְקַטַּח	אַקְטִיחַ	אֲקַטַּח	אֶקָּטַח	אֶקְטַח	1 *c.*	Imperfect.
יִתְקַטְּחוּ	יַקְטִיחוּ	יְקַטְּחוּ	יִקָּטְחוּ	יִקְטְחוּ	*Pl.* 3 *m.*	
תִּתְקַטַּחְנָה	תַּקְטַחְנָה	תְּקַטַּחְנָה	תִּקָּטַחְנָה	תִּקְטַחְנָה	3 *f.*	
תִּתְקַטְּחוּ	תַּקְטִיחוּ	תְּקַטְּחוּ	תִּקָּטְחוּ	תִּקְטְחוּ	2 *m.*	
תִּתְקַטַּחְנָה	תַּקְטַחְנָה	תְּקַטַּחְנָה	תִּקָּטַחְנָה	תִּקְטַחְנָה	2 *f.*	
נִתְקַטַּח	נַקְטִיחַ	נְקַטַּח	נִקָּטַח	נִקְטַח	1 *c.*	
הִתְקַטַּח	הַקְטַח	קַטַּח	הִקָּטַח	קְטַח	*Sg.* 2 *m.*	
הִתְקַטְּחִי	הַקְטִיחִי	קַטְּחִי	הִקָּטְחִי	קִטְחִי	2 *f.*	Imperative.
הִתְקַטְּחוּ	הַקְטִיחוּ	קַטְּחוּ	הִקָּטְחוּ	קִטְחוּ	*Pl.* 2 *m.*	
הִתְקַטַּחְנָה	הַקְטֵחְנָה	קַטַּחְנָה	הִקָּטַחְנָה	קְטַחְנָה	2 *f.*	
——	הַקְטֵחַ	קַטֹּחַ	נִקְטֹח	קָטוֹחַ	*abs.*	Infin.
הִתְקַטֵּחַ	הַקְטִיחַ	קַטַּח	הִקָּטֵחַ	קְטֹחַ	*Const.*	
מִתְקַטֵּחַ	מַקְטִיחַ	מְקַטֵּחַ		קֹטֵחַ	*act.*	Part.
			נִקְטָח	קָטוּחַ	*pass.*	

Hŏf'āl.	Hif'il.	Nif'āl.	Kăl.		
הָטַּל	הִטִּיל	נִטַּל	נָטַל	*Sg.* 3 *m.*	
הָטְּלָה	הִטִּילָה	נִטְּלָה	etc.	3 *f.*	
הָטַּלְתָּ	הִטַּלְתָּ	נִטַּלְתָּ		2 *m.*	
הָטַּלְתְּ	הִטַּלְתְּ	נִטַּלְתְּ		2 *f.*	
הָטַּלְתִּי	הִטַּלְתִּי	נִטַּלְתִּי	regular	1 *c.*	Perfect.
הָטְּלוּ	הִטִּילוּ	נִטְּלוּ		*Pl.* 3 *c.*	
הָטַּלְתֶּם	הִטַּלְתֶּם	נִטַּלְתֶּם		2 *m.*	
הָטַּלְתֶּן	הִטַּלְתֶּן	נִטַּלְתֶּן		2 *f.*	
הָטַּלְנוּ	הִטַּלְנוּ	נִטַּלְנוּ		1 *c.*	
יָטַּל	יַטִּיל	יִנָּטֵל	יָטַּל יִטַּל	*Sg.* 3 *m.*	
תָּטַּל	תַּטִּיל	תִּנָּטֵל	תָּטַּל תִּטַּל	3 *f.*	
תָּטַּל	תַּטִּיל	תִּנָּטֵל	תָּטַּל תִּטַּל	2 *m.*	
תָּטְּלִי	תַּטִּילִי	תִּנָּטְלִי	תָּטְּלִי תִּטְּלִי	2 *f.*	
אָטַּל	אַטִּיל	אֶנָּטֵל	אָטַּל אֶטַּל	1 *c.*	Imperfect.
יָטְּלוּ	יַטִּילוּ	יִנָּטְלוּ	יָטְּלוּ יִטְּלוּ	*Pl.* 3 *m.*	
תָּטַּלְנָה	תַּטֵּלְנָה	תִּנָּטַלְנָה	תָּטַּלְנָה תִּטַּלְנָה	3 *f.*	
תָּטְּלוּ	תַּטִּילוּ	תִּנָּטְלוּ	תָּטְּלוּ תִּטְּלוּ	2 *m.*	
תָּטַּלְנָה	תַּטֵּלְנָה	תִּנָּטַלְנָה	תָּטַּלְנָה תִּטַּלְנָה	2 *f.*	
נָטַּל	נַטִּיל	נִנָּטֵל	נָטַּל נִטַּל	1 *c.*	
	הַטֵּל	הִנָּטֵל	נְטַל טַל	*Sg.* 2 *m.*	
	הַטִּילִי	הִנָּטְלִי	נְטַלִי טְלִי	2 *f.*	
wanting	הַטִּילוּ	הִנָּטְלוּ	נְטַלוּ טְלוּ	*Pl.* 2 *m.*	Imperative.
	הַטֵּלְנָה	הִנָּטַלְנָה	נְטַלְנָה טַלְנָה	2 *f.*	
הָטֵּל	הַטֵּל	הִנָּטֵל / נִטּוֹל	נָטוֹל	abs.	Infin.
הָטַּל	הַטִּיל	הִנָּטֵל	נְטֹל טֶלֶת נְטֹל	Const.	
	מַטִּיל	נִטָּל	נֹטֵל	act.	Part.
מֻטָּל		נִטָּל	נָטוּל	pass.	

Paradigm H. Verb Pē ʾĀlĕf (פ״א). Verb Pē Yôd (פ״י). Para-

Nifʻäl.	Ḳäl.	Hifʻil (prop. פ״י).	Ḳäl (prop. פ״י).
Same as the verb Pē Laryngeal.	אָטַל	הֵיטִיל	יֵטַל
	Same as the verb Pē Laryngeal	הֵיטִילָה	etc.
		הֵיטַלְתָּ	
		הֵיטַלְתְּ	
		הֵיטַלְתִּי	regular
		הֵיטִילוּ	
		הֵיטַלְתֶּם	
		הֵיטַלְתֶּן	
		הֵיטַלְנוּ	
יֵאָטֵל (יֵאָטֵל)	יֵיטִיל	יֵיטִיל	יֵיטַל
תֵּאָטֵל	תֵּיטִיל	תֵּיטִיל	תֵּיטַל
תֵּאָטֵל	תֵּיטִיל	תֵּיטִיל	תֵּיטַל
תֵּאָטְלִי	תֵּיטִילִי	תֵּיטִילִי	תֵּיטְלִי
אֵטַל	אִיטִיל	אִיטִיל	אִיטַל
יֵאָטְלוּ	יֵיטִילוּ	יֵיטִילוּ	יֵיטְלוּ
תֵּאָטֵלְנָה	תֵּיטֵלְנָה	תֵּיטֵלְנָה	תֵּיטַלְנָה
תֵּאָטְלוּ	תֵּיטִילוּ	תֵּיטִילוּ	תֵּיטְלוּ
תֵּאָטֵלְנָה	תֵּיטֵלְנָה	תֵּיטֵלְנָה	תֵּיטַלְנָה
נֵאָטֵל	נֵיטִיל	נֵיטִיל	נֵיטַל
אָטֵל	הֵיטֵל	הֵיטֵל	יְטַל
אָטְלִי	הֵיטִילִי	הֵיטִילִי	יְטְלִי
אָטְלוּ	הֵיטִילוּ	הֵיטִילוּ	יְטְלוּ
אָטֵלְנָה	הֵיטֵלְנָה	הֵיטֵלְנָה	יְטַלְנָה
אָטוֹל	הֵיטֵל	הֵיטֵל	יְטוֹל
אָטֵל, אָטֵל	הֵיטִיל	הֵיטִיל	יְטַל
אֹטֵל	מֵיטִיל	מֵיטִיל	יֹטֵל
אָטוֹל			יָטוֹל

digm I. Verb Pē Wâw (פ״ו)

Hōf'āl.	Hif'il.	Nif'āl.	Ḳāl.		
הוּטַל	הוֹטִיל	נוֹטַל	יָטַל	Sg. 3 m.	
הוּטְלָה	הוֹטִילָה	נוֹטְלָה	etc.	3 f.	
הוּטַלְתָּ	הוֹטַלְתָּ	נוֹטַלְתָּ		2 m.	
הוּטַלְתְּ	הוֹטַלְתְּ	נוֹטַלְתְּ		2 f.	
הוּטַלְתִּי	הוֹטַלְתִּי	נוֹטַלְתִּי	regular	1 c.	Perfect.
הוּטְלוּ	הוֹטִילוּ	נוֹטְלוּ		Pl. 3 c.	
הוּטַלְתֶּם	הוֹטַלְתֶּם	נוֹטַלְתֶּם		2 m.	
הוּטַלְתֶּן	הוֹטַלְתֶּן	נוֹטַלְתֶּן		2 f.	
הוּטַלְנוּ	הוֹטַלְנוּ	נוֹטַלְנוּ		1 c.	
יוּטַל	יוֹטִיל	יוּטַל	יֵטַל יִיטַל	Sg. 3 m.	
תּוּטַל	תּוֹטִיל	etc.	תֵּטַל תִּיטַל	3 f.	
תּוּטַל	תּוֹטִיל		תֵּטַל תִּיטַל	2 m.	
תּוּטְלִי	תּוֹטִילִי		תֵּטְלִי תִּיטְלִי	2 f.	
אוּטַל	אוֹטִיל	regular	אֵטַל אִיטַל	1 c.	
יוּטְלוּ	יוֹטִילוּ		יֵטְלוּ יִיטְלוּ	Pl. 3 m.	Imperfect.
תּוּטַלְנָה	תּוֹטֵלְנָה		תֵּטַלְנָה תִּיטַלְנָה	3 f.	
תּוּטְלוּ	תּוֹטִילוּ		תֵּטְלוּ תִּיטְלוּ	2 m.	
תּוּטַלְנָה	תּוֹטֵלְנָה		תֵּטַלְנָה תִּיטַלְנָה	2 f.	
נוּטַל	נוֹטִיל		נֵטַל נִיטַל	1 c.	
	הוֹטֵל	הִוָּטֵל	טַל, טֵל	Sg. 2 m.	
	הוֹטִילִי	הִוָּטְלִי	טְלִי	2 f.	
wanting	הוֹטִילוּ	הִוָּטְלוּ	טְלוּ	Pl. 2 m.	Imperative.
	הוֹטֵלְנָה	הִוָּטֵלְנָה	טֵלְנָה	2 f.	
——	הוֹטֵל	——	יָטוֹל יָטוֹל	abs.	Infin.
——	הוֹטִיל	הִוָּטֵל	טֶלֶת יְטֹל, טֶלֶת	const.	
	מוֹטִיל		יֵטַל	act.	Part.
מוּטָל		נוֹטָל	יָטוּל	pass.	

Paradigm K. Verb

Hĭθpă'ēl.	Hŏf'ăl.	Hĭf'ĭl.	Pŭ'ăl.
הִתְקַטְּה	הָקְטְה	הִקְטְה	קֻטְּה
הִתְקַטְּתָה	הָקְטְתָה	הִקְטְתָה	קֻטְּתָה
הִתְקַטִּיתָ	הָקְטֵית	הִקְטֵיתָ (ָ ית)	קֻטֵּיתָ
הִתְקַטִּית	הָקְטֵית	הִקְטֵית (ָ ית)	קֻטֵּית
הִתְקַטֵּיתִי	הָקְטֵיתִי	הִקְטֵיתִי (ָ יתִי)	קֻטֵּיתִי
הִתְקַטְּוּ	הָקְטוּ	הִקְטוּ	קֻטּוּ
הִתְקַטִּיתֶם	הָקְטֵיתֶם	הִקְטֵיתֶם (ָ יתֶם)	קֻטֵּיתֶם
הִתְקַטִּיתֶן	הָקְטֵיתֶן	הִקְטֵיתֶן	קֻטֵּיתֶן
הִתְקַטֵּינוּ	הָקְטֵינוּ	הִקְטֵינוּ	קֻטֵּינוּ
יִתְקַטְּה	יָקְטְה	יַקְטֶה	יְקַטֶּה
תִּתְקַטְּה	תָּקְטְה	תַּקְטֶה	תְּקַטֶּה
תִּתְקַטְּה	תָּקְטְה	תַּקְטֶה	תְּקַטֶּה
תִּתְקַטְּי	תָּקְטִי	תַּקְטִי	תְּקַטִּי
אֶתְקַטְּה	אָקְטְה	אַקְטֶה	אֲקַטֶּה
יִתְקַטְּוּ	יָקְטוּ	יַקְטוּ	יְקַטּוּ
תִּתְקַטֵּינָה	תָּקְטֵינָה	תַּקְטֵינָה	תְּקַטֵּינָה
תִּתְקַטְּוּ	תָּקְטוּ	תַּקְטוּ	תְּקַטּוּ
תִּתְקַטֵּינָה	תָּקְטֵינָה	תַּקְטֵינָה	תְּקַטֵּינָה
נִתְקַטְּה	נָקְטְה	נַקְטֶה	נְקַטֶּה
הִתְקַטְּה, הִתְקַטֵּט		הַקְטֵה	
הִתְקַטֵּי		הַקְטִי	
הִתְקַטְּוּ	wanting	הַקְטוּ	wanting
הִתְקַטֵּינָה		הַקְטֵינָה	
———	הָקְטֵה	הַקְטֵה	
הִתְקַטּוֹת	הָקְטוֹת	הַקְטוֹת	קֻטּוֹת
מִתְקַטֶּה	מָקְטֶה	מַקְטֶה	
	מָקְטֶה		מְקֻטֶּה

Lămĕd Hē (ל"ה)   *Feb 4 Zut*

Piēl	Nifʿāl	Ḳal		
קַטָּה	נִקְטָה	קָטָה	Sg. 3 m.	
קִטְּתָה	נִקְטְתָה	קָטְתָה	3 f.	
קִטִּיתָ	נִקְטֵיתָ (ָיתָ)	קָטִיתָ	2 m.	
קִטִּית	נִקְטֵית	קָטִית	2 f.	
קִטִּיתִי, קִטֵּיתִי	נִקְטֵיתִי	קָטִיתִי	1 c.	Perfect.
קִטּוּ	נִקְטוּ	קָטוּ	Pl. 3 c.	
קִטִּיתֶם	נִקְטֵיתֶם	קְטִיתֶם	2 m.	
קִטִּיתֶן	נִקְטֵיתֶן	קְטִיתֶן	2 f.	
קִטִּינוּ	נִקְטֵינוּ	קָטִינוּ	1 c.	
יְקַטֶּה	יִקָּטֶה	יִקְטֶה	Sg. 3 m.	
תְּקַטֶּה	תִּקָּטֶה	תִּקְטֶה	3 f.	
תְּקַטֶּה	תִּקָּטֶה	תִּקְטֶה	2 m.	
תְּקַטִּי	תִּקָּטִי	תִּקְטִי	2 f.	
אֲקַטֶּה	אֶקָּטֶה	אֶקְטֶה	1 c.	Imperfect.
יְקַטּוּ	יִקָּטוּ	יִקְטוּ	Pl. 3 m.	
תְּקַטֶּינָה	תִּקָּטֶינָה	תִּקְטֶינָה	3 f.	
תְּקַטּוּ	תִּקָּטוּ	תִּקְטוּ	2 m.	
תְּקַטֶּינָה	תִּקָּטֶינָה	תִּקְטֶינָה	2 f.	
נְקַטֶּה	נִקָּטֶה	נִקְטֶה	1 c.	
קַטֵּה, קַט	הִקָּטֵה	קְטֵה	Sg. 2 m.	
קַטִּי	הִקָּטִי	קְטִי	2 f.	Imperative.
קַטּוּ	הִקָּטוּ	קְטוּ	Pl. 2 m.	
קַטֶּינָה	הִקָּטֶינָה	קְטֶינָה	2 f.	
קַטֹּה, קַטֵּה	נִקְטֹה, הִקָּטֵה	קָטֹה	abs.	Infin.
קַטּוֹת	הִקָּטוֹת	קְטוֹת	const.	
מְקַטֶּה		קֹטֶה	act.	Part.
	נִקְטֶה	קָטוּי	pass.	

Paradigm L. Verb

Hiθpôʻēl.	Pôʻăl.	Pôʻēl.	Hŏfʻăl.
הִתְקוֹטֵט	קוֹטַט	קוֹטֵט	הוּקַט
הִתְקוֹטְטָה	קוֹטֲטָה	קוֹטֲטָה	הוּקְטָה
הִתְקוֹטַטְתָּ	קוֹטַטְתָּ	קוֹטַטְתָּ	הוּקַטֹּות
הִתְקוֹטַטְתְּ	קוֹטַטְתְּ	קוֹטַטְתְּ	הוּקַטֹּות
הִתְקוֹטַטְתִּי	קוֹטַטְתִּי	קוֹטַטְתִּי	הוּקַטֹּותִי
הִתְקוֹטְטוּ	קוֹטֲטוּ	קוֹטֲטוּ	הוּקְטוּ
הִתְקוֹטַטְתֶּם	קוֹטַטְתֶּם	קוֹטַטְתֶּם	הוּקַטֹּותֶם
הִתְקוֹטַטְתֶּן	קוֹטַטְתֶּן	קוֹטַטְתֶּן	הוּקַטֹּותֶן
הִתְקוֹטַטְנוּ	קוֹטַטְנוּ	קוֹטַטְנוּ	הוּקַטֹּונוּ
יִתְקוֹטֵט	יְקוֹטַט	יְקוֹטֵט	יוּקַט, יֻקַּט
תִּתְקוֹטֵט	תְּקוֹטַט	תְּקוֹטֵט	תּוּקַט
תִּתְקוֹטֵט	תְּקוֹטַט	תְּקוֹטֵט	תּוּקַט
תִּתְקוֹטְטִי	תְּקוֹטֲטִי	תְּקוֹטֲטִי	תּוּקְטִי
אֶתְקוֹטֵט	אֲקוֹטַט	אֲקוֹטֵט	אוּקַט
יִתְקוֹטְטוּ	יְקוֹטֲטוּ	יְקוֹטֲטוּ	יוּקְטוּ
תִּתְקוֹטֵטְנָה	תְּקוֹטַטְנָה	תְּקוֹטַטְנָה	תּוּקַטֶּינָה
תִּתְקוֹטְטוּ	תְּקוֹטֲטוּ	תְּקוֹטֲטוּ	תּוּקְטוּ
תִּתְקוֹטֵטְנָה	תְּקוֹטַטְנָה	תְּקוֹטַטְנָה	תּוּקַטֶּינָה
נִתְקוֹטֵט	נְקוֹטַט	נְקוֹטֵט	נוּקַט
הִתְקוֹטֵט		קוֹטֵט	
הִתְקוֹטֲטִי		קוֹטֲטִי	
הִתְקוֹטֲטוּ	*wanting*	קוֹטֲטוּ	*wanting*
הִתְקוֹטֵטְנָה		קוֹטֵטְנָה	
הִתְקוֹטֵט		קוֹטֵט	—
—	קוֹטֵט	קוֹטֵט	הוּקַט, הָשָׁמָּה
מִתְקוֹטֵט		מְקוֹטֵט	
	מְקוֹטָּט		מוּקָט

Āyin Doubled (ע"ע)

Hif·il.	Nif·al.	Kal.		
הֵקֵט, הֲקֵט	נָקֵט, נָקֵט	קַט, קָטַט	Sg. 3 m.	
הֵקֵטָּה	נָקֵטָּה	קַטָּה, קָטְטָה	3 f.	
הֲקֵטּוֹתָ	נְקַטּוֹתָ	קַטּוֹתָ	2 m.	
הֲקֵטּוֹת	נְקַטּוֹת	קַטּוֹת	2 f.	
הֲקֵטּוֹתִי	נְקַטּוֹתִי	קַטּוֹתִי	1 c.	Perfect.
הֵקֵטּוּ, הֲקֵטּוּ	נָקֵטּוּ	קַטּוּ, קָטְטוּ	Pl. 3 c.	
הֲקֵטּוֹתֶם	נְקַטּוֹתֶם	קַטּוֹתֶם	2 m.	
הֲקֵטּוֹתֶן	נְקַטּוֹתֶן	קַטּוֹתֶן	2 f.	
הֲקֵטּוֹנוּ	נְקַטּוֹנוּ	קַטּוֹנוּ	1 c.	
יָקֵט, יַקֵט	יָקֵט	יָקֹט, יֵקַל יָקֹט	Sg. 3 m.	
תָּקֵט	תָּקֵט	תָּקֹט תָּקֹט	3 f.	
תָּקֵט	תָּקֵט	תָּקֹט תָּקֹט	2 m.	
תָּקֵטִּי	תָּקֵטִּי	תָּקֹטִּי תָּקֹטִּי	2 f.	
אָקֵט	אָקֵט	אָקֹט אָקֹט	1 c.	
יָקֵטּוּ, יַקֵטּוּ	יָקֵטּוּ	יָקֹטּוּ יָקֹטּוּ	Pl. 3 m.	Imperfect.
תָּקֵטֶּינָה	תָּקֵטֶּינָה	תָּקֹטְנָה תָּקֹטֶּינָה	3 f.	
תָּקֵטּוּ	תָּקֵטּוּ	תָּקֹטּוּ תָּקֹטּוּ	2 m.	
תָּקֵטֶּינָה	תָּקֵטֶּינָה	תָּקֹטְנָה תָּקֹטֶּינָה	2 f.	
נָקֵט	נָקֵט	נָקֹט נָקֹט	1 c.	
הָקֵט	הִקַּט	קֹט	Sg. 2 m.	
הָקֵטִּי	הִקַּטִּי	קֹטִּי	2 f.	
הָקֵטּוּ	הִקַּטּוּ	קֹטּוּ	Pl. 2 m.	Imperative.
הָקֵטֶּינָה	הִקַּטֶּינָה	קֹטֶּינָה	2 f.	
הָקֵט	הִקּוֹט, הִקֵּט	קָטוֹט	abs.	Infin.
הָקֵט	הִקֵּט	קֹט	const.	
מֵקֵט		קֹטֵט	act.	Part.
	נָקֵט	קָטוֹט	pass.	

Pôlāl.	Pôlēl.	Hŏfʿal.	Hifʿil.
קוֹלַל	קוֹלֵל	הוּקַל	הֵקִיל
קוֹלֲלָה	קוֹלֲלָה	הוּקְלָה	הֵקִילָה
etc.	קוֹלַלְתָּ	הוּקַלְתָּ	הֲקִילֹותָ
	קוֹלַלְתְּ	הוּקַלְתְּ	הֲקִילֹות
	קוֹלַלְתִּי	הוּקַלְתִּי	הֲקִילֹותִי
	קוֹלֲלוּ	הוּקְלוּ	הֵקִילוּ
	קוֹלַלְתֶּם	הוּקַלְתֶּם	הֲקִילֹותֶם
	קוֹלַלְתֶּן	הוּקַלְתֶּן	הֲקִילֹותֶן
	קוֹלַלְנוּ	הוּקַלְנוּ	הֲקִילֹונוּ
יְקוֹלַל	יְקוֹלֵל	יוּקַל	יָקִיל
תְּקוֹלַל	תְּקוֹלֵל	תּוּקַל	תָּקִיל
etc.	תְּקוֹלֵל	תּוּקַל	תָּקִיל
	תְּקוֹלֲלִי	תּוּקְלִי	תָּקִילִי
	אֲקוֹלֵל	אוּקַל	אָקִיל
	יְקוֹלֲלוּ	יוּקְלוּ	יָקִילוּ
	תְּקוֹלַלְלֶנָה	תּוּקַלְנָה	תָּקֵלֶנָה, תְּקִילֶינָה
	תְּקוֹלֲלוּ	תּוּקְלוּ	תָּקִילוּ
	תְּקוֹלַלְלֶנָה	תּוּקַלְנָה	תָּקֵלֶנָה
	נְקוֹלֵל	נוּקַל	נָקִיל
	קוֹלֵל		הָקֵל
	קוֹלֲלִי		הָקִילִי
wanting	קוֹלֲלוּ	wanting	הָקִילוּ
	קוֹלֵלְנָה		הָקֵלְנָה
	——	——	הָקֵל
	קוֹלֵל	הוּקַל	הָקִיל
	מְקוֹלֵל		מֵקִיל
מְקוֹלָל	מְקוֹלָל	מוּקַל	מוּקָל

Nif'al.	Ḳal (ע"י).	Ḳal (ע"ו).			
נָקוֹל	קַל	קָל קָל	*Sg.* 3 *m.*		
נָקוֹלָה	קַלָה	קָלָה קָלָה	3 *f.*		
נְקוֹלוֹתָ	קַלְתָ	קַלְתָ קַלְתָ	2 *m.*		
נְקוֹלוֹת	etc.	קַלְתְ קַלְתְ	2 *f.*		**Perfect.**
נְקוֹלוֹתִי		קַלְתִי קַלְתִי	1 *c.*		
נָקוֹלוּ		קַלוּ קָלוּ	*Pl.* 3 *c.*		
נְקוֹלוֹתֶם		קַלְתֶם קַלְתֶם	2 *m.*		
נְקוֹלוֹתֶן		קַלְתֶן קַלְתֶן	2 *f.*		
נְקוֹלוֹנוּ		קַלְנוּ קַלְנוּ	1 *c.*		
יִקוֹל	יָקִיל	יָקוֹל, יָבוֹא	*Sg.* 3 *m.*		
תִקוֹל	תָקִיל	תָקוֹל	3 *f.*		
תִקוֹל	תָקִיל	תָקוֹל	2 *m.*		
תִקוֹלִי	תָקִילִי	תָקוֹלִי	2 *f.*		
אֶקוֹל	אָקִיל	אָקוֹל	1 *c.*		**Imperfect.**
יִקוֹלוּ	יָקִילוּ	יָקוֹלוּ	*Pl.* 3 *m.*		
——	תָקֵלְנָה	תָקוֹלֶינָה, תָקֹלְנָה	3 *f.*		
תִקוֹלוּ	תָקִילוּ	תָקוֹלוּ	2 *m.*		
——	תָקֵלְנָה	תָקוֹלֶינָה	2 *f.*		
נִקוֹל	נָקִיל	נָקוֹל	1 *c.*		
הִקוֹל	קִיל	קוֹל	*Sg.* 2 *m.*		
הִקוֹלִי	קִילִי	קוֹלִי	2 *f.*		**Imperative.**
הִקוֹלוּ	קִילוּ	קוֹלוּ	*Pl.* 2 *m.*		
——		קֹלְנָה	2 *f.*		
הִקוֹל, נָקוֹל	קוֹל	קוֹל	*abs.*		**Infin.**
הִקוֹל	קִיל	קוֹל	*const.*		
	קָל	קָל	*act.*		**Part.**
נָקוֹל	קוֹל קִיל	קוֹל	*pass.*		

Paradigm N. Verb Lămĕd 'Ālĕf (ל"א)   *7eb 4 test*

Hiθpă·ēl.	Hif·il.	Pï·ēl.	Nif·ăl.	Ḳăl.		
הִתְקַטֵּא	הִקְטִיא	קִטֵּא / קִטָּא	נִקְטָא	קְטֵא / קְטָא	Sg. 3 m.	Perfect.
הִתְקַטְּאָה	הִקְטִיאָה	קִטְּאָה	נִקְטְאָה	קָטְאָה	3 f.	
הִתְקַטֵּאתָ	הִקְטֵאתָ	קִטֵּאתָ	נִקְטֵאתָ	קָטֵאתָ	2 m.	
הִתְקַטֵּאת	הִקְטֵאת	קִטֵּאת	נִקְטֵאת	קָטֵאת	2 f.	
הִתְקַטֵּאתִי	הִקְטֵאתִי	קִטֵּאתִי	נִקְטֵאתִי	קָטֵאתִי	1 c.	
הִתְקַטְּאוּ	הִקְטִיאוּ	קִטְּאוּ	נִקְטְאוּ	קָטְאוּ	Pl. 3 c.	
הִתְקַטֵּאתֶם	הִקְטֵאתֶם	קִטֵּאתֶם	נִקְטֵאתֶם	קְטָאתֶם	2 m.	
הִתְקַטֵּאתֶן	הִקְטֵאתֶן	קִטֵּאתֶן	נִקְטֵאתֶן	קְטָאתֶן	2 f.	
הִתְקַטֵּאנוּ	הִקְטֵאנוּ	קִטֵּאנוּ	נִקְטֵאנוּ	קָטָאנוּ	1 c.	
יִתְקַטֵּא	יַקְטִיא	יְקַטֵּא	יִקָּטֵא	יִקְטָא	Sg. 3 m.	Imperfect.
תִּתְקַטֵּא	תַּקְטִיא	תְּקַטֵּא	תִּקָּטֵא	תִּקְטָא	3 f.	
תִּתְקַטֵּא	תַּקְטִיא	תְּקַטֵּא	תִּקָּטֵא	תִּקְטָא	2 m.	
תִּתְקַטְּאִי	תַּקְטִיאִי	תְּקַטְּאִי	תִּקָּטְאִי	תִּקְטְאִי	2 f.	
אֶתְקַטֵּא	אַקְטִיא	אֲקַטֵּא	אֶקָּטֵא	אֶקְטָא	1 c.	
יִתְקַטְּאוּ	יַקְטִיאוּ	יְקַטְּאוּ	יִקָּטְאוּ	יִקְטְאוּ	Pl. 3 m.	
תִּתְקַטֵּאנָה	תַּקְטֵאנָה	תְּקַטֵּאנָה	תִּקָּטֵאנָה	תִּקְטֶאנָה	3 f.	
תִּתְקַטְּאוּ	תַּקְטִיאוּ	תְּקַטְּאוּ	תִּקָּטְאוּ	תִּקְטְאוּ	2 m.	
תִּתְקַטֵּאנָה	תַּקְטֵאנָה	תְּקַטֵּאנָה	תִּקָּטֵאנָה	תִּקְטֶאנָה	2 f.	
נִתְקַטֵּא	נַקְטִיא	נְקַטֵּא	נִקָּטֵא	נִקְטָא	1 c.	
הִתְקַטֵּא	הַקְטֵא	קַטֵּא	הִקָּטֵא	קְטָא	Sg. 2 m.	Imperative.
הִתְקַטְּאִי	הַקְטִיאִי	קַטְּאִי	הִקָּטְאִי	קִטְאִי	2 f.	
הִתְקַטְּאוּ	הַקְטִיאוּ	קַטְּאוּ	הִקָּטְאוּ	קִטְאוּ	Pl. 2 m.	
הִתְקַטֵּאנָה	הַקְטֵאנָה	קַטֵּאנָה	הִקָּטֵאנָה	קְטֶאנָה	2 f.	
———	הַקְטֵא	קַטֵּא	נִקְטֹא	קָטוֹא	abs.	Infin.
הִתְקַטֵּא	הַקְטִיא	קַטֵּא	הִקָּטֵא	קְטֹא	const.	
מִתְקַטֵּא	מַקְטִיא	מְקַטֵּא	———	קֹטֵא	act.	Part.
			נִקְטָא	קָטוּא	pass.	

INDEX OF SUBJECTS

[The references are to sections, unless otherwise indicated.]

211